THE CORPORATE
PLANNING PROCESS

THE CORPORATE
PLANNING PROCESS

By MELVILLE C. BRANCH

AMERICAN MANAGEMENT ASSOCIATION

1515 BROADWAY, TIMES SQUARE

NEW YORK 36, N. Y.

Contents

Plates

Figures

About the Author

MELVILLE C. BRANCH has been active in many applications of planning for twenty years and is considered expert in the field. One of his continuing interests has been the process of planning. This book reflects specifically seven years' experience with the Ramo-Wooldridge Corporation and Thompson Ramo Wooldridge Inc. as Corporate Associate for Planning and Member of the Senior Staff (West Coast).

Previously, Dr. Branch was Associate Professor of Planning and Acting Director of the Program of Education and Research in Planning at the University of Chicago; Director of The Bureau of Urban Research at Princeton University; and, earlier, associated with the U.S. National Resources Planning Board in the Executive Offices of the President.

Dr. Branch's education culminated in his receiving the first doctorate awarded in planning (Harvard University). He is currently extending his experience into new areas, on a part-time basis, as a member of the Los Angeles City Planning Commission and lecturer in comprehensive planning in the College of Engineering at the University of California in Los Angeles. Dr. Branch has contributed extensively to a variety of management and professional journals, and has published several books on aspects of planning.

Introduction

By DEAN E. WOOLDRIDGE

Nowadays planning is a term that enjoys universal respect and admiration. No corporate executive would fail to affirm that planning is important and that his company attempts to do it properly. The debates on the subject, insofar as there are any, have to do not with *whether* but with *how* and *how much*.

A case can be made for the point of view that the only thing more dangerous to a company than no planning at all is too much planning. The history of American business provides more than one instance of an executive who has committed his organization to an energetic course of action based on future projections made by his planning group, only to have to beat an expensive retreat later on when events develop in a direction contrary to that anticipated. In corporate management, as in other human activities, a penalty is frequently exacted from those who mistake a work of fiction for a statement of fact.

But the possibility of misuse does not condemn a tool—it simply emphasizes the importance of proper training for the workman who uses it. The corporate planning process does have results that are

DEAN E. WOOLDRIDGE is a member of the Board of Directors and Past President of Thompson Ramo Wooldridge Inc. Previously, he was President, Ramo-Wooldridge Corporation; and Vice President and Director, Research and Development Laboratories, Hughes Aircraft Company. Dr. Wooldridge is nationally known as a scientist-engineer and executive.

factual and can be treated as such. And even the fiction can be valuable, if it is good fiction.

The Immediate Values

The product of corporate planning that can be used at face value as a guide for the conduct of the corporation's affairs is that which consists of translating major decisions that have already been made into the many resulting actions—all interrelated—of departments, groups, and individuals. For a company with 5,000 employees that has decided to move its operations from New York to Chicago, just the listing of all the steps that must be taken can be a formidable task. To insure that such a list is complete is usually an assignment worthy of the highest-caliber planning staff, as is the subsequent establishment of a time schedule for each of the necessary chores that will provide an integrated, coherent pattern to minimize cost, maximize responsiveness to customer requirements during the period of the move, and meet all of management's other objectives in determining on a major relocation.

The result of such an exercise, when it is related to a situation that actually exists and to decisions that have already been made, is a detailed pattern of control for immediate and continuing corporate action. While schedule delays and other unanticipated occurrences will undoubtedly force modification of the plan from time to time, on the whole this kind of corporate planning—if competently done —should provide a picture of the future that is accurate enough to be considered factual and to be used by corporate management as a solid point of departure for speculation about what the still more distant future may hold in store.

The Longer Range

But there is another kind of corporate planning. This consists of attempts to portray the aspects of the future that are of interest to management. Assumptions are made concerning trends which are not yet discernible, circumstances which have not yet crystallized, events which have not yet occurred, decisions which have not yet been reached. Areas in which such assumptions may be necessary include general and particular economic conditions, political climate, government policy, rates of technological change, product demand and market potentials, and competitors' achievements.

If properly employed, such conditional forecasts can constitute a valuable tool. The danger lies in the fact that the details of the planning process, once the assumptions have been made, are identical in this type of imaginative planning with those that lead to a legitimate program of action in, for example, a major move like that just described. It is probably this appearance of reality in the final planning document that accounts for the frequency with which not only the program planners but also the members of top management ascribe more validity to the detailed conclusions than the oftentimes highly questionable nature of the assumptions would justify.

Awareness of this danger causes some executives to be less than completely enthusiastic about the formally organized corporate planning process. This is a situation which the practitioners and proponents of corporate planning must remedy. They must take the lead in protecting themselves and others against improper use of projective studies. Every planning document should start with a statement of the assumptions upon which the analysis is based and, when summarizing the results of the analysis, should restate these assumptions clearly as conditions upon the validity of the conclusions.

If the staff planner and line executive discipline themselves in this way, the habits of thought thus encouraged will produce other benefits. In particular, it is less likely that the planning effort will be carried to unprofitable lengths in terms either of detail or of extrapolation into the future: the pyramiding of assumptions necessary to permit such extended analysis will warn the planner when he is approaching the point where what has hitherto been a solid piece of fiction is about to cross the line into meaningless fantasy.

Growing Opportunities

While most of the pitfalls of planning lie in this area of future projections, so do many of its greatest opportunities for service. Properly conducted advance planning can be of real assistance to top management in its determination of corporate objectives and policy—and in the decision making through which it seeks to implement those objectives and that policy.

Modern corporate activities are frequently so complex that it is impossible for the small group of men who guide the company—however able—to foresee quickly and easily all the important consequences of the decisions they may be contemplating. An analysis of the probable effects of alternate decisions on whatever aspects of the corporate situation the executive has reason to feel may be of key importance not infrequently leads to the choice of a different course of action from the one that superficial judgment might otherwise have favored. It is this support of the executive decision-making process by a competent projection of the probable operational consequences of alternative courses of action that constitutes the most fertile territory for wider cultivation by company planners.

Fortunately, the introduction of electronic data processing into business and industry and the subsequent adaptation of military-originated techniques of operations research and problem analysis have provided new resources for corporate planning. No one can deny the importance of these new resources in the process of tracing through the consequences of a given set of assumptions for a system, such as a corporation, composed of a number of components responding in a more or less determinable fashion in accordance with the assumptions and a set of operating principles that describe their functioning. And this is the kind of activity to which electronic digital computers are nowadays being applied.

As discussed by Dr. Branch in the fourth and final chapters of this book, the processing of information is an essential aspect of planning. Quantities of data are required for the successful operation of many larger enterprises today, with the consequent need for rapid correlation, storage, and retrieval; and the nature of the planning function is such as to qualify it better than most other business and industrial activities for assistance by electronic devices. In fact, the possibilities in this direction are so promising that workers in the field would be well advised to equip themselves with a working knowledge of electronic data processing and take advantage of every opportunity to develop suitable applications of the new techniques.

Toward Maximum Effectiveness

This book is designed to aid the serious practitioner of corporate planning in making his efforts more effective. And we include here not only the staff specialist but top management and the executive down the line in his role as planner.

We have already seen the value of sound advance planning to top management as it determines company objectives and policy and makes the basic decisions which mean success—or failure—for the future. All the more important, then, that top management be generally familiar with planning procedure and, above all, recognize the sort of reasoning upon which planners' analyses necessarily depend. Similarly, the line manager who must plan his own department's operations—and whose plans will influence, and be influenced by, over-all corporate planning—will be much more likely to approach this aspect of his job with competence if he has a thorough understanding of the planning process and his share in it. To sum up, corporate planning flourishes in a climate where line manager and staff specialist respect one another and work harmoniously toward common goals.

The professional staff planner for his part will be alert to the possibilities of the newer technology in his field—specifically, the potentialities of electronic data processing. In short, by the competent performance of his planning function, he will help his company's line management make effective use of its human and material resources.

It is to such objectives that this book is dedicated. In this spirit, it is commended to the reader.

THE CORPORATE
PLANNING PROCESS

Skill in professional management is the next major frontier of business competition, and that management which leads in this work will enjoy a tremendous advantage.—*Joseph A. Grazier, President, American Radiator and Standard Sanitary Corporation, 1961.*

Better planning is, perhaps, the most talked-of need in business today. This is true for many reasons: rapid growth, new dimensions in size, acceleration of change, intensification of competition, and the other increasingly complex problems faced by industry in the atomic age.

Chief among the basic compulsions toward industrial planning is competition. . . . Competition cannot be outguessed; it must be outplanned.

The most important reason for planning, however, is not compulsion but opportunity—opportunity to make a profit from new activities or new ways of doing things. A system of planning is best when it is broad enough to include not merely plans for the solutions of problems, but plans for the discovery and exploitation of opportunities as well.

From the viewpoint of industry as a whole, the survival of the system that permits private enterprise may well depend on company planning.—*Ralph M. Besse, President, Cleveland Electric Illuminating Company, 1957.*

CHAPTER I

Background and Purpose

Planning has been practiced by American business since its beginning. Without at least a minimum of such activity, even the most primitive enterprises of trade and production could not survive and grow. As an inherent aspect of management, planning is part of all business endeavor. A company or one of its units is engaged in planning whenever it sets an objective to be achieved in the future. Policies and procedures are instruments of planning as well as of general management, since guides to thinking and action are established in the first instance and specific methods of implementation in the second. Budgets are more than control devices, because they establish in advance the level of activity expected of an organizational unit during the year and collectively comprise a program of relative expenditure and effort between different elements of the business. To accomplish specific objectives, companies formulate numerous operating plans to carry out particular programs in sales-distribution, production, research and development, physical facilities, personnel, and other functional components.

When added together, these programs constitute a pattern of accomplishment which represents or establishes in itself certain corporate objectives. In many companies, however, these objectives are as much a casual accumulation of current intentions as a purposive formulation for the longer-range future. There is no central analysis of the diverse materials embodying the aims of different units, or review is restricted to financial feasibility and apparent validity.

Divisional reporting is not explicit and comprehensive—sometimes as much informal verbalism as developed statement on paper. Important elements must be assumed or inferred. Comparative analysis is difficult or impossible when such limitations exist, corporate goals and guidelines are not available, or different units are isolated organizationally.

In this book, we are concerned with more deliberate *corporate planning:* explicit rather than implicit, integrative rather than collective in its emphasis. Corporate management initiates as well as reviews in a balanced two-way flow. In terms of the capabilities, conclusions, and desires of respective components, it formulates longer-range goals for the company as a whole and establishes a strategy for their attainment. It integrates the plans of different units with respect to these corporate goals and with reference to each other. Corporate planning is comprehensive and continuous, involving all elements of the company separately and in conjunction. It is deliberate. It is organized. Planning responsibilities are formally assigned within operating and staff units. A procedure and a time schedule are established for the preparation and processing of component plans directed toward agreed-upon corporate objectives. Plans and objectives are modified to meet changes of circumstance and the experience of operating units. The sum total of this organized and regular projective activity is the form of corporate planning we are considering.

The end purpose of this effort by a business establishment is the improvement of profits and return on investment over time by its development as an effective and lasting organism within itself, its field of competition, and the community and nation of which it is a part.

The Changing Context of Business Planning

It was possible in the past for business to prosper with little corporate planning. Profits were easier to make because of the acceleration in demand created by rapid population growth, exceptional national economic expansion, and widespread increase and distribution of personal income. Also helpful were the unique market situations, limited competition, slower-speed production, and other circumstances no longer prevailing. Many companies performed satisfactorily without what the president of The B. F. Goodrich Company called "a planned approach to profitability"—to the extent profits were often determined by comparison of corporate bank balances at the beginning and end of the year.[1]

Perpetuation of these informal methods of operation into the more complex environment of modern times occasionally led to such bizarre results as the discovery by one of our great motor-car manufacturers some years ago that it was losing approximately $75 on each car produced. ". . . None of the Massey factories had anything resembling a modern cost-control system [in 1955]. Costs were determined on a seat-of-the-pants basis, and the seats of the various factory superintendents varied quite a lot."[2] "When I first took over [in 1959], I could not even find out how much some of our products cost. . . ."[3]

Business was less complicated than it is now. Many factors taken for granted today were comparatively unimportant or non-existent not many years ago: in finance-accounting; labor, stockholder, and public relations; tax legislation; governmental regulation and influence; consumer preference; or international political-economic commitments, trade, and competition. Business was also relatively self-sufficient. Raw-material requirements were fewer and mostly available within the immediate region; labor was largely local; much of the machinery and equipment was made by the company itself or procured nearby; energy was produced at the plant; knowledge and information were in large part self-generated. From the resulting position of greater independence and private power possible in the past, business actions were often taken with little concern for their external consequences. The epitome of this attitude, long since abandoned, is William H. Vanderbilt's oft-quoted remark: "The public be damned."

Times have changed. Nowadays, companies are part of and dependent on a vast interdependent network of activities. A specialization and dispersal of economic and cultural activity has paralleled the more widely acknowledged specialization of labor. The individual business today is dependent on private or public utilities for its energy and other vital services, on many suppliers for everything from ashtrays to machines, on a wide variety of transportation and communication systems—none of which it controls. It must reckon with labor unions, public opinion, government authority, and inde-

PLANNING TERMS

[A few planning terms, derived from one or more areas of endeavor and specialization, have been established by common usage. Several of these are employed throughout this book.]

COMPREHENSIVE PLANNING

Comprehensive planning is the continued formulation of objectives for an organizational entity and the guidance of its affairs toward their attainment. Any organization, institution, or establishment with sufficient self-determination to make planning for its future worthwhile is such an entity. Examples include: a company, partnership, or individual enterprise; a governmental agency or service; a professional association; a family—or any subordinate unit within such an entity which has significant autonomy. The Bell Telephone System illustrates an achievement by business which could not have been accomplished without planning comprehensively. In one sense, all planning is comprehensive if the scope of consideration is complete for what is being planned; no significant aspect is ignored. But, to maintain consistent terminology, comprehensive planning means over-all planning for an organizational entity, and functional planning relates to one of its parts. If need be, we can be precisely descriptive within these definitions by characterizing functional plans as comprehensive within their limited range.

> *Corporate* planning is the shorter term designating comprehensive planning by a business enterprise.

FUNCTIONAL PLANNING

Functional planning focuses on an element of the total problem. In a business, this might be manufacturing, finance, or public relations; in civil governmental planning, highways or forest conservation; in military planning, airborne logistics or naval maneuver. Functional planning is segmental in nature, although of course it must fit associated considerations. It may represent several closely related activities, or it may be very narrow in scope but intensive in its depth of analysis.

PHYSICAL PLANNING

Physical planning is concerned with the location, arrangement, and characteristics of three-dimensional features on the land. Although cost and many other factors are involved, spatial design is the central form of analysis and the end product is an areal pattern embodying engineering-architectural solutions. Physical planning is performed by business in industrial location, site selection, and project plans for facilities and three-dimensional operations on the ground.

> *City* and *regional* planning are the best-known applications of this form of partial planning.

GOVERNMENT PLANNING
MILITARY PLANNING
BUSINESS PLANNING

Government, military, and *business* planning refer to the application of the process within these areas of activity. It may be comprehensive in scope, it may be functional in nature, or it may include physical planning. For the most part, therefore, these general designations indicate only who is doing the planning and the broad sector of the economy for which it is intended.

SOCIO-ECONOMIC PLANNING

Although *socio-economic* planning has not been a popular term in the United States because of its association with Socialist governments or the extreme applications of dictatorships, its existence within our democratic society is exemplified by social security, public health programs, unemployment insurance, tax and fiscal policies, fair employment practices, and various regulatory activities by different levels of government. Private enterprise engages in limited forms of socio-economic planning: health insurance and retirement programs, diversification of product to reduce seasonal unemployment, contributions to charities and educational institutions, or political support. For the most part, socio-economic planning, like military planning, is undertaken by government.

pendent consumer preference as never before. It may require knowledge generated in far-off places.

In particular, the rapid growth of the mass media of communication has increased the sensitivity of business to external developments occurring either close by or at great distances. The time lag in the dissemination of information has been sharply reduced. Failure of a commercial aircraft anywhere in the world affects sales in a matter of hours; consumer demand rises almost overnight because of advertising in a national magazine; a new product or raw material quickly obsoletes its competitors; a union agreement in New England influences labor costs in California; a politically inspired tariff eliminates a foreign market; or a significant formula disclosed anywhere on the globe can constitute the handwriting on the wall which portends the abandonment of a widely employed technical process. As a consequence, business operations are highly sensitive to a growing number of factors. Decisions must be made within decreasing reaction times.

While communication has been extended, knowledge and information are being produced at what appears to be an exponential rate. To keep pace with this production has become a digestive problem in itself for the contemporary corporation. There is now available a large quantity of external information pertinent to the operations and longer-range plans of a business, compiled by government, industry and trade associations, research organizations, consultant firms, business publications, and universities. More knowledge is generated internally within the business concerning its own methods, mechanisms, and technological-scientific efforts. The quantity and variety of data involved in current operations have expanded to such an extent that their handling requires a degree of deliberate organization unnecessary in times past. It is, of course, for these reasons that improved office machines and electronic data processing are receiving such attention today.

As a consequence of these pervasive developments in the environmental context of business, each area of functional planning has more to consider and accomplish in both range and depth. *Financial planning* has been complicated by the diversification of ownership and lending institutions, the manipulations required to minimize taxes within legitimate bounds, monetary inflation, and the increased significance of public investment opinion as it affects stock prices or new stock issue. Contemporary pressures on earnings have emphasized cash flow and inventory turnover as never before, and it is now possible to lease rather than own almost any tangible asset. Controllership must contend today with a maze of governmental rules and regulations, more refined cost accounting, the expanding number of discrete units or functions within the business to be continually cost-analyzed, and the heightened tempo of monetary transactions.

Most publicized, perhaps, have been the growing complexity, specialization, and precision of *production planning*—the result of scientific discoveries, new materials and products, mechanical achievements and higher-speed manufacture, and quality control. It is indeed a far cry from the manufacture of a simple, single-model car to the geographically decentralized assembly of the modern automobile in hundreds of combinations of model, accessories, optional equipment, furnishings, and color; from the oil still to huge, intricate, electronically controlled refineries producing a stream of primary and derivative products in various combinations; from many small machines individually operated to integrated batteries of automated machines and transport equipment performing a succession of operations without human intervention. Entirely new technologies are being incorporated in productive processes. Nuclear-power generation and heating, radioactive measurement and isotope tracers, ultrasonics, cryogenics, and automatic machine and process control are familiar examples.

In *sales and distribution*, consumer reaction is far more important than was the case not long ago. Eye-catching and appealing industrial design, visual differentiation from competitive products, gift and "window" packaging, and enclosed corrosion inhibitors or indicators illustrate present-day considerations in packaging which have been added to the long-established criteria of low cost, easy product insertion and inventory storage, and shipping protection. With higher consumer incomes and lower unit costs of manufacture, the disposable product has entered the sales scene. The new media of communication have extended the sales contact, and new knowledge concerning emotional reactions contributes to the consumer sales puzzle. A shift to sales engineers has accompanied the growing number of technically sophisticated products. Sales-inventory control has become such an important cost in many businesses and so complex in its ramifications that the mathematical techniques of operations research are often needed for successful solution. In general, distributive systems have expanded geographically in breadth, and for some products the successive levels of distribution have multiplied. As products become mechanically more intricate, servicing and repair are more difficult to arrange.

During the past 25 years, *industrial relations and personnel administration* have developed into a full-time specialization. In many companies, collective bargaining requires much thought devoted to strategy and tactics, and union relations many hours of management attention. Fringe benefits are now a substantial proportion of total wages, exemplifying the changing environment of work, personal security, and business responsibility. The decreasing demand for unskilled labor is symptomatic of the continued development of machines and the corresponding importance of technical, administrative, and other professional employees. The necessary classification of scientific-technical, technical-support, clerical-stenographic, and managerial-administrative personnel has multiplied many times, requiring more information concerning education, experience, professional activities, and managerial capability. Psychological test and psychiatric interview were almost unknown within business not many years ago. In-service training has expanded. And employee attitudes—once considered relatively unimportant—now comprise a significant part of the personnel picture.

Physical-facilities planning also reflects the complications of our time. The selection, specification, and design of utilities within industrial buildings have become as important as the architectural enclosure—or are even more important. Included in the picture today are different power requirements; heating and air-conditioning; special environmental control of temperature, dust, vibration, and acoustics; telephones, teletype, public address, radio, and closed-circuit television; monitor-control and security-alarm systems; air, vacuum, and various liquid supply lines; elevators, conveyors, and other automatic transport; or recorded music. Especially in the chemical industries, the productive mechanism has so grown in size, complexity, and uniqueness that it has in fact become the "building" and architectural enclosure is very limited. The more rapid obsolescence of productive processes and products emphasizes spatial flexibility and easy rearrangement. At the same time, additional demands have been placed on the planning and design of facilities housing employees by the higher standards of indoor environment brought about by changes in attitude concerning working conditions, the rising proportion of professional-clerical employees, and —most recently—competition in the recruitment of technical personnel. As zoning and city planning become more demanding, and public-community relations significant in corporate success, new requirements of exterior design and site planning are imposed. And, last but by no means least, cost analysis—always important— becomes crucial as facilities construction and maintenance costs continue their steady rise.

Of all the primary areas of functional planning in business, *research and development* has experienced the most dramatic changes in recent times. Budgetary allocations have been increased sharply, many professional employees recruited, new facilities built specifically for this work, and the function represented at the vice-presidential level of management organization in many companies. Technological advances are increasing the rate of physical obsolescence by a much faster development of new processes and products. Further increase in this rate of replacement is encouraged by changing consumer-customer demand more reactive to style and special features than was the case a few years ago. With shortened life cycles, new products must be developed, cost-analyzed, and engineered; their market, sales, and distribution estimated; and many commitments made months or years before production begins. It is now being found desirable and practicable to incorporate a significant degree of procedural planning in this indeterminate area of activity once considered completely incompatible with organized forethought. "Instead of leaving innovation more or less to chance, as was largely the case in earlier days, many industries are deliberately setting out to plan far ahead for the introduction, year after year, of profitable new products."[4]

Since a primary purpose of corporate planning is the integration of different areas of functional emphasis, it encompasses the aggregate of their respective complications. Because its scope of consideration and responsibility is comprehensive and final for the company as a whole, it is analytically more complex and demanding than the functional planning of any of its parts. The corporation is the legal entity and responsible organizational unit. With the increasing average size of companies, decentralization as a frequent management objective, greater geographical dispersion, a multiplication of elements within the business, a proliferation of external factors to be taken into account, the faster tempo and delicate balance of contemporary operations, and acceleration in the quantity of information and knowledge, it is not surprising that business is shifting its attention with respect to planning upward to the topmost level of management. Unless component plans are drawn in terms of carefully formulated, longer-range corporate objectives, their worth is impaired. They may be based on erroneous assumptions through ignorance or misinterpretation, and they are unlikely to be mutually supportive or even consistent. Without organized integration and projection, the different organizational entities and functional activities of a company are most certainly less efficient or even conflicting.

With most companies facing rising costs and reduced profits, there is no longer sufficient tolerance between the two to absorb prolonged inefficiency and costly mistakes. Careful planning is normally required today to develop programs which will reduce operating costs, increase sales, strengthen management, inaugurate foreign operations, identify a sound acquisition policy, or otherwise improve profits over time. As expressed succinctly by the chairman and president of Standard Oil Company (Indiana): "More than ever, the new decade will be a test of management."[5]

It is clear that socio-economic, technological, and political developments in the United States and throughout the world are forcing business to plan more intensively and comprehensively. Thoughtful consideration of corporate planning requires that these underlying trends be borne in mind. They comprise an essential background for a thorough understanding of the comprehensive planning process; they suggest its probable future development; and they are the primary reason for its expansion as an organized activity during the past ten years.

Corporate Planning Today

A number of companies have instituted formal procedures of corporate planning. Planning staffs and working committees of line executives have been established to serve the chief decision makers in charting the future of the business. The activity is organized at the corporate level for the company as a whole, and within each subordinate unit of sufficient size and autonomy to justify the procedure for the better conduct of its affairs. Most of a selected group of medium- and large-size companies contacted several years ago by the National Industrial Conference Board had some special staff support for planning, and business executives report they spend a substantial proportion of their time at the office on planning.[6] The introduction of seminars, workshops, and advanced management training in corporate planning by the American Management Association during the past few years, and its commissioning of this book, reflect this intensified interest and activity.

Much remains to be accomplished, however, in the development of a methodology of corporate planning. As yet, there are few established procedures and techniques. The subject of corporate planning cannot be reduced to simple facts, universal truths, or easy how-to-do-it solutions. This is because we are dealing with a process far more basic and subtle than its simple designation might suggest. As will be made evident in this document, comprehensive planning involves many of the most fundamental operational difficulties and unresolved analytical questions confronting us at this stage of our individual, organizational, and societal development. Since these aspects are inherent in the process we are considering, they cannot be avoided unless we accept superficial treatment tantamount to misrepresentation.

This does not mean, of course, that we are dealing with an unreal or impractical endeavor. To the contrary, as evidenced by the attention being devoted to organized corporate planning, we are concerned with a significant process. It does mean, however, that underlying philosophy, basic approach, and working principles assume special importance. For from the former are derived certain central questions in comprehensive planning which must be approached with understanding caution and careful judgment, since for some time to come they cannot be resolved by scientific method or conclusive logic. How best to make the many value judgments implicit in business activities is a single example. And it is consideration of principles which underlies the selection of specific methods to fit the particular company or situation.

The executive manager so overburdened that he cannot find time for thoughtful reflection and careful analysis is not the man to delve into comprehensive planning. But such executives are the exception. The attitude of American managers has changed significantly in the past several decades. Exclusive involvement in immediate operational detail is avoided to the extent possible. Longer-range planning is accepted as a primary responsibility. And the artificial distinctions between business practicality, theory, and scientific or intellectual analysis are fast disappearing.

In fact, if we accept an extrapolation of present trends, the corporate executive will be concerned with analytical problems of increasing breadth, depth, and complexity in the future. "Management science" is today's most descriptive term for the executive function tomorrow. We are witnessing on the one hand an increasing subdivision of knowledge and professional specialization, and at the same time the early growth of integrative knowledge which is a common denominator of different substantive fields and specific applications. Management science and corporate planning are part of this latter category.

The Purpose of This Book

The purpose of this book is to provide the background of concept, consideration, and procedure believed fundamental to effective corporate planning. It is not restricted, therefore, to the experience of a single company, one type of business, or other limiting situation, but is intended to be generally applicable.

The process and procedure of corporate planning are described, preliminary to subsequent discussion. Corporate characteristics and management attitudes without which there is little hope of success are outlined. A chapter is devoted to methodological considerations to be taken into account in the choice and employment of analytical techniques. There follow chapters on the more recent techniques of analysis, problems and methods of inaugurating a program of comprehensive planning within a company, and some of the differences in organization to be expected in enterprises of different size, nature, and particular circumstance. The cost and contribution to profits of corporate planning are discussed within the limitations of published information and difficulties of measurement. And finally, since corporate planning is evolving rapidly like so many fields of activity today, probable future developments are projected despite the hazards implicit in such predictions. Judgments are made concerning the improvements in technique to be expected, the probable contributions of related fields of research, the form corporate planning will likely assume during the next decade or so, and the requirements of successful executive performance. Because they have not received sufficient attention in the literature of management relating to planning, human factors are emphasized throughout. To illustrate or substantiate statements, examples or references are incorporated.

At first reaction, the contents of this book may appear unusually broad and basic. Treating the process of subjective reasoning, for instance, may seem many steps removed from the practicalities of everyday business activity. The effort to reach toward the roots of the planning process is in part reflective of the importance attributed to corporate planning in the survival of private enterprise. Business will continue to operate within a generally unfavorable context for the foreseeable future. On the one side is expanding government, which year by year exerts greater control through taxes, laws and regulations, political policy, direct competition, subsidy, and purchasing power. On the other side, the body politic demonstrates apathy or lack of conviction concerning the economic function of private enterprise in our form of society and national endeavor. To survive, prosper, and maintain even today's restricted freedom in the marketplace, widespread and intensive planning by business is mandatory. Without organized forethought and management effectiveness of the highest order, business may slowly but surely be ground between unsympathetic forces. This is one reason for the approach of this book, for corporate planning is sound only if it rests on firm foundations of basic understanding.

If this document fulfills its purpose, it will serve as a reference for those who wish to acquaint themselves with the subject of corporate planning. It may also prove useful to executives or professional specialists engaged in business planning who want on occasion to refresh their perspective before undertaking some new planning task. The effort to be basic and inclusive reflects the additional hope that this may be the forerunner of subsequent books advancing a general theory and principles of comprehensive planning for business organizations.

The corporation in the United States is one of the best microcosms available for study and observation of the planning process. It is an entity of such size that thorough analysis is practicable, with relative autonomy and independent management action, and with consistent internal accounting and record keeping. A company of medium or large size displays almost all the elements and aspects of comprehensive planning in our democratic society. It interacts sensitively and continuously with a highly diverse and dynamic environment. It is subject to competitive forces which discourage prolonged inertia or bureaucratic rigidity; no Parkinson's Law operates to make decline less possible than growth. Decisions are made, actions taken, and results obtained in rapid and continual succession. The surplus resources to support organized planning are found or made available over time if they give promise of worthwhile results. Whatever insights are developed here may therefore be useful in other areas of application or fields of study concerned with comprehensive planning as a significant process in human affairs.

REFERENCES CITED

[1] "Steering Toward Profitability," *Business Week,* 7 November 1958 (No. 1575), p. 169.

[2] William B. Harris, "Massey-Ferguson: Back from the Brink," *Fortune,* October 1958 (Vol. LVIII, No. 4), p. 147.

[3] William H. Walters (President, Diamond National Corporation), "Strict Diet," *Forbes Business and Finance,* 1 February 1961 (Vol. 87, No. 3), p. 17.

[4] "The U.S. Invents a New Way to Grow (A Special Report)," *Business Week,* 23 January 1960, p. 12.

[5] Frank O. Prior, *1959 Annual Report,* Standard Oil Company (Indiana), p. 5.

[6] Arthur D. Baker, Jr., and G. Clark Thompson, "Long-Range Planning Pays Off," *Business Record,* National Industrial Conference Board, October 1956 (Vol. XIII, No. 10), p. 1.

Gray L. Carpenter, "The President's Job," *Top Management Handbook* (Chapter 6), 1960 (McGraw-Hill Book Company), p. 171.

CHAPTER II

Process and Procedure

When treating a generic process which is not susceptible to precise definition, and which therefore has various meanings
for different people, an introductory description is a necessary preliminary to the exposition which more adequately explains the subject matter at hand. This chapter is devoted to such a preliminary
description of the process and procedure of corporate planning.

PROCESS

The basic approach of corporate planning is rational. Analysis,
projection, and conclusion are founded on observed data, statistical
measurement, mathematical treatment, and the best available
methods of non-numerical evaluation and deduction. Scientific
method is used to the extent practicable. When facts, figures, and
calculations are available or can be developed, they take precedence

Portions of this chapter are a revision and extension of material presented at
the 3rd Annual Industrial Economics Conference of the Stanford Research Institute on January 14, 1958 in Los Angeles, California, and published in the
Proceedings of this conference and in *Operations Research,* July–August 1958
(Vol. 6, No. 4), pp. 539–552.

over guess, whim, or emotional preference. But it is recognized that most business situations involve significant economic, legal, political, psychological, and social factors which cannot now be quantified or otherwise processed to fulfill the requirements of "scientific method." This does not mean, however, that they cannot be treated successfully or there do not exist preferable methods of dealing with these less tangible aspects of comprehensive planning.

The focus of corporate planning is on the longer-range future. Operating plans may cover as little as several months under certain conditions, normally not more than a year. Intermediate projections are drawn for several years. The corporate plan, which is distributed throughout the higher echelons of management as the formal statement of actions directed toward the longer-range future, is limited usually to three to five years.

The various functional plans which are part of the corporate plan involve a wide range of time periods. The economic life of many physical facilities can be extrapolated more than five years within the limits established by the likelihood of developments which would hasten their obsolescence. Enterprises engaged in the extraction of mineral resources prove out their reserves many years into the future under different conditions of demand. A company engaged in sustained-yield tree farming gears its functional plans for this basic operation to the time required for seedlings to reach maturity. And some of the goals of corporate planning, such as product diversification, the winning of new market areas from strong competitors, or the reshaping of employee attitudes and skills, must normally be programed over an extended period of time. By contrast, the sales of many department store or supermarket items are difficult or impossible to forecast with confidence beyond the near future; and in many instances the sudden cancellation, cutback, or expansion of military defense programs cannot be anticipated.

A basic characteristic of comprehensive planning is that the continuous application of the process is more important than any particular plan. To paraphrase the late Alfred North Whitehead: "The process itself is the actuality." There is a fundamental difference between a *plan* and *planning*, similar as the words may be. Plans are the stationary pictures which program specifically how a certain effort is to be carried out. Planning is the moving picture which constitutes the reality, purpose, and end objective of the sequence of individual "picture plans." Plans are the commitments to a set course of action required in order to realize results. Thus, a building requires precise plans and specifications for its construction, but the process of planning with respect to the building begins with the first intention and continues during and after its completion—usually including an initial determination of requirements, financing, location, design changes during construction, utilization and modification after completion, and eventual replacement. A plan is a means or mechanism of planning, the more static blueprint necessitated by the obvious fact that if everything changed all the time, there could be few tangible accomplishments.

If a business concern is not mindful of this important difference, it is likely to establish a spurious form of corporate planning which invites disappointment. A one-time, static plan cannot solve continuous planning problems. Some companies have developed plans which defined a sound program for a particular period of time, for certain objectives, or subject to conditions remaining constant. Since time, tide, and specific objectives do not remain constant, these companies are disillusioned when they find themselves in difficulties soon after the effectuation of the plans or even before their completion. What has occurred in each case, of course, is that conditions have changed to such an extent that the plan is no longer relevant and acts as a hindrance rather than a help. Unless the planning process itself is the cardinal emphasis and plans are ancillary to it, the business will derive temporary benefit at best. Corporate planning is therefore never static. It adjusts as need be to changing conditions and goals. Fixed commitments to a given objective, procedure, or over-all blueprint of action for extended periods of time are undertaken only when they have been carefully evaluated as desirable.

Comprehensive planning involves so many variables within the business organization itself and so many indeterminate external factors that a complete analysis of the corporate situation in all its ramifications would be out of date by the time it was finished and, therefore, mainly of historical or theoretical interest. There is always more relevant information than it is possible or practical to obtain. If an attempt is made to derive complete and conclusive information, either the real-life situation for which it is intended will resolve itself in the interim or a decision must be made more or less arbitrarily. Furthermore, the cost of such an informational attempt would be prohibitive, probably exceeding the benefits anticipated from the planning itself. When time is of the essence and the advantages of anticipatory action are not to be lost, a partial answer or a scientifically unsupported judgment today may be better than a conclusive analysis next week or even tomorrow. An understanding of the inherent open-endedness of planning, a coming-to-terms with the scientifically indeterminate environment within which it must operate, and the establishment of an effective *modus operandi* are required for successful planning in general and corporate planning in particular. Both reasoned and intuitive judgments are essential ingredients.

A basic task of corporate planning is to visualize the enterprise as it could be five to ten years hence. The projective formulation embodies objectives appropriate to the environment anticipated at this future time. It represents the culmination of a series of achievements in the interim which are feasible extensions of the company's present situation, and therefore within its internal capability, and which relate realistically to the changes in its external environment expected during the interval of attainment. To this end, the business organism is extrapolated into successive stages in future time in accordance with its past, present, and desired development. From this projective examination, current objectives are adopted and a series of actions derived to achieve them. This process is repeated periodically, and objectives and plans are modified as required. Key elements and significant indicators, such as return on investment, sales per employee, the ratio of administrative to direct productive costs, or employee-separation rate, are observed constantly for internal variances and trends which call for readjustment. External developments relating to general economic conditions, technological advances, consumer habits, competition, and many other factors "outside" the business organization are followed, since they may require revisions in planning at any time.

At its best, organized corporate planning provides for as much flexibility as practicable, but at the same time establishes a direction of corporate effort and a program of specific action which increase the achievements of the business over time through a range of necessary or desirable modification. At its least, corporate planning reduces the adverse consequences of unfavorable circumstances beyond the influence of management. Any expectation that it can insure right answers signifies a fundamental misunderstanding of the nature and purpose of the process. Since it encompasses many indeterminate elements, its potentiality is a significantly improved batting *average* of analysis and decision. A perfect record is by definition the result of chance, too restrictive a scope of consideration, or too short an interval of evaluation. A relatively small improvement in this diagnostic and prognostic average, however, has a magnified effect on corporate success and profits over time.

PROCEDURE

The method of corporate planning reflects the continuous nature of the process. Its four phases—objectives, plans, integration-decision, and implementation—comprise a procedural circle of interdependence. Modifications are made as analysis, action, or results in one of these phases call for compensating adjustments in any one or all of the others. Both feedback and feedforward are involved. An unexpected operating decision may require a change of objectives and plan; a sound plan anticipates insofar as possible the problems of implementation. Were it feasible and desirable, all things considered, the procedural system would allow constant adjustment. In businesses dependent on a consumer demand both difficult to predict and discontinuous, such as the manufacture of specialty women's accessories and children's toys, planning is as short-range and readjustable as practical and profitable. A strategy of "riding the wave" of the unstable demand is often adopted. In other enterprises such as insurance and book publishing, longer-range corporate plans normally need only periodic review. In automobile manufacture or private utilities, crucial commitments are made several years in advance of sales because of the lead time required for production tooling in the first instance; land acquisition, facilities construction, and the installation of supply lines in the second. Whatever the particular situation, when corporate planning is applied effectively, the average frequency and amplitude of adjustment are smaller than the more disruptive ups-and-downs which occur without it. And, as corporate planning becomes a familiar part of management, the range of adjustment beyond that inherent in the business environment narrows as the internal inefficiencies to be expected during its initiation are ironed out.

Objectives (Figure 1)

Since the purpose of planning is to provide a rational direction of activities toward established goals, a plan cannot be drawn without objectives. "Within an organization . . . problems seldom come with solutions or clear goals attached. The decision maker must define the specific objective that will yield the larger goals of the enterprise. . . . Such goals are not final; they are instrumental."[1] They may be clearly stated, assumed but not identified, or even unrecognized; in any event, they are implicit in the plan itself. The derivation of corporate objectives involves several steps in logical sequence.

A statement or representation of the recent history of the company and its current situation is composed. It includes information on financial matters, sales, distribution, inventories, products, production, research, personnel, facilities, and other primary elements of the business. Descriptive data are selected to portray as succinctly as possible the comparative condition of the business at different periods in time. Verbal statements explain those aspects of corporate activity which cannot be quantified meaningfully. Important outside influences on the situation of the company are included. In short, an analytical expression is devised, as concise as consistent with comprehensive coverage, which depicts the recent development of the company within its external environment in all essential aspects.

The comprehensive representation of past and present is extrapolated to show the probable development of the enterprise at successive stages in the future if its external environment and internal situation remain the same and no deliberate changes are initiated. This is an extrapolation of existing "momentum," showing what would likely happen if nothing occurred to change current trends and intentions. It establishes a base reference for analytical comparison and extension.

This "artificial" projection is modified to reflect those known circumstances within and outside the business which are beyond its control and will affect its future operations significantly. It shows the probable development of the corporate organism with only those changes dictated by the relatively independent variables to which it must adjust whether it wishes or not. Included would

Illustrative

GENERAL CORPORATE OBJECTIVES

Semiconductor Manufacturer—1961

Remain an ethical manufacturer of semiconductor devices, providing customers with full value and establishing and maintaining a reputation for fair and honest business practices.

Provide a productive and satisfying work environment for employees, offering career opportunities for personal development and advancement.

Maximize return on investment, consistent with growth objectives, and operate to protect that investment. The Company has as its objective 15% profit before tax and 30% return on stockholders' equity and long-term debt. In order to maximize long-term growth and profitability, remain a leader in the semiconductor industry in advanced technology, device development, and engineering.

Maintain a basic technological capability permitting the Company to develop, produce, and market a specific product within one year. Development is directed toward products which will have a significant market within 2 to 5 years.

Attain a sales volume among the top 5 companies in the semiconductor industry, participating with a broad line of products in approximately 75% of all markets, and competing for a minimum of 15% in each of the markets.

Participate in industrial, military, and consumer markets. Although emphasis is on the military market, the percentage of industrial business will be increased. Consumer electronic and entertainment devices will be marketed.

Manufacture semiconductor devices in high quantity and at minimum cost consistent with customer quality and volume requirements. Continue to develop, produce, and market high-performance devices.

Maintain a standard-performance product line which can be produced and marketed at low cost and high volume. This product line will employ the technology developed for the high-performance products rather than depend upon new technology.

Develop a product line evolving from discrete components to solid-state circuits, sub-assemblies, and simple equipment including passive components. These products will include new-type solid-state devices as they begin to displace existing products.

Obtain more contract sales, particularly in areas where contract programs parallel company programs and product plans.

Consider domestic and foreign markets as one integrated world market, with interrelated technical, manufacturing, and marketing opportunities. The Company will exploit the advantages of foreign manufacturing and marketing.

FIGURE 1

be such external variables as general socio-economic and political trends, foreign and domestic competition, technological developments, or changes in consumer behavior. Internal factors to be considered might include trends in costs, replacement of plant and equipment, or average product life. This projection establishes directions of necessary action and provides a partial picture of the limits of possible change beyond which the company would be undertaking objectives inimical to its best interests or beyond its capabilities.

With this more realistic extrapolation as background, the company formulates an image of itself as it would like to be some years hence in order to most successfully fit the situation it anticipates at this future time—with respect to environmental developments and its own best advancement. The importance of this wishful formulation lies, of course, in the greater range of change and speculative consideration it encourages. Any need for a significantly different company in the longer-range future is more likely identified in this way than by incremental extrapolation from the present. The perspective of desirable development portrayed by this optimum conceptualization persists throughout the process of its modification to conform with the potentialities and limitations of the business institution as it is in reality. It reduces projective myopia and unconstructive inhibitions in anticipating the shape of things to come. It promotes the selection of practical paths which permit seizing an opportunity which has been identified in the wishful formulation, if and when it occurs.

By adjustment back and forth between the "ideal" picturization of itself as it would like to be in the future, and the previous projection emphasizing the inescapable "facts of life," the company arrives at a combination of essential, desirable, and possible objectives. The result of this analytical adjustment is the corporate formulation of longer-range objectives and general requisites for their attainment which provides the necessary guidelines for the operational plans of the company's primary units and those functional plans cutting across organizational lines. It represents the desires expressed by these components to the extent consistent with the best interests of the institution as a whole. It is a formal statement of direction and intention, annually reviewed and extended three to five years into the future but subject to revision whenever desirable. Its premises and assumptions are clearly stated, and the framework of integration and alternative choice from which it was derived is explained. This official statement of direction is a cardinal contribution of corporate management to the process of organized planning. It is the procedural cornerstone of the comprehensive plan composed of all the component plans developed within the company in accordance with the goals and guidelines it establishes. Its form and content vary considerably among different businesses and individual companies.

This sequence of analytical steps outlines the logical procedure of formulating corporate objectives for the first time. Only in medium- or larger-size companies is it feasible to prepare separate analyses for each step. In smaller businesses, this deductive sequence is telescoped within the mind and applied subjectively in the simplified analysis of objectives required by limited resources and appropriate to the smaller scale of activities. Once the method is an established part of the management process, the statement of objectives is modified, rather than drastically revised, at most annual reviews. The "ideal" formulation is re-examined only every few years. For unless the business is volatile in nature, unexpected operating situations develop, or there is major change in the external environment, frequent shifts of corporate policy and direction are of course more disruptive than productive of profits. Several years are needed to implement most corporate objectives. Commitments are made involving time, money, and people which are reoriented or abandoned only at considerable cost. The necessity of minimum stability and continuity of organizational effort places a premium on well-organized planning and projective analysis. Business must chart a course between the Scylla of insufficient attention to the future on the one side, and the Charybdis of predictive uncertainty on the other.

At the topmost level of management, corporate objectives are under continual scrutiny. What is the nature of the business desired by the owners and management five or ten years hence? Almost certainly there will be changes, since there is general agreement that a business cannot long remain static in a dynamic economy. Is it a stronger position in the same business with a larger share of the market? Is diversification or some other gradual change in the character of the business in order, such as different proportions of direct-government, indirect-government, commercial, or direct-consumer sales? What may be the impact of scientific and technical advance, of automation, of industrial progress occurring throughout the world? Is the present organizational structure appropriate for the future? If not, what series of cumulative steps will gradually produce the desired change?

To some, because of uncertainties, it may seem impractical to take the long view, but the chances of survival and success are enhanced by a formulation of objectives and programs of accomplishment to achieve them. "During 1958 significant progress was made in the planning effort. Five-year forecasts prepared by the Company's business units were carefully analyzed in terms of the outlook of the industries served and prospects for sales, profits, and use of capital. This work will proceed on a continuing basis and can be expected to result in the establishment of balanced corporate objectives."[2] Perhaps the greatest discouragement to this approach is its difficulty. It is anything but easy to consider the indefinite future, to evaluate shifting factors, identify trends, and somehow correlate many variables. It is much easier to throw up one's hands and turn to immediate matters with the satisfaction of definite answers. Occasionally, the attitude may exist which is epitomized by the remark attributed to a congressman: "Why should I worry about posterity? What has posterity done for me?" Let our successors take care of their own problems. Unfortunately for those who would adopt this viewpoint, corporate responsibilities are related to the institutional life of the business rather than our own span, and most companies are vital to too many people in too many ways to permit such a management attitude. Enlightened management must take the long and the broad view, and wrestle with it as best it can. The planning process makes this easier and more successful.

Plans

In accordance with corporate objectives, each component of the business prepares a plan for the ensuing year, with extensions for each of several additional years. Activities which involve long amortization periods, or for other reasons should be phased over more than three to five years, are extended further into the future. The plan for the forthcoming fiscal year is sufficiently precise to serve as a specific operational target and criterion of performance.

Naturally, the plan projections for each additional year are progressively less definite, although they will include certain positive commitments or precise forecasts which will extend well into the future.

How far down the levels of administration unit plans are prepared depends on the size and type of business, as well as its particular organizational and operating characteristics. If there is no advantage to be gained in efficiency, exercise of responsibility, evaluation of performance, or training, the programs of smaller units are not treated separately but are part of the formal plan of a bigger unit. The larger the number of distinct plans, the more time-consuming their collection, processing, correlation, modification, and subsequent review for variances. There is a point of equilibrium between the advantages of widespread participation in the corporate planning process and the cost, delay, and administrative complications of too elaborate a management system.

Ordinarily, the proposed plans of a smaller unit include such information as the expected volume and value of its product or service; costs and profitability; personnel required; machinery, equipment, and spatial facilities needed; and specific programs of improvement in management-supervision, performance-productivity, morale, organization, and other matters influencing operating achievement. These plans are not limited to activities which can be quantified and expressed directly and immediately in terms of profit and loss. There are many objectives which are important even though they are less tangible, with deferred benefits for which it is difficult to establish a clear-cut correlation of cause and effect. An example is a program to gradually change employee disinterest into a constructive attitude which should in time be reflected in profits. "The other [six months' plan] is a 'word plan,' a verbal analysis of his department's strengths and weaknesses and what he proposes to do about each. ('We think that's even more important than the sales budget. . . .')"[3]

Except for the first year after the system is inaugurated, these unit plans are not composed *de novo*. They are drawn within a framework of objectives, policies, constraints, and commitments established by the planning and operational experience of earlier years; and they are shaped to a considerable extent by the specific experience of the previous year. Was this prior plan too ambitious as shown by its *post facto* comparison with performance? Were certain aims achieved sooner than anticipated, thus permitting more rapid scheduling? Or was some intended program of improvement revealed to be so impractical that it should be discontinued, at least for the time being? Have there been changes in corporate objectives which call for modifications in the current plan? Plans provide a basis for comparisons which are impossible if intentions are expressed informally or not at all.

It is worthwhile at this point in our preliminary description of corporate planning to note the benefits derived by each unit in developing an annual plan and projections. Most of these benefits apply equally to the higher levels of management we shall be discussing shortly. First and foremost, many of the individuals comprising the unit, and especially its responsible head, are stimulated to think ahead. This may seem a formal and elaborate method of promoting forethought, if we assume everyone does this anyway. In some instances, this is certainly the case, but if we review our experience and observations with this characteristic in mind, we find that thinking ahead in a deliberate, organized, and purposeful fashion is as much the exception as the rule. Undoubtedly, most people have thoughts about the future of the organizational unit for which they are responsible; yet not only are these often piecemeal and sporadic, but they may not be translated into a specific program of attainment with a time schedule of cumulative accomplishment. There is a natural tendency to defer anticipatory decisions until the need becomes self-evident and preparatory action is almost forced by the evolving situation. By this time the advantages of forethought are in large part lost. By its very existence, a formal process of organized planning tends to insure that the different units of the business are thinking ahead to the extent of their capability.

Planning also promotes the comprehensive view. The preparation of a unit plan not only necessitates forethought but requires that all significant elements of the unit be identified and considered. Similarly, the corporate plan requires that the various components of the business are integrated and projected in concert. As a consequence of this higher-level examination of interrelationships, the different units of the company are made more aware of what is going on about and above them. This increase of information reduces organizational isolation and confusion, and promotes a constructive identification with the problems and potentialities which are characteristic of the business as a whole.

Plans provide a measure of performance—which, parenthetically, is sometimes the reason for a strong resistance to the idea. The individual or group is asked what it can and should achieve, and its performance is compared periodically with its own statement of feasible accomplishment. This is not a rigid comparative measure, since extenuating circumstances are taken into account, but it is the best practical mechanism now available. Plans tend, therefore, to increase the level of achievement, both because they contribute to efficient management and because unobtrusively resting on one's laurels is made more difficult. They also promote careful analysis, since plans do not normally spring full-blown from the heads of supervisorial Zeuses but are the product of objective evaluation, which takes time and deliberate application.

The next steps in the planning procedure are the formulation of departmental plans from unit plans, and of divisional plans from departmental plans. In larger organizations, divisional plans may be combined into groups. In accomplishing this integration, the responsible managers may have to modify or call for a restudy of some of the unit plans. The cost of the new equipment scheduled by all of them in combination may exceed the money available to the division. Conflicting programs may need to be harmonized, or perhaps a choice must be made between basically different intentions. At this level of conjunction, the departments or divisions are keeping each other in mind, as did the smaller subordinate units of which they are composed in their planning.

As we proceed upward, the responses to over-all corporate objectives become more apparent as they are accumulated. Divisional plans usually present projected data on production, sales-distribution, new products, inventories, and research; costs, income, return on investment, capital expenditures, profit, working capital, cash flow, and total investment; personnel; physical facilities; and other primary elements of the activity. Statements are included describing actions and intentions toward objectives which do not lend themselves to numerical expression. These plans of the major units of the business—departments, divisions, groups, companies, or even groups of companies as the case may be—are forwarded to corporate management.

Integration-Decision

Corporate management performs the final integration and makes the final decisions. First, it must evaluate each of the major component plans. Is it accurate and consistent within itself? Certainly this is very probably the case, but it is the responsibility of corporate management to confirm by review that there are no significant errors or omissions; the probable penalty to the company of a substantial mistake is too great to ignore. Is each component plan in accord with corporate objectives? For example, if a corporate program of product diversification has been decided upon, can the efforts to this end be identified within the plans and projections of the major units? If a gradual reduction in overhead costs has been requested, is this apparent in the cost data shown in the proposed plans? Are the capital expenditures requested *in toto* beyond the current capacity of the business? If so, must suggested budgets be reduced or new financing arranged? Are the intentions of some unit relating to personnel or advertising inimical to the general policies of the company? Certain programs and time schedules may be mutually inconsistent, or combine to produce an undesirable peak load. One decentralized division may want to undertake an increase in wage or salary levels which would, however, create serious personnel problems in other divisions nearby which cannot afford such an increase. Two divisions may have overlooked a cooperative arrangement to their mutual advantage. Or the company may want to build up a smaller division which has the potentiality of profitable growth and would provide a desirable diversification of sales. Besides the funds they would forego because of the increased allocation to the smaller division, other units of the company may be called upon for indirect support. The over-all view and comprehensive analysis required for such a conclusion are not the province of divisional or group managers. Furthermore, the identification, concentration, and competitive drive which contribute to their own successful performance preclude the broader objectivity requisite to such corporate decisions.

The result of corporate integration may call for modification of the component plans. When this is accomplished, they are combined into a comprehensive plan for the business as a whole which is the performance target for the ensuing fiscal year and the official referent for an additional two to four years. As indicated earlier, the process of planning does not stop with the formal adoption of plans, to be resumed a year later. The major components and their subordinate units adjust their shorter-range objectives as experience and circumstances dictate. In this way, planning is continuous, and current data are available at all times in the event an unforeseen development of major significance requires revision of the corporate plan in midyear. And early identification is more likely in the case of important trends which may call for a reorientation of projections at the next formal review.

As has been described, analysis, integration, and decision are applied throughout the corporate planning procedure from the smallest organizational roots. Each unit, department, and division head has worked his way through to his own conclusions and proposed plan. But the most crucial analyses and far-reaching decisions are made by corporate executives—the apex of the triangle, if we visualize the administrative organization in this way. These decisions will affect the operations and profitability of the entire business, both immediately and for the future. Whereas a certain percentage of error in planning at lower levels is less consequential because of the smaller size and more limited activities of the units to which it applies, the same average error at the topmost level can create severe and long-lasting difficulties. As will be discussed at some length in subsequent chapters, the performance of the relatively small group of executives comprising top management is vital.

In today's business world, line executives in high positions are hard-pressed to attend to the hundred and one operating demands on their time. The higher their position, the more frequently they must concentrate on operational matters of such importance that they must be resolved at their level of management without delay. The time available to them for longer-range planning is limited. Except in small businesses, they do not formulate and maintain personally the factual background for corporate planning. A flow of information and a system of analysis are organized, in accordance with procedures they approve, to provide the evaluative materials needed for judgment and decision. More and more, small planning staffs are formed to receive and correlate component plans, distill the most indicative data, integrate and analyze these data, project the resulting information into successive stages of future time, and finally present the composite corporate situation and the probable results of alternative courses of action. At the same time, the corporate planning staff is collecting information, generating special studies, and maintaining selected facts and figures relating to the national economy, governmental policies, financial trends, industry-wide competition, and other developments which comprise the external environment within which business plans are drawn. In this way, the time and energies of the chief decision makers are focused on the most crucial and difficult of their responsibilities: evaluation, choice, decision, and action.

Throughout the organization, there is this combination of line management and staff support. Whereas at the topmost level of a medium-size company a small group may be involved, only one or two people may be devoting full time to staff planning within each division. Staff planning within departments, depending on their size and type of work, is probably a part-time activity combined with other duties. In such an interdependent working relationship, it is self-evident that a constructive attitude on the part of line executives toward planning and the utility of analytical staff assistance is prerequisite to success. If they do not believe in the potentialities of planning, or if they think they can find the time to do it as successfully by themselves, it is probably doomed to failure in the first instance and is significantly limited in the second. There was a time years ago when executive managers could almost fulfill the unrealistic expectation that they know all and do all by themselves. With the increasing complexity of business and industry, the growth of the average size of the corporate unit, and progress in scientific management, the absence of both presumption and expectation is more characteristic of the managerial scene today.

Implementation

Plans are of little value if they are not followed and carried out to the extent practicable. Because of the widespread participation in planning and formal approval of plans already discussed, there is general recognition throughout the company of the operational commitment they represent. Plans are developed and accepted as a basis for the measurement of performance. Each responsible manager has proposed his own program of accomplishment within the context and commitments of the rest of the business. When organized planning is inaugurated, there is likely to be considerable difference between unit plans and performance. With each year of experience, this difference lessens. Before long, the process and procedure are so well understood that there is much less variation between plan and achievement, except when circumstances or decisions beyond the control of a particular component force a change in performance. An efficient flow of information insures that both the need for and the results of such variances are noted promptly and planning projections are modified as need be.

Since organized planning normally sets goals beyond those undertaken without it, productive capabilities are applied to the full for their effectuation. The manager knows where he is heading and can chart his course accordingly. Because his intentions have been correlated with those of others, his plan will less likely be vitiated by mistakes on the part of his colleagues or their failure to look ahead. One of his most difficult decisions in implementation is when and how much to revise his plan when the premises on which it is predicated are modified by circumstance. He does not want to lose the benefits of the commitments and accomplishments already made in accordance with his program of production. On the other hand, if directions have shifted sufficiently, continued achievement along the old lines may turn into serious liabilities in the future. There is no absolute escape from the horns of this dilemma. But the effects of enforced changes of plan in midstream are cushioned by the prior application of accepted principles of sound management, such as the axiom expressed by Publilius Syrus over 2,000 years ago: "It is a bad plan that admits of no modification." If flexibility has been incorporated in the original plan, the impact of radical reorientation is mitigated by the feasibility of at least a minimum turnaround time, and moderate adjustments are often absorbed with less scrapping of what has gone before.

Longer-range predictive certainty is by no means essential to successful comprehensive planning. Of greater significance is the regular reporting of recent history, an integrated picture of the current situation, and the extrapolation of present trends a short time into the future. With these regularly revised, shorter-range projections, the lead time for advance planning and action is reduced, but the reliability of forecasts is increased. If the program of implementation is sensitive to subtle shifts in the wind, if it is organized for rapid modification and adjustments are made when practicable and worthwhile, the basic function and benefits of the process are realized. As with a sailboat beating upwind, although many tacks may be made in accordance with shifts in the wind, the resultant track of the vessel is always generally toward its objective, and a different sailing plan is not required unless there is a major change in the weather. Naturally, the longer-range, more reliable, and more comprehensive the projections, the more definite the planning of business operations can be.

There is sometimes a tendency for those in direct charge of making the business's product to consider themselves the "doers," as contrasted with the planning staff. And it is certainly true that the line manager has his unique capabilities and specific methods of performing his designated task. The staff planner also has his methods of organizing and doing his job. Because they work together, operating executives and those engaged in staff analysis learn each other's special capabilities and emphasis. The line supervisor recognizes that the activities which are his primary responsibility, and therefore naturally his main interest and concern, are affected by objectives, decisions, and events beyond his scope and control. The planning analyst recognizes that planning which does not take operating realities completely into account may be almost worthless and may discredit the process.

COMMENT

The process and procedure of corporate planning may appear at first thought to be complex and paper-heavy, but a fully developed program is not achieved overnight. Rather, it is normally the product of gradual development over a period of several years. As a result, what indeed might be difficult to digest quickly becomes step by step a regular part of the conduct of the business. By the time the fully developed process is in effect, the way of thinking and acting which it represents has become part and parcel of the general corporate attitude, and the procedures involved are familiar and not difficult in themselves. The difficulties involved are those inherent in forethought and anticipatory action, and these are of course inevitable when undertaking anything beyond the minimum or the ordinary.

The system is formal in the sense that there is an organized sequence and time schedule for the formulation of objectives, plan preparation and processing, integration and decision, and implementation. But in smaller businesses particularly, or in special situations, corporate planning is not formalized to this extent. Much of the process is performed within the minds of the primary managers. The essential requirement is a thorough understanding of the approach and process of planning in general. This is fortunate, since small business is more limited in the costs of the administrative overhead it can afford. However, management functions are desirable additions to overhead when they increase sales, decrease expenses, or are otherwise worth their cost. This is never easy to demonstrate, but it applies as much to planning as to other management methods or administrative services.

The question may also have occurred: Does this process and procedure of corporate planning necessitate a high degree of centralization and control? No, it does not, because the function of planning and decision making is shared progressively by many people and can be as decentralized as any other activity. In fact, a greater degree of decentralization is feasible, since plans serve to define the responsibilities and necessary limitations of organizational autonomy. The determination of objectives, the making of planning decisions, and the approval of specific plans can be performed by executive committee as well as single individuals. What *is* necessarily implied by corporate planning is a higher degree of purposeful integration and projection toward agreed-upon objectives for the company as a whole than is otherwise likely. This is certainly to the corporate good.

REFERENCES CITED

[1] Robert D. Calkins (President, Brookings Institution), "The Decision Process in Administration," *Business Horizons,* Fall 1959 (Vol. 2, No. 3), pp. 21, 22.

[2] *1958 Annual Report,* American Machine & Foundry Company, p. 16.

[3] Ralph Lazarus (President, Federated Department Stores), "The First Family of Retailing," *Forbes Business and Finance,* 15 March 1961 (Vol. 87, No. 6), p. 21.

Chapter III

Basic Prerequisites

If corporate planning is a sound endeavor producing improved returns over time, why is it not recognized and applied whenever possible? Why, in some cases, is it flatly rejected? The answers to these questions are contained in the attitudes of the most influential managers or owners of the business toward planning in general, and their acceptance of certain fundamental precepts of the comprehensive planning process. If their attitude is negative because of a misunderstanding of what is involved, disbelief in the value of planning, or reasons of self-interest, the establishment of effective corporate planning will be difficult and prolonged at best. "The most important requirement . . . is that the company's top management must really believe in a forward-planning program."[1]

Without certain prerequisites of compatible policy and constructive acceptance, not only is the effort unproductive but the process itself may be discredited without valid reason until memories of the abortive attempt fade into the past or new leadership is at the helm. There are situations when it is best to postpone the establishment of corporate planning or minimize the activity until an environment is attained within the company which favors its success. "The reasons for [Olin Mathieson's] disappointing showing are wound up in the personalities and management methods of the men who built up and brought together the original two halves of the company. . . . Tensions at the top made it difficult, if not impossible, to work out consistent and effective policies for the new company and its basketful of diverse businesses spread throughout the country and overseas."[2]

IMPLICIT ASSUMPTIONS

Deferred Benefits

It is axiomatic that planning presupposes a willingness to spend time, energy, and money in the present toward results which will not be realized for some time. Furthermore, these benefits are not assured but can only be anticipated on the basis of prior experience and careful consideration of probabilities. Implicit in this approach is the objective of improving profits over time, rather than maximizing immediate return. Clearly, the type and the projective range of planning are quite different for these mutually exclusive alternatives.

Optimization of profits does not mean that maximum possible profits are not sought for a particular product, service, or component within the company. But, as a matter of course, most corporations with an indefinite life expectancy provide a greater assurance of continued profitability in years to come by the utilization of a portion of their current resources to this end. One of the most crucial functions of executive management is to analyze alternative ways in which corporate resources can be employed, and to determine the allocation of effort most likely to improve profits over time. To maintain sales growth, ". . . A&P, with sales approaching $5 billion, deliberately holds its profit margin at about 1 per cent."[3] "[AMF's chairman], looking hard into the future, took a firm step in preparation by setting up the company's first central research staff. This year [1960] AMF is budgeting no less than 4% of total sales [to research and development]. . . ."[4] "I could show you profits tomorrow if I wanted to run this show out of my hat and cut back our research and market development. . . . Since the only thing we'll ultimately have to sell is knowhow, I intend to plow back whatever is necessary to stay ahead."[5] There are, of course, numerous examples of current investment for the future in ordinary business operations: raw-material reserves, new machinery, institutional advertising, depreciation, executive training, provision for facilities expansion—to name but a few.

Except for the speculative entrepreneur and business in a critical situation of survival, an approach of maximum immediate return without concern for the future is rare in the business world today. But the policy of deferred benefits is not universal. There are enterprises with the primary purpose of quick turnover and immediate profit. ". . . Production and merchandising policies were simple: he played by ear. In good years he went all out on production, sold to marginal customers to gain a higher markup and fatter profit. In bad years [he] squeezed out a profit, no matter how small, by stringent economy. . . . But in 1954, as sales fell 14 per cent and profit 64 per cent, it was apparent that increased competition was becoming a serious operating problem."[6] The combine which acquires control of a company to inflate its value and "get out quickly" is not interested in the effectiveness of corporate planning within the captive business. Owners intending an early sale are not inclined to give much attention to the longer-range future of the enterprise. The interest of executives anticipating early retirement often shifts from corporate to personal plans as the date of retirement approaches. Such circumstances do not promote active concern with the type of continuous comprehensive planning under discussion here. Planning activity is present in these exceptional situations, but it is special in nature, it is limited, and it has personal rather than corporate purposes.

Surplus Resources

If the principle of extended benefits is accepted policy, the availability of at least minimal time and effort is a corollary axiom of planning in general and a prerequisite of corporate planning specifically. Not only must funds be available for activities which do not produce an immediate return, but line executives must be willing and able to take a portion of their time from the management of current operations for planning several years ahead. Self-evident as this may seem, we have only to recall from our own experience managers who profess to believe in organized forethought, but somehow never find time to translate their intention into execution.

When a business is in such a precarious position that it must employ its total resources today to insure its survival tomorrow, its planning will necessarily be very short-term, restricted, informal, and in large part intuitive. But time is of the essence in the normal corporate effort. With few exceptions, thinking through the complex questions posed in comprehensive planning cannot be accomplished in a rush or with continual distractions to untrack the mind. As Henry Ford once expressed it in his inimitable way: "If you are always terribly rushed, the trouble with you is that you don't think enough."[7] Analytical achievement is difficult enough in a favorable environment. This is to suggest neither time immemorial nor an ivy-covered refuge, but simply the minimum span of time and undivided attention needed by each individual to formulate and resolve difficult problems.

In medium- and large-size companies, sufficient resources must be available to support some staff personnel who devote most of their time to organized planning. These can be the same people who commonly perform staff functions at the corporate level of management—provided they act collectively in terms of an established procedure of comprehensive rather than functional planning. Usually, however, several new staff positions are needed for individuals with the combination of breadth, insight, and professional capability to perform the analytical integration of the diverse activities and intentions within the company which is the primary purpose of corporate planning.

A company engaged in comprehensive planning evaluates its surplus resources not only in cash and credit but in terms of executive attitudes, management time and capability, the particular characteristics of the business in which it is engaged, and its objectives. From this examination, it can determine the level of effort and expenditure for corporate planning appropriate to its situation and properly related to the potential gains it expects from this organized activity. In this way, it avoids economic waste, disappointment, or disillusionment.

Consideration of the Longer-Range Future

The problems of projecting into the future, well known to every business man, sometimes inhibit the advance decision and prior commitment implicit in planning. If the rewards of projective analysis are to be realized, preparatory action cannot be too little or too late. Risks are always involved, but it is a function of planning to identify these risks and provide a better basis for objective evaluation and subjective judgment than would otherwise be the case. Planning is always a matter of estimating the odds. If it engages in corporate planning, the business enterprise must therefore be willing to act with reference to the longer-range and more uncertain future.

There are companies which choose not to look beyond the immediate future. The situation must be so nearly certain, or the accumulation of evidence so conclusive before decisions are made, that the advantages of anticipatory action are lost. This policy of swinging with the current and not anticipating the tide is usually the outgrowth of several unhappy experiences in the past, more often than not the consequence of unrealistic expectations, wishful forecasting, or unsound projective technique. The conclusion is drawn that forecasting beyond the immediate future is *ipso facto* impossible; therefore, the projective aspects of planning are of little value.

Ordinarily, this attitude is not stated explicitly but is expressed as a desire to leave well enough alone, to preserve the policies and procedures which have yielded satisfactory results in the past, or in other disguises and rationalizations. Needless to say, this position is possible only when the type of activity, business situation, or time period of evaluation permits the making of adequate profits with little analysis and decision. When present, unfortunately, this fatalistic attitude is likely to be maintained and even strengthened until some change in the competitive or market picture suddenly reveals the abnormality of the uniquely favorable business situation —and at the same time the value of longer-range forethought.

By its very nature, planning is the antithesis of the *status quo*. It is a process of examination and re-examination, of continual consideration of the future, of constant searching for more effective methods of accomplishment and improved results. Elements are fixed for varying periods of time, but corporate planning itself is always active and progressive. This is in sharp contrast with the concept of passive stability, of moving only when necessary or when all signs point to a foregone conclusion. There have been times in the history of such American businesses as banking and railroading when management inertia and lack of foresight were all too characteristic of their direction. This attitude prevails in some companies today and undoubtedly will be found in others in the future. Comprehensive planning cannot prosper in such a climate, for it represents so basically different a philosophy of management that it constitutes an unmistakable challenge to any prolonged policy of preserving the existing state of affairs.

Management Abilities and Effort

Corporate planning imposes additional demands upon executive managers both as individuals and as the collective group most responsible for future success. It calls for their best efforts. They must utilize their analytical abilities to the utmost. They must consider and reach conclusions concerning many indeterminate variables. Judgments based on incomplete information are required on important questions one would naturally like to defer until more indicative data are available. Anticipatory decisions must be made well in advance of the time when it will be known whether they were right or wrong. Time must be found for analytical study as well as active management direction, and the procedural steps of comprehensive planning must be accomplished periodically according to the prescribed schedule. In short, it is easier for the individual not to plan than to plan as extensively as is practical and profitable over time from the viewpoint of the corporation as an institution.

Corporate planning is not, therefore, an endeavor for tired management. There are transitional times when a company simply may not have the requisite managerial energy. And certainly, if the managerial spirit is as unwilling as the flesh is weak, the difficulty is compounded.[8] "Until a short time ago, a member of the Finance and Policy Committee privately admits, 'Woolworth had tired leadership, men close to retirement, afraid to try anything.' "[9] When executive attitudes toward the idea and demands of corporate planning are negative for the most part, a limited program of accomplishment is the best that can be expected until its cumulative effect and normal executive replacement permit acceleration. The management group may have to be upgraded or better balanced to provide the individual and composite capability required for comprehensive planning. This too takes time, whether achieved by recruitment or in-service training.

CONCEPTUAL COMPATIBILITY

Absence of Rational Misconceptions

When a company is borne along on the crest of a wave of fortunate circumstance, the potential benefits of longer-range planning are sometimes discounted. Current sales and profits are so promising, and the future apparently so bright, that more deliberate forethought seems unnecessary. The justification usually advanced is that it never pays to rock a winning boat. Why spend money from profits for more management when results are satisfactory?

This conclusion is logically sound *only* for a limited time or for certain components of the business. To be sure, as mentioned previously, no accomplishment is possible if there is perpetual change with no stabilization whatsoever. But the extension of this reasoning to the company as a whole is fallacious, because no favorable business situation is inherently permanent and all elements of the enterprise do not maintain themselves fortuitously in an optimum state of individual and collective equilibrium for any extended period of time. Since both the external environment and the internal conditions of a business change continually, a policy of preserving the *status quo* must produce difficulties sooner or later. The reckoning may be long deferred, but usually the adjustment is correspondingly severe and prolonged.

In hard times, planning may be discounted for different reasons. It is sometimes argued that there is no time for anything but the solution of the immediate and pressing problems at hand. In times of crisis, every effort must indeed be devoted to keeping the corporate ship afloat; however, not only is short-range operations planning required for this emergency action, but some decision based on the longer-range view is usually the key to extrication from a condition of continuing crisis. Comprehensive planning for a business in its infancy or in an immediately precarious position is clearly different from planning under more normal circumstances, but the company which cannot benefit from this activity in any shape or form is indeed unique or *in extremis,* for corporate planning can reduce the losses of involuntary liquidation as well as serve the purposes of growth. It is often forgotten that the value of planning is by no means limited to expansion. In the military sphere, for example, plans for retreat are as vital as those for attack; they spell the difference between retreat and defeat.

Although logically indefensible, a negative attitude toward corporate planning is more understandable under adverse circumstances. The air is tinged with discouragement, personal problems and the possible consequence of continued bad times loom large for each individual, and morale is lowered by the general uncertainty. Under these conditions, the positive thinking needed for constructive analysis and purposeful action directed toward the future is certainly impaired.

Human tendencies in the assignment of credit or causality also act to discount planning. ". . . A man may sometimes be given credit for wisdom and promoted to high rank because he has been infallibly right when in fact he has only been infallibly lucky."[10] The role of chance is often forgotten. An unusually large sale is made, an advantageous purchase becomes possible, or some other favorable event occurs mainly by chance. At the time, the predominant role of chance is recognized and acknowledged by those concerned. As time passes, however, a change occurs. The element of chance is accorded less and less weight, and more and more is attributed to individual acumen. Naturally, this acts to discount the value of organized planning, for the ultimate conclusion is, in effect, that good fortune is the product of personal wisdom; poor fortune is bad luck. Planning more deliberate in nature is not needed in the first instance, and it cannot help in the second. An exaggerated illustration of this attitude is the roulette player with unshakable confidence in his "system." He attributes his successes to its magic, and forgets his losses or ascribes them to bad luck. Once this attitude is implanted in the individual or organization, it is dispelled only when circumstances force a more realistic recognition of the forces beyond the control of the company which affect its success. Not only does corporate planning seek to identify these forces; but, insofar as possible, plans are drawn in terms of the real expectancy of chance events rather than any illusions of cause and effect.

Realistic Expectations

Executive managers carry a heavy load of responsibilities in the business world today. Analytical evaluation becomes more difficult as business becomes more complex, interdependent, and sensitive to a wide range of internal conditions and external forces. Analytical mistakes are more costly as profit margins narrow. There is never enough time to do—or do well—all the things which need to be done. As a consequence, there is a natural tendency to be hopeful about any approach which sounds as if it might provide reliable answers to crucial questions fraught with uncertainty, or any device which purports to remove some burden from overloaded shoulders. Sometimes this hope is extended into overexpectation, or translated into a wishful evaluation of new developments as potential panaceas. The less tangible the development, the greater this tendency to misjudge its nature and underestimate its limitations.

Business history is dotted with examples. There were those who hoped that improved methods of cost accounting might in themselves solve cost problems, or that more deliberate management recognition and administrative representation might eliminate the root difficulties of personnel and labor relations. Others half expected techniques derived from individual and social psychology to provide infallible guides to personnel selection and employee relations. For a while, decentralization was regarded by some as an administrative cure-all. Consultant firms have been retained in costly attempts to obtain from the "expert from out of town" the kind of analytical appraisal and specific recommendation which are so integral a part of the business's operation that considerable internal capability and accomplishment are essential before worthwhile benefits can be expected from external scrutiny. The current emphasis on research and development is misinterpreted by some companies that view it as an automatic master key to corporate success, not recognizing the many problems involved in translating this expensive and somewhat elusive activity into profitable new products; ". . . R & D has become a status symbol in many areas of business today."[11] Such overexpectation is usually associated with general management techniques or broad efforts, rather than specific devices or procedures subject to more precise evaluation.

There is some evidence of unrealistic expectations with respect to corporate planning. The obvious necessity of many forms of functional planning, and the virtual impossibility of challenging the good sense of the endeavor in general, can be deceiving to the extent that they obscure the inherent difficulties of an integrative-projective process as broad in scope as comprehensive planning. In the same sense in which we often conclude that improved "education" is the ultimate solution to so many societal problems today, the word "planning" is similarly deceptive in its semantic suggestion of simplicity. What kind of education? What type of planning? How achieved? At what cost? Frequently underestimated are the time and continuous application required to achieve effective planning, the present limitations in our capability to integrate the many disparate elements involved, and human resistance to its establishment as a formal organized activity. Any assumption that corporate planning in and of itself can bring about dramatic success over and above the potentialities of the business organization and its external environment is of course unrealistic indeed.

EXECUTIVE ACCEPTANCE

The fact that corporate planning is pre-eminently a fluid process engenders its own difficulties of acceptance. Many people prefer to deal with concrete facts and fixed programs which permit positive judgments. Because they are much easier to comprehend and manage than a relatively indefinite and constantly changing process, it is not surprising that there is sometimes a natural reluctance to undertake the more demanding task of continuous comprehensive planning. Collectively, executive management today is in the transitional phase of adjusting its attitudes and methods to the greater fluidity of modern business affairs. Whereas the simpler business problems of yesteryear were more closely definable and comparatively constant, we now recognize not only the more numerous variables to be taken into account in business situations today but the intrinsic inconstancy of these situations. "Nothing is permanent but change."

Neither logic nor experience is in fact a valid basis for executive attitudes discounting the utility of longer-range planning. The real reasons lie hidden in the personal situation of the individual. He may have struggled long and hard to attain his current state of success, be content with matters at present, perhaps anticipate retirement in a few years or otherwise want to relax for a while, and therefore wish as few changes as possible. He may be preoccupied with other interests or intentions, or problems outside the company may be draining his energies. There are executives who adopt the strategy of safety first and avoid activity which by its nature poses difficult questions and uncertain decisions which could endanger personal success. Occasionally, a strategy of defensive inaction is the outgrowth of personal financial overcommitments which demand the preservation of income at any cost. There may be other managers who believe corporate planning would impair their authority, lead to reduction in the size of the unit reporting to them, or otherwise affect their ambitions within the organization. If such attitudes prevail, interest in doing more than the minimum planning necessary is hardly to be expected.

Disinterest or even active opposition to planning can also be a matter of emotional reaction as well as corporate or personal situation. Because he finds it difficult to delegate responsibilities or details, an executive may believe he is so burdened he can only keep up with current problems as they arise. For some unrecognized reason rooted in his past, he may shy away from considering the indefinite future because it intensifies feelings of insecurity which he has transformed into rationalizations against planning. He may avoid intellectually difficult analysis because his most important satisfactions are derived from the hustle and bustle of daily operations. Those who find fighting fires more fun than their prevention are likely to be more effective at handling a given situation than anticipating it. A consuming technical interest can sometimes hide a disinclination to work closely with volatile people as must be done in corporate planning. Or perhaps an emotional need to maintain an unchallenged optimism or freedom of action unhampered by the conclusions of careful study may account indirectly for a distaste of more objective approaches. ". . . Incorrigibly optimistic, [he] insisted sales in the U.S. would soon improve, and the company would then be liquid again. But . . . sales stayed down, inventory continued to climb . . . , and the company faced bankruptcy in a matter of weeks."[12]

Such attitudes exist and will of course continue to exist. Because they are intrinsically human, they cannot be disavowed. Nor are they necessarily unconstructive, for another side of the same man's personality may be highly important to the business. The characteristic which prevents a particular person from planning to the extent generally accepted as desirable may also account for an enthusiasm, drive, or gregariousness quite indispensable in other ways. Each of us possesses constructive and unconstructive elements of character, and our positive potentialities are the result of the two. For our purposes here, the point of emphasis is the importance of favorable executive attitudes as a prerequisite to both the initial acceptance and the operating success of corporate planning.

> . . . The most serious obstacle to long-range planning is not so much the drain on management time, the actual problems of doing good planning, or the danger of revealing company strategy as it is the subtle, but occasionally open, opposition of some executives which appears in the early stages of development.

> Hence top management support is absolutely essential. . . . If you add up all [those] who stipulate top management support in the area of their particular interests, each and every activity appears to need such backing—and that is a physical impossibility. But the argument in the case of long-range planning is overriding, if only because the activity has always been thought of as so distinctly top-level.[13]

REFERENCES CITED

[1] E. R. King (Eastman Kodak Co.), quoted by William E. Hill and Charles H. Granger, *Long-Range Planning for Company Development,* October 1956 (William E. Hill & Co., New York City), p. 11.

[2] "Getting Merged Team in Harness," *Business Week,* 15 April 1961 (No. 1650), p. 147.

"The Fiscal Gluttony of Olin Mathieson," *Forbes Business and Finance,* 1 April 1960 (Vol. 85, No. 7), pp. 19–22.

[3] Robert Sheehan, "Magowan's Way with Safeway," *Fortune,* October 1958 (Vol. LVIII, No. 4), p. 160.

[4] Morehead Patterson (Chairman, American Machine & Foundry Company), in "Second Wind for AMF?" *Forbes Business and Finance,* 15 May 1960 (Vol. 85, No. 10), p. 19.

[5] Fred Zeder (President, Hydrometals Incorporated), in "A Brash David," *ibid.,* p. 39.

[6] "The Mess at Atlas Plywood," *Fortune,* January 1958 (Vol. LVII, No. 1), p. 119.

[7] Henry Ford, *Forbes Business and Finance,* 15 September, 1959 (Vol. 84, No. 6), p. 72.

[8] Frederick R. Kappel (Chairman of the Board, American Telephone & Telegraph Company), *Vitality in a Business Enterprise,* 1961 (McGraw-Hill Book Company), 102 pp.

[9] Carl Rieser, "What's Come over Old Woolworth?" *Fortune,* January 1960 (Vol. LXI, No. 1), p. 93.

[10] Karl W. Deutsch and William G. Madow, "A Note on the Appearance of Wisdom in Large Bureaucratic Organizations," *Behavioral Science* [as reported in *Scientific American,* May 1961 (Vol. 204, No. 5), p. 84].

[11] "Stanford Research: New Strategy for the Sixties," *Business Week,* 25 March 1961 (No. 1647), p. 93.

[12] William B. Harris, "Massey-Ferguson: Back from the Brink," *Fortune,* October 1958 (Vol. LVIII, No. 4), pp. 145–146.

[13] H. Edward Wrapp, "Organization for Long-Range Planning," *Harvard Business Review,* January–February 1957 (Vol. 35, No. 1), p. 39.

CHAPTER IV

Methodological Considerations

Comprehensive planning is a management process, not a science. Its form and content will vary widely among companies of different size and special situation, and with different attitudes and objectives of executive management. In one way or another, all business enterprises collect and organize data, effect their correlation, make schedules and forecasts, and compare performance with intentions, but there is no body of *specific* technique applicable to all companies. In corporate planning, there are at present no standard conventions, such as those in accounting and in financial analysis.

A number of methodological considerations, however, have been established through accumulated planning experience. General conclusions have been drawn which underlie the formulation of a sound structure of procedure and technique for corporate planning purposes, and serve as basic referents in periodically checking the efficiency of this structure as it tends to proliferate and conditions change. Although separately somewhat different in nature, these considerations and conclusions comprise in fact a body of related principles or a common denominator of understanding which necessarily reflects the breadth and depth of the comprehensive planning process itself.

The Decisive Role of Executive Management

While a negative attitude toward corporate planning precludes success, this does not mean it is not needed or would not be worthwhile. To the contrary, there are indications that the companies which do not acknowledge the function need it most. "In the cases of both high-growth and low-growth companies, those that now support planning programs have shown a superior growth rate in recent years."[1] Since World War II, corporate planning staffs have expanded markedly in number and size, and executive titles including the word "planning" are appearing more frequently at the corporate level of management and within the larger subdivisions of companies.[2] Besides the forces requiring greater forethought in business affairs discussed in Chapter I, the rise of professional management emphasizes the operating statements of tangible accomplishment as the most valid measures of satisfactory performance. When business is approached with the analytical objectivity of professional study, and unsuccessful performance is permissible only temporarily under special circumstances, planning is a pre-eminent responsibility of management.

For these reasons, executive management is *methodologically* as well as attitudinally critical in corporate planning. In even the largest companies, the crucial decisions are made by a comparatively small group of line managers at various levels of the organization. Within the context established by action of the board of directors, executive directives, policies, and other guidelines established from above, each manager is responsible for longer-range planning as well as current operations within his jurisdiction. At the apex of the organization, the chief executive officer exercises final responsibility for the present and future of both the company as a whole and its primary parts. He is *de jure* and *de facto* captain of the corporate ship, subject only to his board of directors, the owners, and conditions beyond his influence or control.

Since there is widespread agreement that the president of a larger corporation can no longer be both chief operations officer and navigator-strategist for the business, "admiral of a naval task force" is a more accurate analogy for his role today. Like the admiral, he cannot successfully direct the immediate operations of the corporate ship which is his headquarters, and at the same time plan for the future. Because there are not enough hours in the day for both, current operations are conducted by others. The organizational decentralization which has occurred within business in recent years, analogous to the "management" of a naval task force, is a manifestation of this trend. Management is becoming "more and more a group-command task."[3] One consequence of this development is greater emphasis on coordination, corporate objectives, and organized comprehensive planning as primary responsibilities of the chief executive vital to success. "We feel we have a large job to do in our company to set planning up as a more conscious effort coordinating various functions of our business. It has only recently been a very live subject in our top management."[4] "As president of my company, I can't do anything about what happened last week or last month, and there is very little I can do which will affect operations today or next week. My concern with operations and accomplishments today must bear a relation to where we expect to be tomorrow and the realization of our long-range objectives."[5]

At the same time, it has become increasingly clear that the chief executive requires staff assistance in corporate planning, as he does in traditional areas of functional activity. "The top officers of a company do not have the time, and often not the qualifications, to do the careful, analytical searching and probing to make sure that all pertinent facts have been brought to the foreground in an impartial manner."[6] In companies of medium and large size, he is supported by a small corporate staff, committees of line executives working on specific assignments, and members of the board of directors. Since small business ordinarily cannot afford corporate staff, these functions are performed by line managers to the extent possible as corollary duties. On the smaller scale and within the greater restrictions at successive levels in the larger organization, each line executive fulfills for his area of jurisdiction functions basically equivalent to those of the president at the apex of the organization. Equally high on each man's list of duties is that of planning for the future.

It is the chief executive officer, therefore, and those senior managers reporting to him in a line or staff capacity who constitute the key management group for corporate planning. If their interest in planning is low—but not to the extent of its prohibition—they cannot be circumvented without enormous loss in the effectiveness of the planning program. Nor, in response to their abrogation of the responsibility, can plans be drawn and carried out satisfactorily for them by others.

Three general principles of planning have emerged from these developments in management organization and responsibility. First: the scope of realistic planning cannot exceed the range of activity or consideration of the entity within which it is formulated, for which it is intended, and by which it is implemented. Second: comprehensive planning for any entity is a primary responsibility of its chief executive. Third: without his active support, directly or indirectly applied, it will fail or at best fall short of its potential contribution. It will, in fact, necessarily tend to mirror his concepts and attitudes. He does not, of course, personally formulate the plans in their entirety, but he is the focal point of their preparation and all important decisions and implicit commitments toward the future must be his.

The Open-Ended Context of Planning

Every business institution exists within a total environment much larger than the segment which is its principal concern and with which it maintains direct contact. The operations and planning of a company are tied to many external factors—what may be called macroscopic considerations. The production and sale of its products are related to population growth and composition, general economic conditions, and patterns of demand reflecting the stage of development of systems of production, distribution, consumption, communication, transportation, or national defense. Political and governmental factors are involved in their impact on taxes, labor relations, wages, inflation, interest and exchange rates, and a multitude of laws, rules, and regulations. The actions and plans of competitors, both private enterprise and government-owned and -subsidized, are certainly to be taken into account. And to this illustrative range of external considerations must be added scientific-technological developments and the variety of natural phenomena, such as the weather or geography, which may have a direct or indirect effect on the business. "1959 was a dry year, which reduced our hydroelectric generation. . . . It was also a warm year, which materially reduced gas sales for space heating with an associated loss of many millions of dollars in revenues."[7]

The business enterprise also functions in terms of a more immediate, internal, or microscopic environment. The procurement, training, and management of its employees are related to local economic conditions, laws, customs, and attitudes. To meet the requirements of financial, legal, and regulatory environments, it performs a multitude of internal record-keeping and accounting transactions, combining these into operating and financial analyses at each level of organization. Its continual introspective examination of internal activities to improve profit margins makes use of the knowledge accumulated within the organization in many fields of professional concentration. Public and industrial relations within the immediate community are often as important as those established at a national level, since the position of the company in its environment of human attitudes is derived locally as well as regionally and nationally. Microclimate or microgeology can be as important in a local situation as the more general aspects of these fields are for some businesses on a much broader scale.

These few illustrations exemplify the extent to which any business exists and operates within an environmental continuum composed of a wide diversity of external and internal factors, extending from the macroscopic to the microscopic. This is of course an outstanding characteristic of our time. The surge of knowledge and virtual elimination of geographical isolation during the past half-century have underlined the circular, interactive nature of our physical-human world. In the last analysis, all natural phenomena and human activities are interrelated, and the number of demonstrably significant interdependencies is increasing rapidly.

This environmental fact has important implications for planning. Were we to investigate completely the conditions and considerations influencing our planning for a particular company, logically we should have all available data pertaining to all environmental factors. Practically speaking, if we attempted to develop this range of information, the situation with which we are immediately and directly concerned would change significantly during the time required to collect and correlate so extensive a background of data. We would have to gather and formulate new information, most of which in its turn would be out of date by the time it was available. This differential in real time will restrict our scope of consideration in planning until we are able to develop a more complete sequence of interdependent data, and the means of almost instantaneous correlation which will provide current information for any point in time and averages for various periods. This is beyond both our factual knowledge and our integrative ability at present. It is also prohibitively expensive. Parenthetically, we will of course never achieve comprehensive knowledge and complete information in the ultimate sense. A "principle of uncertainty," roughly comparable to Heisenberg's dictum in particle physics, operates in comprehensive planning.

The open-ended and uncertain context of planning can create difficulties. Sometimes, it is misinterpreted as a logical invalidation; how can you plan if you do not have *all* relevant facts? It inhibits some individuals from concluding, deciding, and acting with dispatch. It tempts others to pursue the intellectual trail of logically related information to the point of losing sight of the practical purpose of planning, the limitations it imposes on the time and money which can be spent constructively, and the level of analytical complexity beyond which further exploration is not worthwhile. Determination of the point of diminishing informational return and selection of the most significant elements of information from the mass of material often available are never easy, even for those with long experience. But effective planning is impossible if delayed until all important questions are answered, since matters can never be resolved to the point of certainty and procrastination is fatal to success.

Several generalizations can be made concerning methodology and the diffusive context of planning. The internal and external environments of the company, or of the specific planning problem, are scanned comprehensively to identify the range of relevant consideration and insure that no area of environmental influence is unrecognized or forgotten. It is almost always necessary to distill from this range and depth of recognized influence those primary factors which relate most closely to the underlying problem of management, and which can be resolved within the time and money available for study. In their selection and analysis, accurate data are obtained and scientific method is used to the extent possible, but subjective judgment is applied without hesitation as required. Since a deliberate procedure of logical analysis favors sound judgments, the method of conducting the examination is as important as the reliability of data. Periodically, the abridgment of environmental factors and the methods of taking them into account are checked by retrospective evaluation.

Scope of Consideration

Of course, it is as necessary in comprehensive planning to assure an adequate scope of consideration as it is to avoid investigations so excessive they are self-defeating. In planning practice, the omission of significant elements is more common than wandering too far afield.

A company manufactures an automobile with a body style so different from its predecessors and prevailing consumer taste that the model is a failure. Production of a toy is discontinued before the breakeven point because of the volume of warranty replacements resulting from a design insufficiently rugged to endure the normal destructiveness of children. At a broader level, a toy manufacturer indicates that his ". . . company has not kept pace with the growth of the market. . . . Long-range planning done five or six years ago would have, without a doubt, brought us into a much more favorable position today."[8] A company is hurt because it overlooks in its articles of incorporation a legal obligation to pay dividends out of accumulated surplus, rather than from earnings when justified, or because pre-emptive rights on new stock issue are not qualified for stock options. Another endures a period of decline because it underestimates the consequences of managerial nepotism, or finds the profits of recent acquisitions reduced for some years by unanticipated problems of integration into the parent complex. ". . . Its hectic buildup never left St. Regis [Paper Company] a chance to catch up with itself."[9] American businesses transplant executives abroad until lack of success confirms the distinctiveness of foreign operations and the desirability of management by resident nationals to the extent possible. And, as a cause of small-business bankruptcy, failure to calculate the capital reserve required as a cushion against temporary adversity is second only to the difficulties of acquiring the indicated amount.

These are perhaps dramatic examples, but every company is familiar from its own experience with omissions in planning which have increased costs, created difficulties, and reduced profits. Sins of omission will certainly be with us as long as there are unknown elements, recognized factors which cannot be appraised reliably, and the average incidence of human error. But they are reduced by the application of appropriate method. To the extent omissions are noted at each successive level of management review and integration, the procedure of corporate planning in itself encourages a broader scope of examination than occurs otherwise. Elements less important in functional planning or missed in a more restrictive approach emerge from the type of analysis implicit in the objective of viewing the situation comprehensively. To this end, enough time is scheduled at each level of review to favor the accumulation of all significant factors. Checklists are included in the procedure. Individuals with different personal and professional perceptions are involved for the specific purpose of lessening the chance an important factor is overlooked. Corporate planning staffs usually include one or more persons selected because of their comprehensive overview and assigned the responsibility of reviewing the scope of analytical consideration.

What can be called the principle of parallel development is helpful. All elements of a plan or problem to be included in its analysis are represented from the beginning—even though their resolution is scheduled and possible only much later in the evolution toward a final solution. This contrasts with the sequential method of introducing each input only when specifically necessary. The advantages of parallel participation in corporate planning are quite clear. It promotes inclusive thinking. Each area of substantive emphasis has a longer association with other components in which to acquire an understanding of the problem as a whole and mature its own jurisdictional analysis and conclusion. Management control is needed, however, to avoid confusion and maintain a procedural priority of first things first.

New product planning is a case in point. It was not unusual some years ago for the research and development of new products to be carried to the completion of a prototype before other vital considerations were introduced into the picture. In general, a sequential procedure was followed. Higher research costs and shorter average product life are forcing abandonment of this procedure in favor of parallel participation. "It takes just as long and just as much money to develop a million-dollar bust as a ten-million-dollar bell ringer."[10] Representatives of market research, business-financial analysis, and sales-distribution-promotion are brought in during the first phases of development. For, at any time during the evolution of a new product, a basic change in the market situation, a rise in projected production costs which cannot be passed on to the customer, or serious conflict with established distribution policy can lead to rescheduling or abandonment of the program. Since ordinarily a choice must be made between proposals competing for research funds, the percentage of new products which are successful and the returns from this important investment are increased by continuous screening from all essential points of view.

It is better to identify too many than too few elements during the early stages of planning analysis. The selection of those to be considered within the restrictions of time, money, and method is sounder if made from an inclusive listing. This list is also a constant reminder of the simplification which has been made and a valuable mental reference for subjective decision. It facilitates recognition of changes in the relative significance of different elements as conditions change.

Information-Communication

Information is the knowledge which makes corporate planning possible, confirmed in its usefulness and validity by factual corroboration, experience, and improved results. It ranges from precise data to highly subjective judgments. Within this broad definition, successful planning may be based in part on inaccurate information. The area of inaccuracy may be insignificant in the total analysis, cancelled out by subjective judgment, or offset by compensating misinformation or error. Irregularly, success is achieved by fortuitous chance. Any realistic definition of information for corporate planning reflects the necessity of proceeding on the basis of the best knowledge available. The difficulties of identifying and measuring the profit improvements directly attributable to comprehensive planning are discussed in Chapter VII. Logically, the benefits of planning should increase to a point of diminishing return as its informational base is strengthened.

Any intensification of planning activity promotes better use of existing data, but effective corporate planning requires a minimum background of information concerning operations within the company and its external environment. The continuous establishment of longer-range objectives and the integration of activities undertaken in this endeavor require more information than is necessary for shorter-range operations separately considered. This is one of the reasons why comprehensive planning takes time and money. Informational requirements naturally vary with different businesses and their particular situation; however, Figure 2 lists the categories of data normally needed in the larger-size enterprise. Although it appears voluminous when brought together in this way, most of this information is maintained within well-managed companies.

Apart from these needs for corporate planning, several developments already mentioned in different connections promote more and better internal information. Governmental actions impose a growing load of record keeping and periodic reporting. More data are required as the production of goods and services becomes technically more complicated, with an expanding number of interdependent participants from material suppliers to insurance specialists making administrative management more difficult. As declining profit margins and increasing investment requirements magnify the consequences of wrong decisions in lost money, time, and reputation, available facts are neglected to the corporate peril. The faster tempo of business operations today is both cause and consequence of the extended informational capability within business made possible in large part by the improved means of collecting, storing, processing, and disseminating data.

Forces are also operating which advance the quantity and quality of external information concerning the business environment. As they grow in size and scope, governmental bodies compile more data relating to private enterprise. There is an increasing output by trade associations, financial institutions, business and news publications, professional societies, consulting and research organizations, universities. And, as business responds to governmental scrutiny, diversified ownership, more widespread and continuous financial appraisal, and general public opinion, its own external reporting is more extensive. "More and more facts are being crammed into annual reports to stockholders every year according to a survey by the American Institute of Certified Public Accountants."[11]

The employment of electronic computers emphasizes the classification and compatibility of data, and their speed permits calculations otherwise impossible. But the age-old pitfalls of information processes still exist and require careful attention. Human minds and emotions are always involved at different stages of automatic data processing. People provide, supplement, or interpret the initial information; they write the instructions which direct the precise manipulation of the data within the machine; and they interpret, evaluate, and determine the end use of the processed information. More important, much of the information vital in planning at the higher levels of decision making is qualitative and procedural in nature, encompassing areas of substantive knowledge which cannot yet be quantified meaningfully and involving integrations beyond the scope of present-day scientific-mathematical method. "Even our present primitive knowledge of the decision process in organizations suggests that any attempt to view it as a system of information processing is grossly misleading. A complex interplay of human attitudes and values is involved. . . . Accounting, sales, finance, and production often share both complementary and conflicting interests in a series of decisions. . . . The substitution of mechanical for human processing devices is likely to yield unanticipated, often unsatisfactory, results."[12]

Corporate planning requires established procedures of collecting and processing information which are designed to maximize human contributions and minimize human limitations, as well as employ mechanical handling to the extent practicable and profitable. Since information normally passes through many hands and heads, accepted ground rules of accuracy are important. The nature and source of data are described, if not unmistakably implicit in the data themselves. Reference is made to significant assumptions and interpretations incorporated in data, thus avoiding undetected changes in the meaning of information when it is progressively reinterpreted and cumulative adjustments are not identified. The range of accuracy or the percentage limits of significance are stated clearly. Insignificant figures are dropped. Above all, not only are data defined but direct comparisons are made only between equivalents. Subjective information is treated with comparable care by including the experience of the source in the area of judgment, the representative validity of a sampling of opinion, or the logical analysis underlying a deductive conclusion.

Self-evident as such precautions of informational accuracy may seem, it is surprising how often they are honored as much in the breach as in the observance. Companies employ percentage returns on investment without defining investment. The potential profitability of different projects is expressed and compared by undefined return-on-investment figures which can vary by as much as 100 per cent, depending on whether initial investment, average investment, or discounted cash flow was employed.[13] Overhead and development costs are expressed differently by different units within the same company, often without the explanation of their derivation necessary for meaningful comparison. A few random opinions are inflated into a consensus as a consequence of informational carelessness, vested interest, or the overemphasis often engendered by successive restatement. Organizational groups are sometimes as prone as individuals to accept numbers as intrinsically more valid than unquantified judgment, without checking their origin or statistical validity. And executives have been known to insist on simplification of reporting to the point where the figures are conveniently few, but only half-meaningful in themselves because significant details have had to be dropped in the condensation.

There are fundamental questions of descriptive accuracy and informational procedure still unresolved or dependent upon the particular corporate situation. What are valid measurements of the profit performance of operating divisions? How is the performance of staff units best evaluated? What is the best method of identifying and measuring the return on investment in research and development? Is there a valid method of calculating an optimum expenditure for advertising? How should the liability incurred by leased assets be determined and stated in the balance sheet? Is there a practical method of depicting the financial structure and behavior of the business for corporate planning purposes which will show more clearly than the traditional accounting statements the dynamics of what is occurring and why? In the opinion of one group of critics, ". . . the people who by inference are custodians of value think in terms of figures which are bound in a 'strait jacket' of accounting and cost techniques . . . unsatisfactory as a medium to control a *dynamic* running management that has changed so drastically in needs the past few years."[14]

Since producing and processing information take time and money, excessive reporting and analysis are obviously wasteful. The dangers of needless paperwork are familiar to every executive. Companies can overproduce self-descriptive information to the extent of impairing the profitable production of the salable end product. "[Planning] can help a company or it can get the entire organization so snarled in red tape that you spend all of your time planning and none of your time doing."[15] At the other extreme, an enterprise cannot operate efficiently, appraise its true situation, or engage successfully in longer-range planning without adequate management information.

Several generalizations can, in fact, be made from the viewpoint of corporate planning. No information is developed without a specific purpose. It is in the simplest, least ambiguous, and most easily understood form which fulfills the purpose. Duplication is avoided. To the extent feasible, information is consistent and directly comparable throughout the company. Its source, date of issuance and applicability, derivation, and range of significance or accuracy are shown. Any limitations of use inherent in the data are specifically stated. Ratios and other combinational designations are employed—provided no significant aspect of the information is lost in the special indication, which must also be meaningful and generally understood. Key data are used whenever experience proves they are descriptive of broader areas of consideration which would otherwise require more extensive reporting. The body of information systematically employed in corporate planning is appraised periodically to confirm its continued usefulness and validity, and identify desirable improvements.

In contrast with current practice, the informational responsibilities of staff personnel, in addition to the knowledge of company operations commonly expected, are spelled out in the descriptions of corporate planning positions. Illustrations of such intelligence might include the activities and plans of business competition, new management methods, the state of the art in a technical or professional area, candidates for corporate acquisition, or international political-economic developments.

Since information is the product of one or more of many forms of communication, and at the same time is dependent for its reality and usefulness on communication within oneself and with others, information and communication are inseparable in theory and fact. Even biologically innate information or "knowledge" is communicated from generation to generation by inheritance. And the sensory information we receive constantly by eye, ear, nose, or touch achieves its reality through one of the many systems of communication incorporated within the human body. There are many illustrations of this interdependence in management practice. Graphic information does not lend itself to verbal transmission by telephone. The information exchanged verbally between two persons face to face is modified by their visible behavior, and subtle intelligence concerning attitude is communicated unconsciously. High-speed computers could not perform their special kind of complex internal intercommunication if the information were not expressed in binary or other symbolic form. And, since such abstract information is neither generally meaningful nor communicated interpersonally in itself, it must be re-expressed as words, numbers, or graphic patterns after electronic processing.

In management and corporate planning, it is more practical to consider information and communication as separate but closely interdependent. Information is the knowledge transmitted, communication the means of transmission. In this sense, communication has received increased attention within management circles in recent years. The relationship between fast, reliable information and efficient, profitable operations has been expounded. The benefits of a sound structure of formal intercommunication have been emphasized to the point where small staff units concerned with "organization" or "systems and procedures" have been established in many larger companies. Informal means of transmission such as the grapevine have received attention, and the mass media of communication have been studied to determine the combination most effective for advertising and other external public relations.[16]

Communication is the procedural lifeblood of corporate planning. The executive decision makers and professional staff most concerned rely almost entirely on data prepared by others. They have little time and opportunity to acquire informational raw material at its source. The essential requirement is the continuous communication of the information they need for corporate planning purposes at the lowest practical cost. "The adequacy of problem solving within organizations depends upon the adequacy of communication as well as upon the skills available."[17] The organization of different informational channels varies, of course, with their function. Some must operate with minimum delay. Sales, costs, profits, inventory, employment, and other financial factors are communicated quickly for continual comparison with projected trends, milestone events, and longer-range plans—as well as their many implications for current management. Environmental intelligence which might modify objectives is transmitted with equal dispatch, since delay in its evaluation and any consequent adjustments in plan can be competitively disastrous. Examples of such intelligence include an engineering development foreshadowing the obsolescence of a productive process, the decision of a powerful company to compete in a product area, or the passage of governmental tax, labor, or defense legislation affecting the corporate future. Some categories of information are communicated less frequently. Except for payroll accounting, union labor relations, and immediate situations involving key employees, the transmission of personnel data reflects the longer time interval normally taken in planning and implementing programs within this area of functional activity. Similarly, research and development is a gradual process with an extended time scale and less immediacy.

To the extent possible, the same reports employed in current operations are used for comprehensive planning. Any additional requirements of coverage, reliability, correlation, simplification, or method of presentation are identified and arranged. Informal channels of supplementary information are established as needed— usually between staff personnel. A schedule is formulated which provides for the consistent transmission and use of corporate information; for example, data are communicated only as often as they can be used effectively, or in such form and at such times as simplify their correlation for the same time period. Ways of representing and communicating corporate planning information are developed which facilitate executive decision. This usually involves the distillation of essentials in special representations of exceptional conceptual clarity, portraying correlations, the analysis of alternatives, and composite projections into the future. Dissemination of the components of the corporate plan as formally adopted takes place through the same reporting channels used for their submission. And the informal or staff channels of communication which supply supplementary information for corporate planning are employed for the follow-up clarification and modification of plans that are almost always required during their implementation.

Human limitations to efficient communication have only recently begun to receive the attention they deserve. There are managers who communicate as little as possible as a means of extending their influence by having people come to them for information, or who needlessly complicate the material in order to increase their personal indispensability. Others exaggerate the need for data to serve their ambition for an organizational "empire." Information must be extracted from another type because, for reasons of their own, they do not realize the crucial importance of communication in the management and operations of every enterprise. By their nature, some people think in terms of communication far more than others. Every company has the problem of different organizational units repeating the same mistakes, usually because of lack of communication, sometimes because of unwillingness to be guided by the experience of others. Channels of disruptive rumor are established between persons with similar susceptibilities to misinformation. Any organizational pathway for the transmission of subjective judgments is sensitive to the personalities of the individuals who comprise it; the initial input is often changed as optimism, pessimism, disagreement, unconscious misunderstanding, or any one of many emotional reactions influences its successive interpretation.

Awareness of the more subtle human aspects of communication is useful mainly as an element of personal understanding on the part of executives responsible for planning. In an institution such as the corporation, with long life and the requirement of profitability for survival, the practical application of this understanding by the executive is limited to personnel selection, job assignment, and his own intercommunication. Ability to communicate is clearly essential in the choice and use of people directly active in the corporate planning process. But any attempt by the company to delve into individual characteristics of personality or incorporate psychological mechanisms into communication procedures will almost certainly magnify individual problems and compound organizational difficulties.

The Role of Reason

Planning presupposes the dominance of purposive reason, as contrasted with unthinking action, irrational reaction, emotional irresponsibility, or random chance. To the extent possible, situations are analyzed, conclusions reached, and actions taken on the basis of sound rational thought. The implications of this fundamental assumption are neither simple nor self-evident.

A feature of human evolution has been the slow but steady control of reflexive reaction and the growth of rationality. Before *homo* became *sapiens,* involuntary instinctual response served the purposes of biological survival. Each progressive stage in the evolution of man has been marked by an increase in his capacity and control of reason, and a corresponding increase in the complexity of his social, economic, and technical environment. From the interplay of these two developments have emerged both the capacity and the necessity for improved planning. But the long way we have to go before we achieve any "triumph of reason" is evidenced on all sides in worldwide political strife, social and personal tension, ethical conflict, and mental-emotional confusion—to name but a few of many manifestations. We are in what appears to be a significant phase of our transition from instinctually dominated to rationally balanced beings. The cultural precepts of our society and the complexities of our modern environment preclude an intelligent denial of the rational approach and the necessity of organized planning, but we are only beginning to understand how to apply our mental-emotional capabilities effectively in this endeavor.

Planning activities encompass the rational and the non-rational. Scientific method—the epitome of the rational approach—is limited in its scope by definition. Its aim is the inclusion of more and more phenomena within its range of experimental observation and calculative certainty by discovering laws which govern their behavior. But, at present, truly scientific method can be applied only to certain segments of comprehensive planning, because many of the different elements of the total problem are variable, some cannot be expressed meaningfully with numbers, the units of measurement of others are not comparable, and the laws of operation of another group are unknown. If we confined ourselves to those phenomena which can be quantified and expressed with predictive certainty, numerous activities vital in real life would be excluded. Not only is this true for elements and aspects relating to human behavior and value judgments; but, as executives know, even an area as predominantly numerical as financial accounting involves alternatives of purpose and method which produce different sets of quantitative data.

"Science, in itself, is not the source of ethical standards, the moral insight, the wisdom that is needed to make value judgments, though it is an important ingredient in making value judgments. Social, political and military decisions are made on grounds other than those in which science is authoritative."[18]

The limitations of scientific method in corporate planning do not, of course, suggest that the only alternative is pure chance or capricious fate. As discussed specifically in the next chapter, there are procedures which contribute to the necessary synthesis in corporate planning of many types of information of varying precision and reliability, different forms of objective analysis, and numerous subjective judgments. Despite its crucial role in the comprehensive planning process, the nature, potentialities, and limitations of rational thought often do not receive sufficient attention and sometimes are misunderstood.

The human mind consists of two basic parts: the conscious and the unconscious. The conscious is the receptor of external stimuli and perceptions. It retains the information we can recall and the thought processes we can apply as needed in organizing this information for intentional purposes. Some of this material is not available immediately upon demand, but comes to mind with delayed recall from a portion of the conscious called the preconscious.

The unconscious is the reservoir of instincts, sensory impressions, emotional drives, and the information we cannot recall at will. Research suggests that most, if not all, of the discrete stimuli we receive through our sensory system are recorded and stored in the unconscious from earliest infancy. Its content is unorganized, reflecting primitive instinctual patterns, emotional contrasts and conflicts, and random information.

A third primary element of the mind determines the respective content and contribution of these two basic parts. Acting as a control, this censor transmits the external perceptions received by the conscious to unconscious storage. It retains within this reservoir the many impulses and items of past information which are inappropriate to our present environment and which conflict with conscious purposes. It filters into our awareness those inputs from the unconscious which are emotionally acceptable and relate to conscious concerns. From such controlled interactions between the two basic components of the human mind emerges a balance of intuition and rationality which constitutes human reason in the full sense of the word.

Although the unconscious is a basic component of the mind, its role is frequently underestimated or misunderstood. Not only does it influence our reaction to current events and situations, but it is involved in the thinking we label objective, rational, and scientific. For included in the mental "data processing" we perform consciously and deliberately are informational materials drawn by the censor-control from the extensive storage accumulated unconsciously through the years. Because the unconscious is a fundamental part of personality which cannot be isolated and controlled beyond a point, its most characteristic emotional features influence our rational thought whether or not they are logically consistent.

Understanding the general nature of mental-emotional processes is essential in determining how human reason is best applied in comprehensive planning: in procedural organization, policy formation, and the selection and utilization of the individuals most directly concerned with the corporate future. Theoretical abstractions which purport to eliminate subjective judgment and provide exact answers to *comprehensive* planning questions reflect a lack of recognition of the scope of corporate planning, the limitations of intellectualism and scientific method, or the nature of the human animal. In any event, before they are considered seriously, they should be reviewed critically in detail and their validity confirmed by experimental application, without artificial limitation, to current and past operating experience.

Intuition and Its Validity [19]

Intuition is the insight stimulated by unconscious material. Purposive deliberation triggers the censor-control to admit to conscious awareness material from the unconscious which bears upon the matter "in mind." This additional stimulus-information acts to confirm, extend, or challenge the conscious conclusion. It provokes re-examination and contributes forgotten but relevant information to the intellectual process.

Because of the nature of the unconscious, the material provided by intuition is less subject to the inhibitions, limitations in scope of perception, and restrictions on imagination often present in deliberate analysis. It is especially illuminating with respect to people and the intangible aspects of situations. It is more a feeling than a rational deduction supported by clear-cut reasons and a coherent chain of premise, evidence, and conclusion. Usually, intuition is a sudden insight or conviction, often penetrating the essence of the matter at hand.

Keen intuition is characteristic of many successful business men. It may be discounted by the skeptical as personal luck, random chance, or fortunate circumstance. It may be mistaken for superior intelligence or exceptional analytical ability. Sometimes it is obscured because individuals disclaim judgment only partly supported by logical analysis, or the corporate atmosphere demands some *pro forma* rationalization for all conclusion. In both instances, artificial justification may be manufactured in a self-deceptive attempt to corroborate intuition.

As part of the "power of comprehending and inferring," intuition is necessarily involved in comprehensive planning. Appropriately employed, it is a powerful companion of conscious and deliberate analysis. It assumes added importance when data are lacking and quantitative calculation is inconclusive. Executives engaged in corporate planning must constantly apply intuitive judgments in management deliberations and decision making, especially when there is not enough time for thorough study. ". . . The humble private individual business of being 'on guard' and using 'common sense' . . . is largely an 'intuitive' rather than a logical process. In the aggregate it is the most important of all known processes of foresight, and the least respected."[20]

Of course, not all intuition is sound. We recognize areas of reaction and judgment in which our own insights are more accurate than in others. Also, there are probably certain areas in which our intuition is in fact less reliable than we believe. This is partly the product of personal experience and emotional development, and partly a consequence of knowledge and training. There are people whose intuition is consistently wrong.

The validity of intuitive judgment depends on what can be called the condition and circuitry of the mind. Significantly crossed emotional wires can short-circuit the mental process of intuitive resolution and produce false or biased answers—not necessarily from the viewpoint of the individual who thinks and acts as he does for some compelling reason, but because judgments in the best interests of a business institution normally require as much objectivity as possible. In these instances, the censor-control is transmitting material from the unconscious which supports urgent demands of emotionality rather than the requirements of better-balanced reason. If this disequilibrium is extreme, unconscious material may be either blocked or so overwhelming that rational insight is absent.

For most business men, this intuitive circuitry is best evaluated by the sound conclusions it produces, and by comparison with intuitive minds of demonstrated capability. Unfortunately, it is difficult for most of us to recognize and admit limitations in this respect and to restrict our intuitive convictions accordingly. Fortunately, corporate planning provides a sufficient expression of judgments by different persons at successive stages of the process to enable each to check his insights with comparable opinion. And those areas in which our judgments are impaired repeatedly by unconscious factors are likely to be identified in the analysis of past performance which is also part of planning. To illustrate: any reiterative over-optimism or undue pessimism which is a consequence of unrecognized influences is likely to show up in the historical record, and is compensated for by others if we do not learn to do it ourselves. At the topmost level of management, self-acknowledgment of what the record reveals, business competition, other forces of circumstance, or the reaction of board of directors, stockholders, or financial community must be relied upon to correct sooner or later any significant and continuing errors of subjective judgment.

Synthesis of Man and Machine

Men and machines have been joined in a working relationship since earliest times. The Technological Revolution has extended the machine capability developed during the Industrial Revolution by incorporating physical phenomena previously unknown or little understood. Far-reaching advancements in the application of machines and in the refinement of their operations are represented by radio, radar, television, jet-engine aircraft, gasoline refinery, atomic reactor, electron microscope, or microtransistor. A new level of versatility, precision, reliability, and subtlety is attained in the performance of such mechanisms. Comparable advances have been made in control devices and data-processing equipment: automatic telephone switchgear, automated machine tools, military fire-control devices, and electronic computers.

Within business enterprise, these scientific-technical achievements have influenced the management process as well as engineering-production. Electric typewriter, dictating machine, telephone, teletype, adding machine, desk calculator, punch-card equipment, and microfilm are part of present-day administration. As the most recent arrival on the corporate scene, with proven value in scientific research and complex military systems, the electronic computer is in process of evolution as an instrument of management.[21] Because of the number now employed in business and the widespread use to be expected with further reductions in cost, they can be accepted as an established tool of management. "By 1965, U.S. and Canadian business men will be spending over $1 billion annually in rental for computer systems. Retail value of computer systems produced for business and scientific use will climb from $470 million in 1960 to more than $1 billion in 1965."[22] Without question, computers are the most significant recent development in the synthesis of man and machine for corporate planning purposes.

In considering electronic computers, objectivity is important since these devices elicit exaggerated responses. On the one hand, scientist-engineers sometimes suggest in their enthusiasm that computers will in time outperform man in most of his functions. On the other hand, many business men, social scientists, and laymen are unduly skeptical. There is a tendency to regard computers as *dei ex machina,* or to harbor an unexpressed or unrecognized fear that they will supplant man. Others are concerned lest they cause permanent unemployment. For our purposes, the salient fact is that computers are here to stay. Their use would expand even were it delayed for political-economic reasons; no technological development of such import could be retarded deliberately for long.

Because of their speed, electronic computers can accomplish calculations impossible or impractical for man. Numerous examples have been published of data processed by these machines in a few minutes which would require human lifetimes of laborious computation. By ultra-high-speed addition, they perform multiplication, subtraction, division, and many combinations and extensions of these basic mathematical operations, such as correlation and integration. When self-checking routines are incorporated in the program of instructions, they are many times more accurate than humans performing the same calculations. Moreover, almost instantaneous feedback is a significant feature of electronic computers. So quickly can the results of data processing be fed back to modify the next increment of input that the computer can perform calculative operations with a refinement of control otherwise impossible. Small rates of change in the output of a high-speed machine, pipeline, electric wire, or almost any device transporting a material substance or physical force can be signaled back in time to modify subsequent inputs. In this way, a steadier flow is maintained, reducing the difficulties which ordinarily will accompany greater fluctuation.

Feedback can also be applied to the purely calculative analysis of organizational processes. In a company, it can be employed to show almost immediately the impact of a change in the forecast rate of sales on production, inventory, cash flow, or probable profits. The method can be reversed to compute by feedforward the many consequences of a decision to expand production and the pattern of sales required to support the increased capacity, maintain profits, and meet other required conditions. ". . . When we ask it, it tells what will be the effect of various changes in emphasis. Thus, when we do make a decision, we know we are making the best one."[23] Of course, the value of such calculations depends on the soundness of the premises which they represent.

The second general capability of computers is their memory. Information in the language form employed by the machine can be stored, filed, or "remembered" in enormous quantities. Without this feature, high speed is patently impossible. The limits to this storage are established by practical considerations of access time and cost which are being reduced steadily, with significant advances very likely still to come. Stored information can be classified in many ways, replaced or updated automatically as new data are available, and reformulated into new combinations. This ability to record and process large quantities of data extends business analysis in several ways. More data can be used concerning a single activity, a broader range of information can be examined for significant correlations, and a much larger volume of historical data can be maintained for comparison, trend-identification, and projective purposes. Statistical reliability, analytic scope, and the informational basis for inference and judgment are strengthened accordingly.

The third descriptive characteristic of computer systems is their capacity for receiving and processing information from mechanical sensors which respond to light, sound, movement, and numerous electromagnetic and chemical properties. For example: thermometer, speedometer, scale, microphone, lens, photoelectric cell, pH meter, accelerometer, barometer, pressure gauge, electron tube, or electroencephalograph. Many of these sensors record phenomena beyond the range of human detection, or measure those also detectable by man with greater precision than is possible with his conscious sensory apparatus. The attachment of such compatible input devices extends greatly the scope of operations to which the computer can make a substantial contribution. But this extension is more significant in process control, automated production, military and space projects, or weather monitoring than in corporate planning analysis, which receives its direct inputs for the most part from various forms of office machines.

The first two of these basic abilities enable a computer system to perform analytical calculations which improve administration, general line management, and planning. In management words rather than computer terminology, the machine can store, classify, and maintain current data relating to inventory, production costs, overhead, sales, personnel, or any one of the many business operations usefully described by numbers. This information is available on call with far less delay than with traditional recording, filing, and accounting procedures. To accomplish this organized storage, the computer scans, identifies, and groups data which have the same characteristics or are similarly coded. "The Bank of America . . . automatically processes 1.7 million checking accounts each night. . . ."[24] By reversing the procedure and programing the computer to search stored information for correlations, unforeseen interrelationships and more useful classifications may be found. In an area of functional planning: "Computers at American Cyanamid Co.'s Bridgeville, Pa., plant 'remember' some 24,000 items of maintenance history" which are analyzed for new insights into preventive maintenance.[25] Similarly, in corporate planning it is possible to identify unexpected factors within or outside the company which affect profits.

The computer also integrates information. It can combine the basic financial data of separate operating entities in a small fraction of the time otherwise required. It can be programed so that it will quickly integrate a series of related probabilities into an over-all probability, and will perform the logical analysis required to derive the outcome of a sequence of interdependent propositions. Or it can provide continual extrapolations of data in accordance with assumptions either fixed or selected by the machine itself from prior calculations. Thus, sales projections may be derived from a long list of relevant factors by automatic machine selection of the 10 to 20 elements, in priority order, which have correlated most closely with actual sales and sales forecasts in the past—with recent history more heavily weighted.

Electronic computers are uniquely useful in simulation. For example, the financial balance sheet is a simplified representation of the corporate condition. Since the relationships between the different items of the balance sheet are known at those points in time when the books are closed, and within limits during intermediate accounting periods, the repercussive effects of a change in cash flow on the other elements of the balance sheet can be simulated in a few minutes. Similarly, the separate and collective effects of refinancing debt, leasing rather than owning fixed assets, setting a higher objective in return on investment, or expanding production can be calculated quickly and expressed as revised balance sheets.

An illustration of simulation in functional planning is the application of the technique by the maintenance division of a railroad to inventory warehousing at different depots along its trackage. A method of calculating what items should be stored at which locations was tested by applying a mathematical model to five years of recorded experience. By means of an electronic computer, it was concluded that the more scientific method would have provided equal or better availability of maintenance items during these past years at an annual saving of several hundred thousand dollars. Subsequently, the method was confirmed in practice.[26]

Undoubtedly, the electronic computer has added a new dimension to corporate planning. Its capacity for high-speed correlation, integration, projection, and simulation permit a level of analysis previously impossible because of the time required to process the data. It is now possible to identify developments more quickly; learn more about the complex interactions of business operations; determine the diverse consequences of a trend or event more broadly, reliably, and specifically; and maintain a projective simulation of the company which permits the evaluation of various alternatives by revealing the probable results and corollary requirements of a specific course of action. Input sources may be widely separated geographically: "A noteworthy development during the year was . . . linking several of the refineries with a large computer at the Company's San Francisco headquarters. . . . The computer is able to supply, in a matter of minutes, solutions to technical problems, as well as directions for operating refinery process units with maximum efficiency and profitability."[27]

At present, cost is the principal determinant of practicality. From this point of view, an electronic computer system consists of five parts: the computer itself; the input-output devices required to transpose information into the language of the machine and to retranslate it into useful form for the purposes of management; professional personnel to write program instructions and monitor the machine; spatial enclosure to meet environmental and maintenance requirements; and supplementary storage for historical and other information which is used infrequently and therefore not contained within the continuously operating capacity of the computer. Whether owned, leased, or purchased from an outside service organization, electronic computation is expensive. It is justified only when the cost of a higher order of data processing and analysis is more than offset by improvements over a period of time in current efficiency or projective management.[28] Ordinarily, this means an enterprise medium or large in size, with one or more of the operating complexities normal to American business. In many companies, the computer is also used for engineering computations, mathematical simulation of new production processes, research, or particular functions such as inventory control, payroll records, or personnel data. "In 1960 the accounting for materials handled by 185 storerooms throughout our system was converted to computer operation. Programing is now in progress for conversion to electronic processing of payroll and plant accounting. The computers have also been utilized to make numerous engineering and statistical studies."[29]

In these cases costs are shared. Occasionally, computing capacity in excess of internal demand can be sold outside the company.

It is not surprising that the electronic computer is an approximate image of the central nervous system of man. The functional parallels between the two are well known. Memory, conscious recall, reasoning, and the human senses approximate information storage, access, calculation, and mechanical sensors in machine systems. In considering the composite analytical process of men working with machines, their differences are more important than their similarities. Sooner or later, machines are used for those operations they perform as well or better than man. Witness the employment of the abacus, balance scale, slide rule, adding machine, desk calculator, or mechanical differential analyzer. And of course the world today is filled with examples of the much greater extent to which we are employing mechanical apparatus to perform physical operations in our behalf. The computer will therefore be utilized to the fullest extent practical and profitable in corporate planning.

Man applies his capabilities to make the combination of men and machines most effective for analytical purposes. He must direct or operate mechanical instruments of analysis. He must evaluate their performance with respect to the internal and external environments of the enterprise as a whole, which he alone can see and experience. He redirects their general and specific use as conditions change. Regardless of the degree of reliability or the extent of self-checking incorporated in the mechanism, he is the final monitor of its accuracy. He must decide how mechanically derived data are used, and exercise his responsibility of questioning or disregarding the results of such analysis. In shaping his role, man recognizes his unique capacities and those areas in which his own analytical performance is extended by mechanical means.

Despite remarkable advances in inanimate devices, current fascination with the electronic computer, and the potentialities of synthetic biology, the intelligent mental-nervous system remains the ultimate and most impressive instrument of cognition. The human mind can remember and manipulate a great variety of information: visual images, sounds, tastes, odors, tactile sensations, memories, impressions, feelings, fantasies, and a wide range of words, numbers, graphical material, and other abstractions. This assimilation demands no particular order or sequential consistency. It can be transposed from one form to another almost instantaneously in that, for example, physical or numerical relationships can be reconceptualized as graphical or written expressions. The combined storage capacity of conscious and unconscious minds is large. As discussed briefly in the previous section, not only are most if not all sensory impressions recorded, but many of them are continuously affecting conscious thought. From this synthesis emerge our patterns of reasoning, subjective judgment, and emotional reaction. It underlies the extraordinary richness, subtlety, and uniqueness of human communication through language and other forms of expression.

Considering the range of information it processes, the central nervous system is very fast in action—although some areas of receptivity and conclusion may be slow or even completely blocked from conscious access for emotional reasons. Its informational and procedural flexibility is extensive and remarkably rapid. A conceptual approach or line of thought can be changed several times in an instant, from one form to others distinctly different. The mind possesses a keen sense of real time. For the most part, the information we receive and its mental processing are automatically differentiated according to its applicability and meaningfulness for past, present, and future. We are conscious of the significance of real time in thought and action. These mental capabilities combine to provide a wide range and sensitivity of critical check or error detection—not so much in minutiae as with respect to basic elements and interrelationships.

Human perception is more comprehensive than mechanical observation. Not only are the five human senses individually alert, but they function in concert through the central nervous system. A bad taste is amplified by a bad smell; the visual image of a person is modified by what we hear. We can knowingly focus one or several of these senses in a deliberately perceptive effort. Our biological sensors, in combination with the unconscious, constitute the "sixth sense"—our capacity to record and respond to an object or situation without conscious awareness of the specific reasons or process of conclusion. This intuitive capacity is especially acute and reliable in some people, and continuously operative in all of us. It accounts in part for the flexibility of the human mind, its ability to continuously adjust our line of reaction and thought as the external situation changes. Feedback is characteristic of the human central nervous system. Its expression may be mainly physical, as in the automatic and immediate compensating movements we make when we lose our balance. Or, in deliberate mental analysis, it is expressed in our reconsideration of method and conclusion as the factors change.

Man is analytically unique in other ways. He can proceed without knowing; he can search and progress without supportive information. He is not restricted to the next increment of logically progressive advance; "quantum jumps" of awareness or mental "breakthroughs" are possible. Proof is developed later. In this way he is creative, having the capacity to add more than is immediately implied by the known "state of the art" or situation. By definition, man alone can determine human values; he must make the ultimate choice of human objectives in response to human needs. Imagination is unique to man. With this projective ability, he can pictorialize freely within his mind, conceptualize abstractions or events very different from existing experience, fantasy within the realm of conceivable reality. And, difficult or impossible as it may be to define, he appears the only organism with the sense of consciousness.

The impressive capabilities of the mind as an instrument of conscious reasoning are represented in the range and depth of human knowledge. Man applies his intelligence to solve problems by different forms of logical analysis: inference, deduction, analogy, experiment, mathematical method. He is inclusive or restrictive in this reasoning as the case may be. In value judgments involving indefinites, the range of mental consideration is broad; supporting proof is correspondingly weak or impossible. In mathematics, the range of consideration is restricted, logical structure strong because it can be formulated with numerical precision and quantitative coherence. The outstanding potentialities of human reasoning in corporate planning are its scope and flexibility, its ability to encompass elements of very different nature, certainty, and stability and nonetheless arrive at a deductive conclusion.

It is in this area of greatest potentiality, however, that man needs assistance. Most persons do not consciously scan a situation in all important aspects to identify its many different elements and considerations. The frequent assumption that this awareness is widespread ignores our innate tendency to focus on those aspects with which we are most familiar through experience and professional concentration, or toward which we are oriented by our mental-emotional personalities. For most people, the comprehensive view requires deliberate effort or special stimulation. We are also limited in the number of sequential correlations we can follow without becoming lost. For example, deriving the outcome of a succession of many interdependent conditional interrelationships requires mathematical knowledge. The average person is also limited in his ability to comprehend and manipulate abstractions. Our inherent preference is for real-life, concrete images rooted in the vast unconscious storage of experiences we have observed directly. In contrast, a characteristic of formal analysis is its dependence on the abstract symbols of statistics, mathematics, and logic. The analytical appraisal which is increasingly essential in corporate planning involves these mental activities we perform more effectively with assistance.

Electronic computing devices are tailor-made for this support. Their outstanding capabilities coincide with the areas of the human mind's greatest limitation. By their judicious employment, man extends greatly his own restricted potentialities of numerical analysis, preparatory to his role of non-quantitative integration, judgment, intuition, decision, and purposeful action. At the same time, he upgrades his creative contribution to the continual advancement of the process of business management and corporate planning in general.

In time, human capacity to scan, correlate, and deal with abstractions may improve with educational advances, the effects of our ever-changing environment, and continued evolutionary development of the human mind itself. We know how readily children absorb new concepts with which their parents have great difficulty. It is possible that entirely new methods of conceptualization and analysis may be found which will extend those areas in which we are now cogitatively weak. But we can hardly wait for evolution or an uncertain intellectual breakthrough. We must accept the existing state of affairs described in succinct fashion by Sir Winston Churchill:

> The whole prospect and outlook of mankind grew immeasurably larger, and the multiplication of ideas also proceeded at an incredible rate. This vast expansion was unhappily not accompanied by any noticeable advance in the stature of man

either in his mental faculties or his moral character. His brain got no better; but it buzzed more.[30]

For some time to come, we must rely on those aids to our mental functioning now available. Perhaps it is the more efficient utilization of these which will most likely trigger some fundamental methodological advance.

To summarize from this prerequisite background of understanding: management determines the scope and objectives of the analytical effort in comprehensive planning and the extent to which it is mechanized. The responsible executive formulates the procedure of collecting and processing corporate information and directs the activity. Insofar as practical and profitable, quantitative operations, repetitive functions, and numerical computation are assigned to machines. Professional personnel instruct the computer and related mechanisms in what they will do and how they will operate, and monitor their performance. Instruction and monitoring are simplified by incorporating selective "self-instruction" and automatic "self-checking" in the machine programs. To the extent feasible, the computer is programed to utilize its great speed and large capacity to "discover" new facts, interrelationships, and solutions. Management considers the results and decides the end use of mechanical analysis. Through appropriate delegation, it evaluates and improves the design and operation of the computer system and the over-all synthesis of men and machines for planning purposes.

Although such systems are generally limited to larger institutions at the present time, it is important to remember that the process of collecting, analyzing, and utilizing information is essentially the same in a small business with only the telephone and typewriter available. The difference is in the relative employment of men and machines. In the simpler business operation, people accumulate data, do simple arithmetic, file, and remember; the manager accomplishes the necessary analysis in his head or with pencil and paper. As mechanical devices are incorporated into the process, people operate the machines and perform progressively higher-level analytical and managerial functions requiring their special capabilities. In every case, the most effective system and best employment of men and machines represent a balance between the informational needs of the company, its organizational capabilities, and the "net worth" or profit value of the analytical activity.

Circular Process of Periodic Adjustment

In accordance with long-established principles of management, operating information is transmitted upward through the successive levels of administration or chain of command. The policies and decisions of top management are communicated in a reverse flow. Since these are also the formal channels of corporate planning, they are even more dynamic and vital with this extension of coordinative-projective activity.

The procedure of comprehensive planning is therefore "circular" in an organizational sense. The sequence of communication and responsibility is up and down in a generally circular system of interaction. For example, longer-range objectives are established by corporate management to give direction to component plans. A divisional opportunity representing a considerable departure from previous experience may require simulation of its consequences for the company as a whole before its desirability is confirmed. An unanticipated development of major proportions anywhere in the company may lead to modification of corporate objectives. The different levels of management participate in the resolution of most corporate planning matters, such as criteria of profit performance, coordination of labor relations and policies, capital expenditures, company advertising policy, or product diversification. Each organizational level contributes its input toward final analytical determination and, subsequently, its action toward implementation.

The procedural logic of transmitting, processing, and using information is also circular in nature, comprising a closed loop of feedback and feedforward. By rapid reporting and analysis of operating data, trends are identified at an early stage of development which call for an immediate adjustment of current activities and corresponding changes in the programs of production, use of physical facilities, or recruitment of personnel incorporated in plans for the intermediate future. Similarly, by feedforward, trends are projected in concert to simulate what the company will be like some years hence if it continues in the same direction, and to anticipate specific requirements such as working capital, machines and equipment, or distribution facilities at different future times. By analysis and adjustment back and forth between past, present, and future, a realistic balance is derived between current commitments and desired goals. Although history never repeats itself exactly, retrospective evaluation of historical trends is of course often revealing and specifically suggestive for the future. Two conspicuous illustrations are the behavior of wage rates and other costs, and the percentage success of new product research and development over time. ". . . It takes some 40 ideas . . . to yield one successful new product. . . . The record shows that for every five products emerging from research and development departments as technical successes, there is an average of only one commercial success. . . . Even between major companies in the same industry, efficiencies range from less than 1% to over 50%."[31] By analytical feedback, such experiential trends are maintained with relation to both time and their correlation with external economic conditions and other environmental factors. The communication and processing of information is as continuous as it is worthwhile, since it can be collected as background analysis for periodic application.

The revision of plans is a third form of procedural recycle in the process of organized comprehensive planning. As mentioned earlier, there are practical limits to the frequency of this regular revision; an interval of stabilization is necessary to realize results. The benefits of quantity production, for example, are never attained if modifications are made in unbroken succession. The official, periodic revision of shorter-range plans takes place only as often as required by the nature of the enterprise and improved profit performance over time—usually quarterly. Longer-range plans are revised once a year, but adjustments brought about by current events are accumulated and formal revision is made in the interim if indicated. Normally, corporate goals are changed gradually rather than suddenly since they reflect careful study rather than uncertainty of purpose, analytical procrastination, or change for change's sake. Changes of objective are also limited, of course, by financial obligations and investment in programs of accomplishment partly realized. Occasionally, external situations develop, targets of opportunity arise, or internal facts are revealed in corporate planning which call for immediate revision of the entire framework of both short- and long-range intention.

A significant restriction on the frequency of adjustment in planning is human tolerance. Man cannot produce in a state of perpetual analytical motion, nor manage successfully in response to continuously changing information. Periods of relative stability are required to comprehend the existing situation, to formulate and implement managerial actions, and to consider the future. There are psychological limits to the number of continuous variables which the mind can handle, and physical-nervous limitations to the active response of people to constant change. Natural resistances arise within the individual to limit his responsive sensitivity to never-ending change in the real world—or ulcers and nervous breakdowns occur. These individual boundaries are circumvented in part by dividing the responsibilities of following rapidly changing elements of the business, and by restricting the display of new data to the rate of absorption and best managerial performance of those concerned. The problem is most crucial for the small group of executives who examine the corporate condition in its entirety, for at this level of ultimate synthesis, projection, and decision the largest number of continuous variables are relevant and the possible combinations almost infinite.

The practical outcome of considering these regenerative characteristics of the comprehensive planning process is a sounder organizational structure, efficient informational procedures, and a schedule for the regular revision of corporate plans—neither so often nor infrequently as to impair their function—with sufficient communication and continual analysis to provide interim surveillance and enough flexibility to permit revision at any time.

It is sometimes contended that "operational" and "developmental" plans are intrinsically different. If so, the correlation of operating programs for the present and developmental plans for the longer-range future is impossible or presents unique difficulties. Is there an analytical incompatibility between current operations, the short-term or annual plan, and longer-range plans? The question occurs often enough to merit clarification.

The spectrum of comprehensive planning includes past, present, and future. Commitments made yesterday or years ago are restrictive or suggestive for both present and future. The repayment of long-term debt and the use of existing plant and equipment are familiar examples. Past investments have developed corporate capabilities which are current or potential assets, such as a strong sales or service organization for certain products. Accumulated experience comprises a continuing background affecting present operations and planning. Extrapolations, forecasts, and other analytical projections all have their roots in the past. "What is past is prologue."

Past achievements and future intentions are vital aspects of a company's standing and prospects, but neither has meaning except with relation to present action. What is being done here and now is the most significant reality. It is the time of tangible accomplishment, of most accurate measurement and operational adjustment represented by precise production schedules, sales orders on hand, actual inventory, more exact cost data, going interest rate, or vacant managerial positions. Profit performance has its greatest impact.

The future is tomorrow in a strict sense, and one, five, or ten years hence in business practice. It is the province of probabilities, ranging from the definite to the indefinite and unpredictable. The replacement of personnel is as certain as life and death, the obligation of repaying debt as sure as human nature. Because many political-economic events are unpredictable, the value of the dollar with which the long-term debt will be repaid is uncertain. As every company knows, sales forecasts are subject to considerable variation from the best estimates. Product demand can evaporate unexpectedly owing to lower-cost competition, change in consumer taste, or technological obsolescence. The future is the constant challenge of business, the forthcoming period of multiple uncertainties for which some projection, forecast, or guess is either implicit in every decision or made deliberately as a basis for purposeful action. Rarely can the future be ignored.

If viewed in this way, operational and developmental plans are programs of activity for different periods within a continuously progressing span of time and uncertainty. This span rarely exceeds the range of human interest represented by the mature lifetime of the individual in business—40 years at the most. Because of predictive and practical limitations, the average span of active consideration influencing present conclusions is closer to ten years. Within this range of time, today's operating plans become tomorrow's history, and developmental plans for the longer-range future evolve slowly but surely toward operating programs for the present. The fact of today ultimately becomes a historical interpretation, and with the passage of time the forecast is transmuted into present fact. To be sure, the passage of time may bring such variances between forecast, present fact, and retrospective evaluation that their identity is anything but obvious.

Corporate plans comprise a continuous gradation from specific programs for current operations to more general statements of action directed toward the future. They schedule the activities necessary to realize current targets and attain agreed-upon objectives by successive stages. Naturally, the plan for the present period is most detailed and precise; it is also more subject to changes forced by immediate circumstance or crisis. But a portion of this current activity was "reserved" earlier for application toward specific needs foreseen in the future, and toward general achievements which should enable the company to maintain or improve its performance within the environment anticipated five or more years hence. This allocation of effort for the future is made possible by the surplus resources and policy of optimizing profits over time discussed in the previous chapter.

As operations are modified by immediate circumstance, variances occur between current plan and actuality which require the consequent adjustment of future activities and intentions. There is regular readjustment between reality as it develops and plans for the future. A year of unexpected difficulties and no profits of course calls for reconsideration of plans based on the use of this anticipated return. The entire program of intention may be shifted further into the future until the financial requirements of profitability have been met and these resources are once more available, or plans may be revised because the year's postponement changes certain timing considered critical.

Operational and developmental plans are not different in kind but are inseparably interrelated. There is no logical discrepancy nor unique problem of correlation. One is the feasible or at least conceivable extension of the other. Difficulties of correlation are methodological rather than generic. Until recently, the regular readjustment required by variances between plan and actuality was impractical or impossible for most businesses. Processing the necessary volume of data was prohibitively expensive, or the circular procedure of feedback-feedforward was too complicated and slow with existing office machines. There was less interest in established corporate planning. With electronic computing equipment, feasible analytic adjustment has been extended in range and frequency. The process and outcome more widely accepted today are conceptualized in Figure 3. Although sharp variances can occur between plan and outcome, the course of corporate progress over time is significantly closer to chosen objectives than is the case without flexible direction.

Incorporation of Flexibility

The incorporation of flexibility is a cardinal principle of planning. Any attempt to be all-inclusive and rigid in the formulation

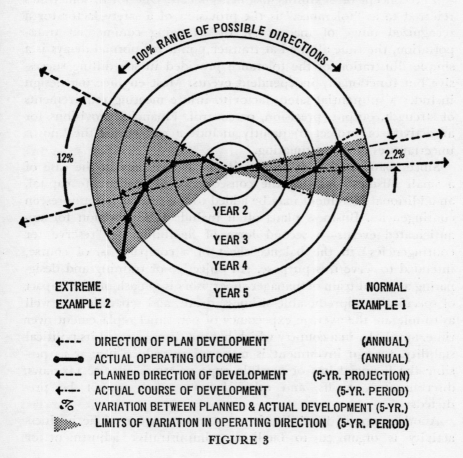

Conceptualization of Two Illustrative Variations in
Operating and Plan Direction

CORPORATE COURSE OF DEVELOPMENT

←---	DIRECTION OF PLAN DEVELOPMENT	(ANNUAL)
•—•	ACTUAL OPERATING OUTCOME	(ANNUAL)
←--	PLANNED DIRECTION OF DEVELOPMENT	(5-YR. PROJECTION)
←·--	ACTUAL COURSE OF DEVELOPMENT	(5-YR. PERIOD)
.%	VARIATION BETWEEN PLANNED & ACTUAL DEVELOPMENT (5-YR.)
▷▷▷	LIMITS OF VARIATION IN OPERATING DIRECTION	(5-YR. PERIOD)

FIGURE 3

of plans, or to persist in their implementation as originally drawn regardless of interim developments, almost invariably leads to unfortunate consequences. "[Safeway] might almost be called 'the classic situation' of modern American business, . . . a corporation . . . built to greatness by the fierce competitiveness and individuality of a single leader, and then suddenly [finding] itself held back by that leader's principles and unwillingness to conform to the realities of a more dispassionate, more up-to-date philosophy of management."[32] The corporate policy of Montgomery Ward during the decade following World War II is probably the most publicized confirmation that flexibility is not always accepted and applied as a guiding rule of management.

The concept of flexibility has many facets. One form, sometimes referred to as "tolerance," is the provision of a safety factor for a recognized range of inaccuracy. In arranging commercial transportation, the time allowed at transfer points for normal delays is a simple illustration of the tolerance provided in scheduling successive but functionally independent events. Most engineering design includes a substantial safety factor to insure meeting requirements of strength, output, precision, or control. Financial provisions for an activity or project frequently include a reserve for the known uncertainties of cost estimating.

Since abandonment of an activity, or bankruptcy in the case of a small business, may be the consequence of inadequate capital, an additional increment may be added to the reserve for unforeseen contingencies. Business plans often include this provision for unanticipated events—a second form of flexibility. A "reserve for contingencies" in the balance sheet of a company is, of course, intended to serve this purpose. An objective of training and designating a second team of manager-supervisors is to cushion the impact of specifically unpredictable sickness, death, and separation, as well as to tolerate the average expectancy of personnel replacement over time. Similarly, in a country which has not demonstrated its political stability, foreign investment is managed to reduce insofar as possible the financial loss of possible expropriation, adverse tax laws, discriminatory tariffs, and other factors which cannot be predicted.

Another type of flexibility is structural in nature. The business activity is organized to facilitate administrative adjustment or physical-spatial rearrangement. This is less a matter of specific provision for expected and unexpected events than an organic flexibility incorporated as a general principle of sound management. A system of administrative organization which channels all communication and decision through a single executive position is less flexible than one which spreads responsibilities, encourages individual initiative, and permits a greater range of autonomous action. In facilities planning and plant engineering, buildings, machines, and equipment are organized in space to provide a general physical flexibility considered worthwhile in the long run, even at the expense of some loss of immediate efficiency. It may be used for any one or a combination of possible purposes: expansion, rearrangement, safety, operating and maintenance access, inspection, supervision, insurance advantages, amenity. In the same sense, multipurpose machinery and broadly written policies are structurally more flexible than special-purpose machines and policy statements so narrow they allow no variation of method in their implementation.

Several aspects of flexibility are especially relevant in corporate planning. The longer-range its projections, the greater their flexibility to allow for increased uncertainty. The deferred commitments intentionally incorporated in each projected year are reduced progressively as planning approaches the present, and the flexibility of the total projection is retained by an equivalent extension into the future. The extent of flexibility in a plan is therefore in part a function of time: progressive commitment for the present and near term, greater freedom of action for the intermediate and longer-range future. Maintaining this principle requires deliberate attention. A company is committing itself continuously in many different ways through debt, product selection, manufacturing methods, sales contracts, distribution system, leases, industrial location, labor policy, employment contracts, or organizational structure—to name an illustrative few. Both the nature and the extent of these commitments change as they lapse, are abandoned or revised, and new obligations are undertaken. They represent necessary decisions or desirable arrangements, but at the same time they constitute in the aggregate a limitation of flexibility. "The flexibility of the budget in any current year . . . is small compared with the possible impact of program decisions this year on budgets for future years."[33] Not all obligations are unalterable, of course, but their change normally means a loss or cost of some sort. It is important in corporate planning to know the pattern of commitment for the future, and the residual areas in which adjustment can be made more easily. This pattern is rarely obvious and sometimes surprising when revealed.

The requirement of surplus resources for effective planning is a type of flexibility; current demands cannot be so consuming that there is no freedom of action or strategic choice with respect to the future. And the process of periodic revision of corporate plans presumes the possibility of adjustments. Inevitably, however, this leeway is reduced as shorter-range plans are specified, operational decisions made, and specific programs implemented. A basic principle of comprehensive planning is to maintain at all times a degree of structural flexibility somewhere within the total business organism. The area of adjustment may shift over time from one division to another. While impossible to provide now, it may be practical in a year or two if planned. It may be foregone temporarily, to be regained at a later date. Some corporate functions are by their nature less flexible than others. Usually there are more limitations to change in certain areas of finance and physical facilities, for example, than in personnel-employment and public relations.

The future is the constant challenge of business largely because of the twin problems of flexibility and commitment. Corporate planning provides the analytical background needed for executive determination of how much structural flexibility is desirable, in what areas of functional planning and programs of operation, and when various capabilities of adjustment are to be attained and relinquished. A balance must be reached between the extremes of excessive flexibility, which reduces near-term operational efficiency and dilutes the present use of corporate resources by lack of specification, and short-term commitment so complete and restrictive of future adjustment that success is dependent on conditions remaining unchanged. Flexibility in the form of safety factors must also be examined. These provisions can accumulate by progressive addition until undue costs are incurred for needlessly defensive features, or a policy is so watered down it is not very useful. If everybody adds his own tolerance for adjustment, the total allowance for flexibility is likely to be both excessive and more random than planned.

There is wide variation in the extent to which individuals can adapt to changing conditions, and in their capacity to conceptualize and think in terms of continual adjustment. For some, these attributes are a natural outgrowth of personality and circumstance. For others, they are difficult or even impossible to acquire. Since comprehensive planning is a process of adjustment in which human judgment is the most critical ingredient, personal adaptability and analytical flexibility are characteristics required of those most concerned with the activity.

Allied Endeavors

Occasionally, the relationship of several allied endeavors to corporate planning is misunderstood. Their function is misinterpreted, or commonly accepted definitions are expanded to the point where they are comparable with that of comprehensive planning. Brief explanation of these related activities will eliminate any possibility of confusion. No attempt will be made to provide complete definitions or to describe the various meanings which exist in some cases for the same term. The intent is, rather, to emphasize the difference between these component activities and corporate planning as discussed in this book.

As estimates of a future situation or condition, *forecasts* are part of planning (Figure 4). The background role of such projective analyses as population growth, national economic development, or use of income is widely recognized. Equally basic for most businesses are the expected size and characteristics of the market for the company's product, or the probable pattern of competition. A wide variety of general and specific forecasts may be worthwhile for different purposes within a company. For example, long-range planning at Standard Oil (Indiana) ". . . involves three kinds of capital expenditure forecasts. One of these is a detailed one-year projection for operational purposes, another is a five-year forecast for budgetary control, and the third is a 15-year forecast for expansion planning."[34] Forecasts may lead to operational changes which require several years of careful planning before they can be realized. A forecast of the existing situation may be unacceptable to management and call for planned action which will create new corporate prospects. Forecasts are not plans, therefore, because they do not in

MANAGEMENT PERSONNEL: ANTICIPATED NEEDS

Lockheed-California Company

[by H. Lockwood, Supervisor, Management Selection, Training, & Research]

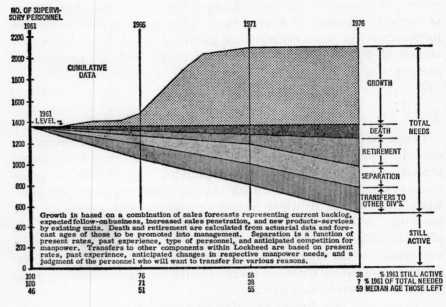

FIGURE 4

themselves establish specific company objectives or encompass the range of consideration required in developing programs of purposive action.

In some companies, short-range forecasts by operating units are used as formal statements of their most realistic expectations based on existing conditions. Extrapolations of such key elements as sales, production, and profits highlight variances between current outlook and plan projections previously developed and adopted. For example, the forecast of sales derived from the immediate outlook every week or month is compared with the plan which is normally reviewed quarterly or, in some businesses, less frequently. These short-term forecasts are available before the time scheduled for re-examination of existing plans. They provide a current reference for management during the interval which is deliberately provided between plan reviews for the reasons presented earlier in this chapter. Because they are limited to a few key indicators, they do not involve the greater expense and administrative effort of complete planning analysis.

This series of operational forecasts, successively replaced by actuals, is at hand for any immediate action it suggests, and comprises a record of variances between short-range intention and performance when plans are formally reviewed to decide whether they should be retained or revised. Usually, these variances average out close to the plan projection. When a significant difference between performance, forecast, and plan projection persists, they must of course be adjusted sooner or later to a closer coincidence. As corporate planning becomes an established process, the variance between operational forecast and plan projection diminishes, and the procedure of comparison serves mainly to identify exceptional interim developments.

A *budget* is a method of analysis and control which describes anticipated requirements of money, relates level of activity and cost, or formally limits permissible expenditure. It is a near-term operational device and a partial measure of performance expressed in dollars, which defines neither the longer-range objectives nor the more inclusive plans of which it is only a part. Budgets are an important instrument of planning, but they are subject to change both in the total amount made available and in the specific utilization of a given allocation. These changes are the consequence of the more inclusive activity of comprehensive planning.

Profit plan is a term used occasionally to focus attention on the dual importance of profits and planning. It is often associated with a concerted effort to improve performance in particular areas of functional planning such as sales and production. Employed in this way, it can lead to overemphasis of short-term profits at the expense of greater gains over a longer period of time. Research and development, and the complete overhauling of potentially profitable operations which have been mismanaged, are cases in point. Profit objectives are the foundation of every business plan. If it is desirable to include the word "profit" as a constant reminder, and if profit plans are considered as broad in scope as corporate plans, the two terms mean the same thing. To avoid confusion, only one should be adopted. Not only is "corporate planning" more expressive of the full range of consideration in planning comprehensively for business, but "profit planning" is available for more precise description. It might define, for instance, that portion of a comprehensive plan which specifies profit capabilities and intentions separately.

> An important part of the Profit Planning Department's work is preparing estimates of costs and profit returns on each individual size of each variety produced and/or marketed by the company. An estimate of product cost and profit for each size of each variety is prepared at the beginning of the year as an integral part of the budget for the year. Then, throughout the year, these product cost and profit estimates are revised to show the effect of significant changes in material unit costs, labor performance, yield performance, overhead absorption, selling prices, discounts, etc.[35]

In seeking to establish the potential demand or possible penetration for a product or service, or for a family of related products and services, *market research* is clearly intended for planning purposes. It can be broad in its analytical coverage, including consumer survey, customer evaluation, costs, pricing, sales methods, distribution, product repair and maintenance, financing, technological life, governmental regulations and attitudes, acceptance by union labor, or other determinants of the true market situation. When thorough market study is undertaken, it usually involves most functional activities within the company before it is concluded. But market research does not itself establish the corporate objectives with which it is closely related, the area and extent of investigation, and many of the factual inputs which are collected from sales, production, finance, and other components of the company. These elements are determined within the broader context of corporate planning, and consequent decisions are based only in part on market research.

Operations research employs mathematics and the techniques of the physical and social sciences for the quantitative-numerical solution of problems which can be solved by scientific method. Its general approach involves observation; the derivation of a mathematical model describing the phenomenon under study; controlled experiment; adjustment of the model to incorporate understanding developed by the experiment; and, finally, application of the acquired knowledge to the direction and control of the phenomenon in question. To date, operations research has been heavily mathematical in its approach, often requiring electronic computers for the necessary calculation.[36]

In the decade and a half since operations research was first employed for military planning during World War II, this field of specialization has been responsible for significant advances in the methods of analyzing certain business operations and functional planning. Examples include the inventory level which compromises most satisfactorily such conflicting criteria as availability, cost, investment, and cash flow; the least costly pattern of distribution by existing transportation routes; means of scheduling the flow of different components in production assembly to increase output; and the most effective use-distribution of available cash among different operating units. Operations research is also interested in larger systems such as the corporation as a whole or the total endeavor of defense against submarines by different military means. It seeks methods of accurate measurement and calculative comparison between alternatives since ". . . it is interested in providing executives with the soundest possible basis for evaluating the activities under their control so that necessary decisions may be made."[37]

There are those who maintain, however:

> The manager has often found that management science [i.e., operations research] did not deal with his most urgent problems; it has not learned to take into account the variables he knows to be important; it is not cast in a language with which he is familiar. . . . The attitude is that of an exercise in formal logic rather than that of seeking useful help in real problems. For most of the great problems, mathematical solutions fall far short of being able to find the "best" solution. The misleading objective of trying only for the optimum solution often results in simplifying the problem until it is devoid of practical interest.[38]

> This leads to an ailment that might be called mathematician's aphasia. The victim abstracts the original problem until the mathematical intractibilities have been removed (and all semblance to reality lost), solves the now simplified problem, and then pretends that this was the problem he wanted to solve all along. He expects the manager to be so dazzled by the beauty of the mathematical results that he will not remember that his practical operating problem has not been handled.[39]

Whichever viewpoint prevails, operations research is not now equivalent with corporate planning as described in this book. Besides substantive limitations such as those cited, it does not encompass the processes of subjective judgment and the mental-emotional factors which are essential aspects of executive management and the great majority of the organisms to which it is applied. The attitudes and personalities of most professional practitioners of operations research today are very different from those of line managers; not infrequently, their concepts of the realities of business enterprise are poles apart. Few of the two groups have shared similar experiences, and a modification of respective attitudes is characteristic of these exceptions.

For the present and foreseeable future, operations research will make a worthwhile contribution to certain specific activities and areas of investigation within the broader context of corporate planning. It combines several of the many forms of analysis which can be applied profitably in the appropriate situation. But it does not now share with corporate planning the same objectives, scope of consideration, or range of methodology. By its emphasis on mathematical-quantitative precision, operations research will exert a beneficial pressure on corporate planning to develop and incorporate scientific method to the extent feasible. In time, the two fields may converge, the former becoming more inclusive and the latter more scientific.

REFERENCES CITED

[1] N. R. Maines, *Why Companies Grow* (Stanford Research Institute, Menlo Park), p. 4.

[2] Charles E. Summer, Jr., "The Future Role of the Corporate Planner," *California Management Review*, Winter 1961 (Vol. III, No. 2), pp. 17–31. William M. Freeman, "Big Job Is Open: 'Looking Ahead,'" *New York Times*, Sunday 7 August 1960, p. F5.

[3] Frederick Harbison and Charles A. Myers, *Management in the Industrial World* [reported in *Business Week*, 2 January 1960 (No. 1583), p. 60].

[4] N. R. Maines, *supra*, p. 6.

[5] Charles B. Thornton (President, Litton Industries), quoted by William E. Hill and Charles H. Granger, *Long-Range Planning for Company Development*, October 1956 (William E. Hill & Co., New York City), p. 5.

[6] John G. McLean (Vice President, Coordinating and Planning, Continental Oil Co.), "The Development, Operation, and Organization of Central Research Staffs in Industry," address (mimeo) before the Business Research

Section, Southwestern Social Science Association, Galveston, Texas, 27 March 1959, p. 9.

[7] *1959 Annual Report*, Pacific Gas and Electric Corporation.

[8] N. R. Maines, *supra*, p. 5.

[9] "Change of Heart," *Forbes Business and Finance*, 1 February 1961 (Vol. 87, No. 3), p. 32.

[10] Booz, Allen, & Hamilton, *Management of New Products*, 1960, p. 18.

[11] *Business Week*, 7 November 1959 (No. 1575), p. 167.

[12] Melvin Anshen, "The Manager and the Black Box," *Harvard Business Review*, November–December 1960 (Vol. 38, No. 6), p. 89.

[13] John G. McLean, "How to Evaluate New Capital Investments," *Harvard Business Review*, November–December 1958 (Vol. 36, No. 6), pp. 59–69.

Edward A. Ravenscroft, "Return on Investment: Fit the Method to Your Need," *Harvard Business Review*, March–April 1960 (Vol. 38, No. 2), pp. 97–109.

[14] Fred V. Gardner, *Profit Management and Control*, 1955 (McGraw-Hill Book Company), p. vii.

Bernard Whitney and Marion S. Israel, "A Working Model of the Financial Dynamics of a Business," *Operations Research*, July–August 1958 (Vol. 6, No. 4), pp. 573–579.

[15] Don G. Mitchell (Vice Chairman, General Telephone & Electronics Corporation; formerly, Chairman and President, Sylvania Electric Products), quoted by William E. Hill and Charles H. Granger, *supra*, p. 9.

Perrin Stryker and the Editors of *Fortune*, *A Guide to Modern Management Methods* (Chapter Eleven, "A Slight Case of Overcommunication"), 1954 (McGraw-Hill Book Company), pp. 177–186.

[16] Keith Davis, "Management Communication and the Grapevine," *Harvard Business Review*, September–October 1953 (Vol. 31, No. 5), pp. 43–49.

M. Joseph Dooher and Vivienne Marquis, *Effective Communication on the Job*, 1956 (American Management Association), 278 pp.

[17] Victor A. Thompson, "Hierarchy, Specialization, and Organizational Conflict," *Administrative Science Quarterly*, March 1961 (Vol. 5, No. 4), p. 500.

[18] Polykarp Kusch, "The Role of Science," *The Wall Street Journal*, Wednesday, 15 March 1961 (Vol. LXIV, No. 51), p. 12 (extracted remarks to the Pulitzer Prize jurors, 1955).

[19] Ralph R. Greenson, M.D., and Hilda S. Rollman-Branch, M.D., personal communication, 1961.

Karl A. Menninger, *The Human Mind*, 1953 (Alfred A. Knopf), 517 pp.

[20] Chester I. Barnard (President, New Jersey Bell Telephone Co.), "Methods and Limitations of Foresight in Modern Affairs," address delivered at the Thirtieth Annual Convention of the Association of Life Insurance Presidents, New York, 4 December 1936, p. 4.

[21] George P. Schultz and Thomas L. Whistler (Editors), *Management Organization and the Computer*, 1960 (Free Press), 257 pp.

[22] Joseph P. Lovewell (Stanford Research Institute, Menlo Park), personal communication, 26 February 1962.

[23] Seabrook Hull and the Board of Editors, "The Polaris Program: An Interview with Vice Admiral W. F. Raborn, Jr., USN," *Missile Design and Development*, January 1961 (Vol. 7, No. 1), p. 58.

[24] Richard West, "Computers Solve Vast Paper Work," *Los Angeles Times*, Sunday, 5 February 1961, Section E, p. 7.

[25] Ralph E. Winters, "More Firms Cut Costs by Fixing Equipment Before Breakdowns," *The Wall Street Journal*, Tuesday, 7 March 1961 (Vol. LXIV, No. 45), p. 10.

[26] 3rd Annual Industrial Economics Conference (How Companies Grow), sponsored by Stanford Research Institute, Los Angeles, January 13–15, 1958.
James C. Hetrick, "Mathematical Models in Capital Budgeting," *Harvard Business Review*, January–February 1961 (Vol. 39, No. 1), pp. 49–64.
Harvey N. Shycon and Richard B. Maffei, "Simulation—Tool for Better Distribution," *ibid.*, November–December 1960 (Vol. 38, No. 6), pp. 65–75.

[27] *Annual Report 1960*, p. 13; *Bulletin*, April 1961 (Vol. XL, No. 2), pp. 9–11, Standard Oil Company of California.

[28] E. W. Martin, Jr., "Practical Problems of Introducing a Computer," *Business Horizons*, Fall 1960 (Vol. 3, No. 6), pp. 4 ff.

[29] *1960 Annual Report*, Pacific Gas and Electric Company, p. 6.

[30] *A Churchill Reader*, 1954 (Houghton Mifflin Co.), p. 381.

[31] Booz, Allen, & Hamilton, *Management of New Products*, 1960, p. 3.

[32] Robert Sheehan, "Magowan's Way with Safeway," *Fortune*, October 1958 (Vol. LVIII, No. 4), p. 114.

[33] Charles Hitch, in "Applying an Economist's Yardstick to Defense," *Business Week*, 4 March 1961 (No. 1644), p. 65.

[34] W. D. McEachron, quoted by William E. Hill and Charles H. Granger, *supra*, p. 4.
Forecasting in Industry, Conference Board Reports—Studies in Business Policy No. 77 (National Industrial Conference Board, Inc., New York City), 76 pp.

[35] R. Burt Gookin (Comptroller, H. J. Heinz Co.), "III. Responsibilities of the Comptroller's Division (The Profit Budget Plan)," *How H. J. Heinz Manages Its Financial Planning and Controls*, Financial Management Series No. 106, 1953 (American Management Association), pp. 18–37.

[36] Andrew Vazsonyi, *Scientific Programming in Business and Industry*, 1958 (John Wiley & Sons), 474 pp.

[37] *Information on Operations Research and the Operations Research Society of America*, February 1958 (ORSA, Baltimore), 16 pp.

Operations Research Reconsidered: Some Frontiers and Boundaries of Industrial OR, Management Report No. 10, 1958 (American Management Association), 143 pp.

[38] Jay W. Forrester, *The Impact of Feedback Control Concepts on the Management Sciences,* FIER Distinguished Lecture, 27 October, 1960 (Foundation for Instrumentation Education and Research, New York City), 24 pp.

[39] Herbert A. Simon, *The New Science of Management Decision,* 1960, (Harper & Brothers), p. 18.

CHAPTER V

Techniques of Analysis

By ELDRED C. NELSON and MELVILLE C. BRANCH

Corporate planning involves two broad categories of analysis: mathematical-statistical method and human judgment. The first is scientific, the second "subjective," in nature. The first seeks data and a quantitative expression of their interrelationships which is factual in the sense that if the process is repeated, the results conform to the descriptive statement. The second is to a greater extent the product of mental and behavioral mechanisms not yet

ELDRED C. NELSON is a recognized authority in the field of mathematical-statistical techniques. Now associated with Space Technology Laboratories, Inc., he was formerly Director, Intellectronics Laboratories, Ramo-Wooldridge Division of Thompson Ramo Wooldridge Inc.; Associate Director of the Computer Systems Division of the Ramo Wooldridge Corporation; and Head of the Advanced Electronics Laboratory at Hughes Aircraft Company. He has been a member of the faculties of the University of Chicago and the University of California at Berkeley.

Dr. Nelson is principal author of the first part of this chapter, entitled "Mathematical-Statistical Method."

sufficiently understood for systematic treatment and comparable predictive accuracy.

Since people perform or direct quantitative-scientific observation, calculation, and experiment, this dual division is arbitrary. Actually, scientific "fact" and human psychology are interconnected. But, because of historical development, educational emphasis, professional identification, and the practical benefits of simplification, this general separation will continue useful until it is replaced by new categorization or some form of expression which combines the quantitatively precise and behaviorally inexact. Until this occurs, the synthesis of the two kinds of analysis is so important that the last section of this chapter is devoted to its discussion with reference to corporate planning.

MATHEMATICAL-STATISTICAL METHOD

As in most areas of endeavor, any quantitative-scientific technique is employed in corporate planning which is feasible, has demonstrated its validity, and serves the needs and purposes at hand. Many methods have been used for years: standard accounting practices, inventory and production scheduling, extrapolative forecasting, statistical sampling, and numerous engineering or financial calculations. Some are relative newcomers to the business scene. If not employed directly by the executive, they are reflected in one way or another in the material which he reviews and on which he bases his decisions. Increasingly, he must use them himself in his own comprehensive analysis of current problems and planning for the future.

> . . . Top management itself often fails to participate in the training programs that it sponsors for its subordinates. In some countries . . . it is considered an insult to suggest that a successful top manager might benefit from exposure to information about scientific management and some of the newer management techniques. . . .[1]

Most readers are generally familiar with many established methods of analysis. The intent of this section is to scan the more important quantitative techniques for corporate planning, some of which are only recently developed and whose employment in business is just beginning. Each is described briefly, comments are made concerning its present and potential use in business, and specific examples are given. In each case, reference is made to material which provides a more complete introduction to the method than is possible here.

As scientific techniques are improved in their reliability and coverage, the general manager must keep pace. Clearly, he cannot absorb every one in detail, but he can acquire sufficient familiarity to comprehend the approach and general method, ask perceptive and significant questions, and decide on the modification, extension, and use of the material. Certain techniques he will employ constantly in his own personal analysis. Others are basic to the analysis prepared for him by staff personnel. And new techniques are in the offing which will require study by younger managers today and expanded training for those of tomorrow. Reluctance to come to grips with mathematical-statistical technique is becoming an increasingly serious handicap for the general manager. ". . . The accent has shifted, . . . from initiative to systematic scientific thinking."[2]

Probability and Statistics

Business is filled with situations in which the things that are known are not sufficient to determine the outcome exactly. *Probability* is the branch of mathematics employed to resolve many of these situations of uncertainty and incomplete information. The situations which it tests and to which its use is restricted are *statistical* in nature: each event is considered with relation to the outcome in a large number of directly comparable occurrences. Statistical methods were first used extensively in the natural sciences; the quantitative treatments of heat, atomic structure, and radar are among the many areas of physical science dependent on this approach. In fact, few if any areas of science have not made use of probability. Similarly, in the social and behavioral sciences, the actuarial tables for life insurance rates, as well as public opinion survey by selective sampling, are based on the probabilities which can often be developed from accumulated statistics. Most business men today are aware of statistical likelihood as an important aspect of numerous business situations, although comparatively few have had occasion to study its specific derivation and use as an analytical technique. Many people are aware of the importance of probability in gambling, and some of the notions of probability are often explained in terms of games of chance.

Predicting in advance which side of a coin will appear after it is tossed is one of the simplest situations of uncertainty, since the outcome of the toss is not known in advance. If a coin is tossed *n* times and heads appear *m* times, the ratio *m/n* is called the *relative frequency* of occurrence of heads. As the number of tosses (*n*) is increased, the relative frequency approaches a fixed number. This number, approached by the experimental relative frequency, is the probability that heads will turn up when the coin is flipped. If the coin is perfectly balanced, so thin that its lighting on edge is impossible, and the toss is made in an unbiased manner, the probability of obtaining heads is *1/2* and that of obtaining tails *1/2*. Since, in this example, the occurrence of one of the two possible kinds of events (heads) and the occurrence of the other (tails) are equally likely, the situation is expressed numerically in the equality of the two probabilities. The sum of these two probabilities (heads and tails) is *1/2 + 1/2 = 1*. This is the probability that either heads or tails will occur in the toss, and the value *1* indicates that one of the two is certain to occur.

Probability is therefore a number with a value between *0* and *1*. Zero signifies that the event having that probability will never occur. If there are *n* kinds of events, each equally likely to occur, the probability that a particular one of these events will happen in one trial is *1/n*. If the set of events is tossing a die, the probability that one of its six sides will be face up is *1/6*. In many situations, certain equally likely events are not separated but grouped together. For example, a pair of dice has 36 combinations of faces, each of which is equally likely to occur in a single unbiased toss of the dice. Although the probability that a particular combination will occur on a single toss is therefore *1/36,* most dice games do not differentiate between the various ways in which the numbers on the different faces are combined to produce the same sum. Thus, for the eleven possible sums of the two numbers in the range *1* through *6,* the number of ways in which each sum can occur is:

Sum	2	3	4	5	6	7	8	9	10	11	12
No. of Ways	1	2	3	4	5	6	5	4	3	2	1
Probability	.0278	.0556	.0833	.1111	.1389	.1667	.1389	.1111	.0833	.0556	.0278

The probability of each sum's occurrence is the number of ways that sum can occur, multiplied by the probability of occurrence of each way (*1/36*).

A list of numbers such as the above is the *probability distribution* for the occurrence of the sums. It is the mathematical expression which quantifies what is known and what is not known about an uncertain situation. Since it may comprise a long and complicated list of numbers, certain numbers computed from the distribution have been found especially useful and are frequently employed to represent or describe the entire array. One of these (the sum 7 in the example above) is the *most probable* sum, because it has the largest probability. Another is the *mean* or *average* value, sometimes called the *expectation* or *expected* value (computed by multiplying the value of the variable being averaged by the probability of occurrence of that value, and adding these products for all possible values). Also important is the *dispersion* or *standard deviation*, which provides a measure of the "width" of the distribution—that is, the extent to which different values are scattered about the mean value (computed by taking the square root of the "difference" between the "mean of the square" of the variable, and the "square of the mean" value of the same variable).

The purpose here is to suggest something of the analytical technique of probability for those who have only a casual acquaintance with this branch of mathematics. Thousands of volumes have been written on the matter, and many more are to come. Since the likelihood of events occurring in the future is basic to planning, statistical analysis is fundamental to most forms of quantitative projection. As important as its use, however, is the realization of when it cannot be employed. If the events for which probabilities are sought are not sufficiently similar for the accumulation of significant statistical experience, the numbers calculated are meaningless. Many events and situations in business are composed of so many factors or vary so widely with each "occurrence" that mathematical formulations are not available to describe them reliably. Frequently, the most important business events and the more significant questions underlying comprehensive planning must be so simplified or altered to fit the requirements of valid statistical treatment that the mathematical answers are of limited or even dubious worth.

But, with this caution in mind, it can be said that the use of probability is expanding rapidly in business planning; and there is every indication that this trend will continue as corporate information is gathered in more uniform or comparable form, new mathematical methods are developed, and more managers are versed in the technique. As mentioned earlier, it has long been the foundation stone of insurance. In addition, it is widely employed in the quality control of manufactured products, providing the schedule of selective sampling which yields a given average and range of product quality.

The manufacturer cannot completely control the factors which affect the quality of an assembly-line or process-flow product. Consequently, the product units, whether they are separate or parts of a continuous "stream," are not of exactly the same "quality value." Because these values are distributed about a mean value, the precise quality of any single product unit cannot be predicted in advance. The manufacturer controls production so that the mean value is a specified value, and the dispersion is kept within specified limits. To test product quality, he tests a sample, selected by statistical techniques, and from the test values infers, again on the basis of statistical methods, the distribution of manufactured values. When the test distribution differs from the desired distribution, corrective measures are applied in the manufacturing process.

Probability also lies behind information used by business. Construction companies often adjust their concrete-pouring schedules to fit weather forecasts, recognizing that the weatherman will be wrong in a certain number of cases but right in a sufficiently large percentage to make the adjustment worthwhile. Interim population censuses, on which many businesses rely for marketing data, are derived from a scientific sampling of a portion of the total population selected by statistical methods.

Any measurement or experiment is, in general, subject to uncertainties because it is impractical or impossible to control the measurement process to the degree necessary to obtain an exact result. Hence the result of any measurement or data-collection activity is not a quantitative absolute in itself but must be interpreted statistically. A serious and surprisingly frequent omission in numerical results submitted to corporate management is any indication of the percentage limits of accuracy. Without this important information, the manager may not know whether a difference of several or even 10 per cent between figures is significant or not. Probability theory is a tool which can serve this purpose precisely. Its practical contribution is further increased when it is used not only in after-the-fact analysis of data already at hand but in planning and designing the data-collection process. By such *experimental design*, the measurement and collection of data may be so carried out that the factors which are controlled are known and those which are uncontrolled vary in such a way that the data as a whole form a meaningful statistical distribution. From this designed distribution, the desired numbers and their statistical confidence can be computed. Utilization of probability and statistics in this way usually reduces the cost of gathering data and increases the likelihood of their being as useful as possible under the given circumstances.[3]

Concepts of probability can also be applied very broadly by corporate management in the formulation of subjective judgments: recognition of the compound effect of separate interdependent risks, a realistic estimate of a situation, or awareness of the statistical chances against hopeful exception. Such attitudes are sometimes helpful in avoiding serious mistakes at the top:

> One is led to conclude that . . . top management failed to recognize that the new age of advanced technology demands advanced management techniques. . . . It pursued a "double-or-nothing" policy, risking greater and greater losses in the hope that one more commitment would square all accounts. This, in short, is the story of a great corporation that got out of control.[4]

Models

Thinking about any subject is done within the framework of a conceptual model representing each person's knowledge of the subject. Most of these mental models are vague and ill-defined; some are logical structures formed in a systematic way. *Mathematical models* are an extension of this latter category into definite, quantitative terms. Because of their precision, they are finding increasing use in business.

Managers employ various conceptual constructs in conducting business operations. Some are visualized in the mind; some are intuitive, based on experience but not consciously formulated. Others are formalized on paper: organization charts, the balance sheet, or a set of standard operating procedures. An accounting system is a model of certain fiscal aspects of a company with some of the features of a mathematical model. Because it deals with numbers and uses them in a series of arithmetic operations, it is mathematical; but most of the interrelationships among these various operations are treated verbally rather than mathematically.

Most of the models used in business today are of this latter type; the concepts on which they are based and the detailed interrelationships among the different elements of the model are expressed in words. Since verbal descriptions tend to be long, complicated, and vague, it is difficult for a manager to comprehend a dynamic business operation thoroughly by reviewing a written description such as a procedures manual. In contrast, mathematical descriptions are compact, definite, and quantitative. For the mathematically informed person, they facilitate and extend understanding of the operation. They disclose immediately or make possible the uncovering of interactions among different aspects of the matter under study which are neither apparent in a verbal description nor attainable by discussion. They permit the development of calculative procedures, such as computer programs, to obtain numerical results and perform exploratory computations.

A model for the cost of a single project in a company conducting many projects illustrates the derivation and use of mathematical models in business. In this simplified example, most of the properties could be expressed verbally, but the mathematical form is more compact and reveals more about the nature of multi-project operations. In particular, it highlights the relationships among some of the different ways commonly employed to describe this type of operation. For this illustration, project costs include labor and material used directly on the project. All other costs are combined as overhead and distributed among all the company's projects in proportion to the cost of direct labor on each. Model formulation is comparatively easy in this instance, because all of the elements involved are available as numerical quantities in the form of costs.

The cost of direct labor of project j is denoted by symbol D_j, the letter symbol D representing the numerical cost and the subscript j designating the project. For example, if the direct labor cost of project 17 for the period under consideration is \$10,000, D_{17} is 10,000.

The cost of material on project j is represented by another symbol, M_j, and total project cost by C_j. Total overhead cost throughout the company is designated B, and this total cost is allocated to each project in proportion to its direct labor cost.

To compute the overhead allocated to project j, it is of course necessary to compute the ratio of D_j (cost of direct labor of the project) to the

PLATE I.　THE CORPORATE REPRESENTATION

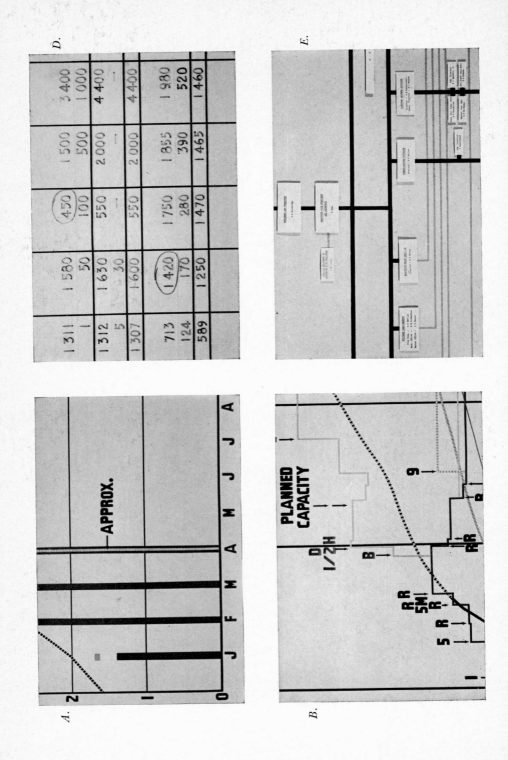

F.

FRONT OFFICE	JAN	FEB	MAR	APR	MAY	JUN	JUL	AUG
MIL. REQUIRE.	16	16	16	16	16	17	17	18
	5	5	5	5	5	5	5	5
DIRECTOR	9	9	9	10	11	11	11	11
CONTROLLER	63	72	75	80	83	84	86	89
CONTRACTS	6	6	6	6	6	6	6	6
FACILITIES	91	104	109	114	116	118	124	126
JAN. UTIL.	65	75	79	84	85	85	87	90
MATERIEL	60	63	69	73	78	83	85	87
OFFICE SERV.	42	50	56	59	60	67	69	71
UTIL.	27	29	29	33	35	37	37	38
PERSONNEL	36	39	43	44	47	47	48	50
SECURITY	125	145	159	159	159	160	166	171
GUARD-RECEP	110	128	140	140	140	140	145	150
TECH. SERV.	5	5	5	7	9	10	14	15
ADMIN.&FINANCE	437	493	531	552	569	586	609	626
ESS	29	32	36	38	39	39	39	44
ERL	4	4	6	8	8	10	11	12
ARL	8	11	18	21	23	24	26	28

C.

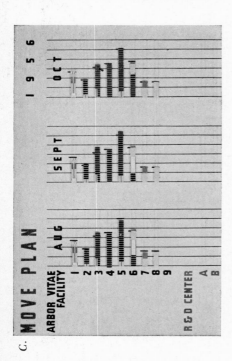

PLATE II.   METHODS OF FLEXIBLE MAINTENANCE AND DISPLAY OF INFORMATION

A. *Bar Chart.* Masonite panel with grid; applied stick-on letters of different color; applied tape of different color.

B. *Graph.* Masonite panel with grid; applied stick-on letters of different color; applied tape of different color.

C. *Movable Bar Chart.* Magnetic panel; movable cardboard segments with magnets on back; tape and stick-on letters applied on magnetic panel.

D. *Tabular Chart.* Plexiglass panel with applied grid and opaque coated back; erasable ink, applied tape divisions.

E. *Organization Chart.* Magnetic panel; movable paper segments with magnets on back; tape of different colors applied on magnetic panel.

F. *Tabular Chart.* Display board; inserted plastic numbers and letters; elastic cord divisions.

PLATE III. ANALYTICAL DISPLAY EQUIPMENT

total direct labor cost of all projects (which is represented by another symbol, D):

$$D = D_1 + D_2 + \ldots D_n$$

where n is the total number of projects in the company.

The fraction of direct labor expended on project j is

$$\frac{D_j}{D}$$

and the overhead cost allocated to project j is

$$\frac{D_j}{D} B.$$

Thus, the total project cost is

$$C_j = D_j + \frac{D_j B}{D} + M_j.$$

This formula may be used to calculate the cost of project j, but it is more convenient if translated into another form. Since D_j is common to the first two terms, it is factored out to provide the new form:

$$C_j = D_j \left(1 + \frac{B}{D}\right) + M_j. \qquad \text{The quantity} \frac{B}{D}$$

which occurs conspicuously in the new form of the equation, is the ratio of the total overhead cost throughout the company (B) to the total direct labor cost of all projects (D). It is usually called the overhead rate, and is designated here by the symbol R.

$$R = \frac{B}{D}. \qquad \text{Substituting } R \text{ for} \frac{B}{D}$$

in the new equation gives

$$C_j = D_j (1 + R) + M_j.$$

This final equation defines a rule of calculation employed by many companies: the cost of a project (C_j) is computed by multiplying its direct labor cost (D_j) by 1 plus the overhead rate (R), and adding the result to the cost of the material on the project (M_j).

Simple as it is, this illustration incorporates most of the important steps in developing a mathematical model. The *objective* of project cost was selected. The *elements* involved in determining project cost were identified. In this case, all of these elements were available costs reliably expressed by numbers; in other cases, the elements of the problem must be simplified, condensed, or re-expressed in *quantitative terms* which can be compared and otherwise processed *mathematically*. *Symbols* were chosen to represent the cost elements. *Rules* for calculating the desired objective—individual project costs—were defined and expressed mathematically. After an initial mathematical formulation, the *equation* was translated into a new form more convenient and conceptually clearer than the original version.

Once a model has been constructed, it is tested to establish its validity. By means of operating data from the business itself, actual and calculated results are compared. The test may confirm the representative reliability of the model and establish confidence in its use. It may disclose certain inaccuracies or inadequacies which are analyzed and corrected. Or it may reveal that the model is so far from depicting the actual situation it cannot be used.

The value of mathematical models depends on how they are employed. First and foremost, only those elements can be incorporated which are represented accurately by numbers or other symbolic terms permitting mathematical manipulation. There are, of course, many important aspects of business which cannot now be expressed or measured with this precision: employee morale, individual management capability, fluctuations in stock value, legalities, or organizational efficiency. Furthermore, the variables in a given business problem or situation may be so numerous and different that mathematical formulation is impractical or impossible. A judgment must be made as to whether the use and benefits of mathematical models are worth the cost of their formulation and maintenance. Managers must be willing and able to use them.

It cannot be expected, therefore, as a few overenthusiastic proponents suggest, that models will permit the automatic operation of a business. Models are but an abstraction of certain elements of the business, with intrinsic limitations. Within these limitations, however, they provide a well-defined conceptual framework which improves the detailed planning of certain activities and the operating decisions which must be made continually by executive managers. Like any other analytical technique, they must be used intelligently, with an understanding of their applicability and the results to be expected.[5]

Physical models are also found in business planning. Among the most common uses are scale models for the arrangement of machines, men, and equipment in manufacturing; master-plan models of complex construction projects; and mockups and study models of products ranging from aircraft and automobiles to consumer goods and their packaging. Like mathematical models—although different in form—these are *analytical* models which are reshaped easily as various aspects are studied or circumstances change, rather than *presentation* models constructed as a final, finished display which is replaced rather than altered. The potential value of physical models is not limited to traditional uses. Whereas picturing organizational interactions is limited on paper by its two-dimensional nature, three-dimensional physical models provide the extra dimension which can extend the conceptualization significantly. Interrelationships can be shown and comprehended which would be too confusing on paper. In large companies with complex organizational and informational interrelationships, such models may be worthwhile when extensive administrative-managerial reorganization is under study. Also, the time will come when physical and mathematical models are tied together in a manner which cannot be specified now, but can be imagined as a reasonable outgrowth of present trends.

Control Theory

Management is responsible for controlling the corporate complex of men and machines organized to provide products and services in order to earn the profit required by the company's owners and the financial community. Since businesses do not produce satisfactorily without direction, and profitability can hardly be taken for granted, executive management controls company operations. Some executives with technical backgrounds have called attention to the similarities between the problems of controlling machines and those encountered in directing company operations. They suggest extension of this analogy by applying some of the techniques developed for controlling machines to corporate management. Explanation of how these techniques might be used is facilitated by preliminary illustration of several simple, well-known control mechanisms.

The thermostat is a familiar example of a mechanical control, maintaining the temperature within an enclosure at a specified value. Its thermometric sensor measures the temperature within the enclosure. This temperature, expressed as an electrical or mechanical signal by the sensing instrument, is compared with the desired temperature which has been set into the thermostat. If this comparison shows a difference between the two temperatures, a signal is transmitted to a control actuator which adjusts the heat flow or refrigeration to equalize the temperature within the enclosure at the desired temperature.

Other examples of mechanical controls are governors regulating the speed of machines, automatic chokes controlling the mixture of gas and air in automobile engines, aircraft autopilots, and radar trackers. The biological world includes many comparable devices. In the human body, the hypothalmus regulates the body temperature in a manner very similar to that of the mechanical thermostat; and pupillary contraction is part of the automatic mechanism controlling the amount of light admitted into the eye.

In each of these examples, the general sequence of operations is the same. First, there is a *sensing mechanism* which measures the *existing situation or performance.* There follows a comparison of this measured performance with a *standard or desired performance.* The thermostat compares a single temperature reading with the desired value. More complex mechanisms, such as fire-control devices, integrate a set of different readings into a single quantity representing present performance. Similarly, the standard with which they are compared may be a single measurement or the result of several simultaneous or different readings. The comparison between existing and standard performance may be a difference in magnitude, as in the case of the thermostat, or it may measure the rate of change or even the acceleration of the difference.

On the basis of this comparison between existing and desired values, *control actions* are taken. The autopilot adjusts the control surfaces of the aircraft; the hypothalmus triggers a change of blood flow through the skin. This measurement and the corresponding adjustment of control are termed *feedback.* Since the entire process of sensing, measuring, comparing, and controlling takes time, control actions are based on performance measurements taken before the control can be exercised. This *time lag* limits the precision of control which is possible and practical. If the delay is sufficiently large, operating conditions may change to such an extent that the calculated control action will no longer bring performance closer to standard. Unstable operation results. Considerable effort has been devoted in the development of control theory to problems of stability.

Another important element of control is measurement. Errors may be due to inaccuracies in the sensing instrument itself, or to the fact that the sensing equipment is recording extraneous signals along with the quantitative measurement of present performance. A familiar example is the static which usually accompanies radio navigation signals and at one time greatly impaired radio reception in the home. *Noise* is the term for the total of such disturbances, whether they are the result of measurement inaccuracies or extraneous influences. Noise in the system naturally makes control more difficult, and it has an important effect on the stability of control. Probability theory and statistical techniques are used to deal with noise.

Such concepts of mechanistic control can be applied in business management. In corporate planning, the measure of present performance is provided by the information collected throughout the company, combined and analyzed for executive managers. Data processing may be entirely manual, culminating in the usual balance sheet and operating statements, or in larger companies it may involve electronic computation and a variety of special analyses and presentations. Current performance is compared with the standard or desired performance for the business, which may be in the form of return on investment, sales goals, or normally a combination of criteria. On the basis of this comparison, management initiates actions to alter performance.

In comparing current and desired performance, trends are as important as the absolute difference at the time of measurement. If sales have been increasing slowly, the corrective action needed to bring them up to a higher standard is usually less than if they had been declining. Time lags and noise, present in business control systems as well as mechanical controls, may be significant and cause serious problems.

Some department stores capitalize on temporary but strong consumer demand by point-of-sale recording. Sales are centrally classified and processed as they are entered in the cash register. When unusual weather, an advertisement or story in a national magazine with a large circulation, or an unknown cause or coincidence creates an unexpected surge of buying in a specialty item, orders are placed immediately to replace dwindling inventory as quickly as possible. As long as the curve of sudden buying is upward, this accelerated replacement continues. As soon as it levels off and begins to drop, the pattern of reordering is changed. In effect, the system is designed to permit "riding the curve" of sudden demand.

If the time lag is excessive between the recording of sales, their totaling, and perhaps comparison with previous experience, there is not enough time to order and receive a new supply before the buying surge may be over. Since time of occurrence, volume, and duration cannot be predicted for this type of demand, the maintenance of heavy inventories to meet exceptional peaks is uneconomic. If the time needed for delivery is too long and demand is heavy but brief, replacement stock arrives too late. If noise in such a fast-acting and finely tuned system garbles or delays information, the consequences can be equally unfortunate.[6]

Although automatic process control is concerned with manufacturing-production rather than the company as a whole, recent advances in technique are suggestive for corporate planning. These new systems extend older methods by integrating profitability with mechanical efficiency. In a chemical plant, for example, the mix of different ingredients is a function not only of physical efficiency— process adjustments as the precise characteristics of raw materials vary or environmental conditions change—but of the most economic and profitable operation in terms of market conditions, product prices, and the particular situation of the company. In time, it may be possible to apply this kind of extended control of continuous production to the much broader range of consideration pertinent to corporate management. The process will be less exact, but it should be useful in revealing unforeseen interrelationships and the most important and sensitive elements of managerial control.[7]

Theory of Games

In the competitive environment within which companies operate, managers are concerned not only with external conditions and internal operations but also, obviously, with the actions of competitors. These actions are determined by other managers, similarly motivated toward profits and related considerations. Some 30 years ago, the outstanding mathematician J. von Neumann noted the analogy between competitive actions in business and those in games: in deciding their course of action, managers behave in many ways like the players in certain games. By developing a mathematical theory of games, he introduced new insights into competitive situations in private enterprise and made possible the extension of our understanding of an important aspect of economic behavior.

The rules of different games are well defined, explicitly stated, and understood by the participants. They establish what the players can do, what moves they can make, how the scoring is done, what specific rewards there are, and when the game is won. The moves they *can* make within the rules, and those they *should* make for their own advantage, depend on the preceding moves made by opponents. In games of pure chance such as penny matching or roulette, the behavior of players does not influence the outcome. The interest lies in observing the unpredictable outcome of each move and the consequent gain or loss. Of course, as described briefly in the prior section on probability and statistics, the average outcome of a long series of tosses or bets can be predicted with close accuracy.

Of greater interest to business are games in which what the players do affects the outcome of the game. In poker, for example, each player develops a *strategy* based on the rules of the game, past actions by opponents, and his anticipation of their future behavior. This strategy guides the play of each participant and his reaction to different situations. The method may be carefully worked out and consciously employed, or it may be an intuitive expression of experience. Ticktacktoe illustrates some of the properties of this class of games.

Two players employ *O* and *X* as their respective marks. The "board" consists of nine areas formed by two pairs of separated parallel lines, intersecting at right angles. Each player, in turn, places his mark with the objective of attaining three of his marks in any straight line. At the same time, he blocks attempts by his opponent to do the same.

Players soon learn by experience the best first moves to make and the most effective ways of countering the opponent. They develop a strategy of play. Because ticktacktoe is a simple game, all possible moves and situations can be calculated. This analysis shows that it is possible for the player with the first move to choose a sequence of play which prevents his losing; dependent on his opponent's moves, he wins or draws. It also shows he cannot formulate a sequence of moves which leads to his winning regardless of his opponent's actions; the sequence of moves which permits his winning requires that his opponent make certain moves in the given situation. The complete strategy of the game is therefore known, and if both players are informed and alternate first moves, they will come out more and more exactly even as the number of games is increased.

Similar to ticktacktoe, but much more complicated, are checkers and chess. In principle, it is possible to tabulate all possible moves and situations for these games and thus determine the best strategy. But the number of possible combinations and moves is so large that they have not as yet all been calculated even with modern high-speed computers. Although study of these more difficult games has been valuable in the development of game theory, its contribution to business strategy has been minimal—mainly because all the facts about the playing situation are known to both players and each move is immediately known to the opponent. Not only is this rarely the situation in business life, but there are usually more than two competitors.

Games like poker, on the other hand, which include elements of concealment and larger numbers of players, approximate actual business conditions more closely. It is from the successful analysis of these games that principles applicable to business may be derived. In its formal treatment, game theory translates the rules of the game into axioms and definitions expressed in mathematical terms; it employs probability to treat the uncertainties of the situation. One important product of these explorations is the *mini-max* concept, which is concerned with the selection of the best strategy after all possible strategies available to the opponent have been defined and analyzed. The apparent choice of selecting the strategy which maximizes gains under all possible circumstances turns out to be impossible because of moves by the opponent. The strategy producing the greatest gains when the opponent follows one pattern of play may result in losses when he plays in a different fashion. The most successful strategy which can be defined mathematically fulfills the mini-max criterion: the mode of play which maximizes the minimum gains possible when all strategies available to the opponent are considered.

Game theory has also described more exactly the important difference between games with two participants and those with three or more players. In the latter, two players can agree to jointly select strategies which insure their winning at the expense of opponents operating as individuals. This analysis of player combinations in multi-player games further defines some of the characteristics of combines of competitors and cartel arrangements.

The contribution of game theory to corporate planning is limited at present to several such concepts which may help the manager generally in his subjective decision as to what he is going to do in difficult competitive circumstances. It also indicates that the highly important strategic aspects of private enterprise are susceptible to quantitative analysis. But scientifically derived answers to problems of corporate competitive policy do not appear likely in the foreseeable future, because the rules of business behavior and interaction are not explicit, complete, or precise. Furthermore, the complexity of real-life competitive situations, as well as the many enterprises and individuals usually involved in different ways, makes mathematical formulation enormously difficult.

Models of business operations have been developed as games for executive training. The consequences of each decision or move by the manager for his company and its situation are derived in minutes from computer programs representing the postulated circumstances. By this rapid simulation, many situations and the effects of decisions are compressed into a fraction of the time which would be required for comparable experience in the normal course of business. A similar method has been used for years in training and "refreshing" commercial pilots; all manner of routine and emergency conditions are feigned so realistically in an aircraft simulator that the reactions of the individual are very close to those experienced in the real thing.

Another kind of game relates to one method of decision making. Since the manager of a business operation is the single participant, it is a game akin to solitaire and competition is excluded. An electronic computer develops the information which represents the operational situation presented to the player. He examines this information and makes his move or decision: selection of a set of actions to be taken. The consequences computed for this move are next examined, and another set of decisions is made. The game is continued until the information disclosed by the computer is satisfactory to the player. By successive decisions and resultant information at each step, he reaches a solution which he might not otherwise have attained—almost certainly not by a single move incorporating a more extensive set of actions. In addition, the sequence of moves can be examined in a post mortem to reveal ways in which the same results might have been achieved more quickly, directly, efficiently, and profitably. This process of limited trial and consequence step by step is a familiar method in business when the situation allows and feedback of information is rapid. As a technique of studying problem solving, game theory may help in developing more precise answers concerning the inherent requirements and limitations of this managerial method and the best way of conducting it.[8]

Information Theory

Information is essential to all organized activity. A single individual in an isolated place employs the information derived from observing his surroundings in deciding his course of action. When two or more persons engage in any joint effort, advancement of their common purpose depends on information concerning their respective actions as well as the physical environment. In a company employing hundreds of people engaged in producing and marketing products and services, an extensive and complicated flow of information is clearly necessary for efficient operations.

A theory quantifying such informational interrelationships has been developed in the field of *electronic communications*. Although still in its infancy, it has produced definitions and measurements applicable and potentially useful in business planning. Information is knowledge about a situation previously unknown to the individual or group. Lack of knowledge about a situation is not knowing which of several *alternative descriptions* applies. Information theory deals with the selection among alternative descriptions and the rejection of the remainder; repetition of what is known is not considered information. From this general description, information theory develops a quantitative definition of information in which the *number of possible descriptions is used as a measure of information* in messages which tell something about the situation. From facts already known, the boundaries of the unknown are established. A list is formulated of all possible relevant messages, and to each is assigned a probability which indicates the likelihood that the correct message is this particular one.

If two ordinary dice are lying on the table and the numbers on their uppermost faces have not been observed, information concerning these numbers is contained in a message which gives their sum. This *incomplete* information discloses that there are 11 alternative descriptions: the total possible combinations of numbers which we know, from our knowledge of the normal construction of dice, could appear.

Of these 11 possible messages, one telling us the number is 7 conveys less information than one disclosing it is 3, since it was *a priori* more probable that the sum is 7 rather than 3. We know from our prior knowledge of the dice that the probability of the sum of the two unknown numbers being 7 is 1/6, whereas the probability of its being 3 is 1/18. More generally stated, it is less of a "surprise" to learn the sum is 7 than to find it is 3, because we know there are more combinations of numbers on the dice which total 7 than there are adding up to 3.

In developing a quantitative definition of information, one was sought which would correspond with intuitive concepts relating to the quantity of information. Our natural tendency, based on experience, is to relate quantity of information with the number of words in a message. We recognize that some messages are lengthy without conveying much information; but, in general, the more words the more information of one sort or another. Ways of coding messages were studied to find a method by which repetition of information or *redundancy* could either be eliminated or be measured quantitatively. When all messages are *a priori* equally probable, one such method of coding is to assign a number to each message. If the numbers selected begin with zero and continue in numerical sequence, the number of *digits* in the code number is a measure of the amount of information which corresponds with our intuitive notion of the number of *words* as a measure of information. A mathematical function of this code number, which is equal to the number of its digits and in other ways reflects our intuitive concepts, is the *logarithm* of the number.

It is most convenient to use logarithms to the base 2 to measure information. This is equivalent to expressing the number of alternative messages in the *binary number system*.

If the number of messages describing equally probable situations is 8, the logarithm to the base 2 of 8 is 3, because it requires 3 binary digits to represent 8 things. It also means that a message stating only that either situation 4 or 5 had occurred would have less information than a message stating that situation 4 had occurred: less by the amount of information in selecting between the two situations 4 and 5. This demonstrates the utility of the logarithmic function, for

$$log_2 8 - log_2 2 = 3 - 1 = 2.$$

Information theory has made significant contributions to communications systems. Besides providing quantitative definitions, it has shown how to increase the amount of information which can be sent over given communication channels, taking into account noise within these systems. Because of the obvious importance of an efficient flow of information among employees who in effect constitute a company, efforts will be made to develop information theory to the point where it can provide quantitative guides for general management in comprehensive planning. From identification of different information sources and channels, and more exact description of their characteristics, purposeful redundancy can decrease wasteful repetition, and the disruptive disturbance of the system by rumor, exaggeration, or methodological confusion can be reduced. Much of the current attention being given to information flow in business is concentrated on the use of computers in data processing. Although this purpose does not necessitate an attempt at formal application of information theory to the entire system of intercommunication within a company, concepts derived from the theory shape this special analysis for data processing in ways which should make its substantive expansion and practical application to the corporation as a whole easier in the future.[9]

Mathematical Programing

Quantitative techniques for planning which employ mathematical models are referred to generally as *mathematical programing*. Program models have been developed for a wide range of existing and potential applications. One of the most commonly employed of these, *linear programing,*

> . . . has been successfully applied to the study of such diverse problems as production smoothing, traffic control at toll booths, investment scheduling in an electric power industry, job assignment, transportation and warehousing of commodities, railway freight movements, blending of aviation gasoline, optimal crop rotation, Air Force contract bidding and the scheduling of aircraft maintenance, plastic limit analysis of structures, chemical composition at equilibrium, and many others.[10]

The formulation of a mathematical program follows the pattern described in an earlier section of this chapter for quantitative models. First determined are the *objectives* of the program. Since the program must fit the policies and capabilities of the business, *limiting parameters* are defined with sufficient precision to permit their mathematical expression and incorporation into the model. For example, a production plan must obviously be within the capacity of the plant to produce, whether existing, expanded, or supplemented by subcontracting; or purchased parts must be available in the postulated quantities and on the specified dates of delivery. A mathematical program which meets environmental limitations and requirements realistically is a *feasible program*. The details of the program are worked out in a manner similar to those employed for other mathematical models.

Linear programing makes use of *linear relations* between factors affecting the operation under study: it treats quantities which can be defined by adding multiples of certain other quantities. Squares, cubes, transcendental functions, and other *non-linear* relationships cannot therefore be incorporated in the model. In general, linear programing makes use of *inequalities* rather than equations, because most planning programs seek results which fall within certain limits, rather than a precise quantitative objective; business planning usually sets upper and lower limits rather than exact targets. In addition, there are almost always different ways of attaining the objective.

The in-plant production of a quantity of product x to meet a sales forecast, which requires milling operations, must naturally be planned within the capacities of the individual milling machines at hand. But the production plan certainly does not require that all available machines be employed continuously and simultaneously at maximum capacity. In fact, it is well known from experience that any one of several different integrated schedules, with individual machines operating at less than all-out utilization, is normally more efficient.

Since a set of linear inequations does not have a unique solution, there are *numerous solutions* or linear programs which satisfy the inequations representing the situation; these are the feasible programs referred to in the two preceding paragraphs. Any one of these solutions will work, in that each defines a way in which the intended effort can be carried out within the specified restrictions or limiting parameters. But a possible program is, of course, by no means necessarily the desirable solution, for it may be needlessly expensive or prohibitively high in cost. Therefore, a final condition is imposed as the basis for choosing the "best" or *optimum* solution among the many available. Normally, this is the criterion of *minimizing costs or maximizing profits.*

A classical example of linear programing is the transportation problem. A manufacturing firm operates factories and warehouses at many different geographical locations. Each warehouse has certain requirements for goods produced by the factories, determined by the inventory it must carry to meet sales and delivery dates within the region it serves. Each factory also has a particular output rate at which it is producing.

One requirement in the efficient management of production and distribution is to devise a plan of shipment from the various factories to different warehouses which minimizes transportation costs. One technique of solution is the *simplex* method. This provides, first, a simple way of finding a feasible but not necessarily desirable solution. Next, it incorporates a system of proceeding from this feasible solution to another more desirable from the viewpoint of the criterion of optimization—in this case, minimizing transportation costs. The process continues until the optimum solution is derived. Since most such methods of linear programing require extensive numerical computation, digital computers frequently are needed to develop the solutions.

Although many planning problems can be defined in terms which permit the use of linear programing techniques, many others require non-linear mathematical formulation. Mathematical programing includes both linear and non-linear situations, with or without optimization. In many instances, useful mathematical models of operating problems can be constructed even though the criteria of optimum solution are not apparent. Feasible solutions are derived which—although not demonstrably the "best"—are often better than "practical" solutions which turn out not to be feasible because they fail to meet schedule requirements, require new plant capacity, or otherwise bring about unexpected and unwanted corollary consequences. The basic difficulty in non-linear problems, therefore, is to choose between a feasible but not necessarily most profitable solution, derived by mathematical programing, and a purely experiential or judgmental scheme whose consequences can only be guessed and which may turn out unsuccessfully.

> At the present time, research in many aspects of mathematical programing is continuing at a rapid rate. . . . Since difficult and unsolved problems are found to be perennially attractive to mathematicians, it is eminently reasonable to be optimistic about the future development of the mathematics of optimal choice under conditions of constraint.[11]

Systems Engineering

Many businesses involve a complex of different operations which must take place in particular sequences and interrelationships: an automobile assembly line, a gasoline refinery, a telephone system, a large bank, or a newspaper with its numerous participants, communication deadlines, high-speed production, and fast distribution. In addition, some are large in size, with hundreds or thousands of employees and annual sales in millions or hundreds of millions of dollars. Many produce a variety of products and services. In all of them, different aspects of production, finance, sales-marketing, and competition interrelate in so many ways that it is difficult or impossible for a single person to comprehend the total *system of interaction* which constitutes the functional life of the company.

> *Systems engineering*—the invention, the design, and the integration of the whole ensemble, as distinct from the invention

and design of the parts—is an old and always present part of practical engineering. But the term "systems engineering" has become in recent years virtually a new one because the engineering systems with which we are now concerned are so much larger, more complex and difficult to engineer. This is partially because today our desire is to take huge steps in the technology rapidly. A typical, new large engineering system depends much more than was the custom in the past on immediate exploitation of the newest discoveries in pure science. Furthermore, the relationships between the engineering and economic, military and even sociological considerations have become increasingly important. In these times, in which technology is altering our world so rapidly and in which government and industry must continually adjust to these changes, systems engineering has accordingly become a topic of almost semipopular interest.

Strangely enough, this enormous interest in systems engineering has not provided us with a flood of scientific articles to help us understand what systems engineering is and how it is to be improved.[12]

Systems engineering is concerned with the *integration* of the many components which comprise a complicated productive operation. It seeks to arrange and organize these component activities or *subsystems* into an over-all system of interaction which yields the desired result in as efficient and profitable a way as possible and practicable. As its name connotes, it focuses primarily on physical or engineering operations, although increasingly economic, financial, social, psychological, and other "non-physical" aspects are included as methods of incorporating them meaningfully into the total consideration become available. The expression of interrelationships and of the system as a whole is in mathematical-statistical form.

An important and now familiar example of a highly complex operation in which systems engineering has been effective is the guided missile. The missile itself is of course composed of many subsystems: rocket engine, vehicle, guidance, warhead, and fire control—each with its own considerable complexity and numerous elements. There is the launching site, with its ground or sea support equipment involving storage, fueling, positioning, firing, tracking, and ground control including self-destruction of the missile in the air. Information and communication are vitally tied into the picture with relation to early warning of hostile action, time and occasion of firing, and the precise aiming point selected on the basis of the nature of the target and knowledge concerning its exact geographical location. Each of these principal subsystems is complicated in its own right, requiring special technical-professional capabilities. The total system is correspondingly more difficult and substantively complex.

A central telephone station or electronic computer is made up of basically simple elements and circuits. But these "building blocks" are combined, recombined, and interconnected to comprise an entity which will perform the end task for which it is designed. To accomplish this construction, logically complex combinations of circuits must be carefully studied in exact detail.

As the number of interconnected elements increases, the number of interrelationships increases exponentially. At the same time, the input, output, and auditory or display devices essential to the end product or service are integrated into the system.

Systems design commences with an *objective,* and a concept of its possible solution which states the general character of the technical application, the particular techniques to be used, and environmental factors influencing the design. Any or all of the mathematical-statistical techniques described previously in this chapter may be employed. The objective may be modified as systems study discloses unpredictable limitations and potentialities, but the basic intent must of course be fulfilled. Otherwise, the system is of little or no value as an answer to the stated need, however many interesting features it may possess or even if by chance it turns out useful in a different connection. Because complex system design is costly, constant attention to the end purpose is imperative. The *numerous components* which make up the system are identified, and their *interconnections* are treated as elements as fundamental to the system as the components themselves. Therefore, the *logical organization* or functional arangement of parts is the essence of the task.

The *general functions* to be performed are stated in precise operational terms. Each of these is interpreted as a *technical function* which defines the performance requirements of equipment. To simplify the system as much as possible, technical functions common to different operational elements are combined whenever feasible. Such design exploration refines and sharpens the conceptual statement of the system and its constituent functions. It may show that certain functions are difficult or expensive to perform as formulated; and, by technical modifications which do not reduce the efficiency of the system as a whole, it may be possible to specify equipment less expensive or more reliable. Or it may reveal that additional operational functions can be incorporated at little extra cost and no impairment of system reliability and stability.

On the basis of the statement of technical functions as finally developed, the over-all *organization of equipment* is defined, and the characteristics of different *items of equipment* and *operating procedures* are specified. Equipment is designed, fabricated or purchased, tested, and installed.

Many systems include both people and machines: military command control, automobile assembly, or large-scale construction. In these, machines are designed and organized so that their interrelationships with people are as mutually efficient as practicable. In the case of the machine, this may mean design which facilitates human operation or control, an informational output readily understood by the human viewer, or, in close reciprocal interaction, machine design carefully tailored to the physical and mental-nervous characteristics of the human being. In the case of the human being, he may have to retrain himself to perform unnatural manipulative actions easily, because change in equipment design is more costly, disruptive of system efficiency, or impossible; he may have to acquire new comprehensions for the same reasons. The training of astronauts is a case in point. Human engineering—a combination of engineering and psychology—concerns itself with such interrelationships. In system design, the functions to be performed by people are defined, together with the specific skills and training required. Usually, personnel and equipment needs and characteristics are formulated in concert from the start; occasionally, a "personnel subsystem" is defined and designed in parallel with the equipment subsystem.

Because of their intrinsic complexity, systems are unlikely to function properly when first put together. Trial-and-error procedures are an integral part of their design. Equipment units and subsystems are *tested* both separately and partially combined. Finally, the entire system is operated on a schedule of trial runs to determine whether equipment and procedures are indeed functioning as anticipated, and whether the output of the system is what was intended. A proper test program begins during the early phases of design; system design must therefore permit testing which is continual, reasonable in cost, and revealing. Frequently, tests are conducted successfully by simulation on an electronic digital computer.

Errors in systems engineering are of two general types: developmental and conceptual. In any such complicated endeavor, there are bound to be human mistakes in formulation, calculation, transmittal of information, copying of data, and other procedural steps. There are also errors or inadequacies of conceptualization. The manager or even his technical chief may formulate what he wants the system to do in clear terms at its inception, only to find later that the product of its preliminary testing is not what he had in mind, or that he now sees it should be modified. Often, it is impossible to visualize in advance all of the elements and operational ramifications of an intricate system which may sensibly call for subsequent adjustment of the original objectives.

Systems engineering applied to a number of principal activities or major segments of a company requires the same over-all and projective view of men, money, machines, and facilities which is necessary in comprehensive planning. System objectives are established, and operating plans developed to attain them. Products and services are defined and planned; competition, markets, customers, and environmental factors are investigated; and the human, physical, and financial resources to effectuate the stated purposes are determined. The interactions between the activities and organizational components of the company under systems study are analyzed. And, finally, the entire system of shorter- and longer-range plans is appraised to evaluate the likelihood that it will in fact produce the stated goals and desired profits. Except when forming a new company, the application of systems engineering to a business enterprise and to a missile system is different, although there is greater similarity with military command control operations. Since the corporation is normally a going concern, systems engineering must carefully take into account history, tradition, past commitments, established procedures, and other factors which not only limit the extent and rapidity of feasible change but shape the form of realistic and profitable systems planning.

For some time to come, it will not be possible to apply systems engineering to the point where it is synonymous with corporate planning as described in this book. The corporate organism is still insufficiently studied and understood for scientifically systematic, quantitatively consistent treatment. Consequently, system designers cannot identify, describe, and conceptualize all significant elements and relationships. Knowledge concerning some of these elements is today too limited for accurate definition and prediction of performance. This is especially true with respect to people—individually and in groups—and human interactions. In addition, present-day mathematical-statistical statement must be extended considerably before it can measure and encompass the multitude of elements, variables, and indeterminates to be taken into account in comprehensive business planning.

The important potential of systems engineering lies in its capability of providing quantitative solutions for those aspects of the enterprise which can be treated with scientific precision. Such partial answers are helpful, not only as factual contributions to the over-all corporate planning problem, but in the further definition of those elements which are indeterminate and must therefore be dealt with differently. Systems engineering is a significant analytical-planning tool for certain subsystems within the company, such as manufacturing and large-scale construction. And its basic concepts are useful to executive managers in their general thinking, diagnostic resolution, and decision.

SUBJECTIVE JUDGMENT

Although candidacy for higher positions in management usually signifies that sound judgment has been demonstrated in practice, it is sometimes difficult to estimate this capacity from the record—to distinguish elements of luck and unearned credit. The record tells far less about the young man early in his career than about the executive with an extensive background of experience. More important, the possibility of strengthening existing methods of evaluating judgment and improving individual judgment itself is often discounted by business because it is assumed the subject is too elusive for purposive action.

Rather than perception within a special area of concentration, general judgment is the quality under consideration: the comprehensive acumen involved in resolving such matters as longer-range objectives, the desirability of expansion abroad, industry competition, new product selection, sales strategy, a critical personnel problem, advertising policy, or form of organization. This capacity for analyzing scientifically indeterminate situations from many points of view is much in demand within the business world and especially important in corporate planning. Practical techniques which help to identify persons with superior judgment, develop individual capacities, and improve procedures of reaching sound subjective conclusions are of definite value.

Identification

Judgment is the product of knowledge, experience, and personality. A strong indication of the extent of this ability is provided by the formal record of education and business achievement. This is supplemented by the opinions of superiors and associates, discounted for any discernible bias in their views. Record and reputation are confirmed by interviews in which specific judgments are elicited. Not only is the individual's method of deriving subjective conclusions revealed at least partly in this way, but occasionally the discernment attributed to the person from his record is disclosed to have been provided by others, or to be more a consequence of fortunate coincidence than competence.

Sound judgment is not necessarily revealed in the operating record even of those most active in corporate planning. Decisions or recommendations may have required little alternative choice. They may represent concurrence in analysis by others rather than independent reflection and conclusion. More often, the accuracy of judgments at the time they were made is obscured by subsequent developments and soon forgotten. Usually, sound executive judgment is either conspicuous by its presence and successful application, or taken for granted and less well established than management may admit. Better identification calls for procedures which supplement *pro forma* performance.

A record can be kept of the more important judgments of an individual at the time of decision. Thoughtfully reviewed in retrospect, it assists in appraising the scope and reliability of subjective analysis by revealing areas in which perception is outstanding and others in which it is comparatively weak. Maintaining such a record for more than several persons would of course consume too much time. If it were elaborate, it would be administratively impractical. A file of dictated observations serves the main purpose. With this simple aid, memory is less likely to be factually unreliable with the passage of time and modification of original judgments by all concerned. And it is less prejudicially selective in recalling mostly successes, failures, or a particular category of discernment.

Since supervisory and collaborative impressions accumulate in any event, an informal procedure of notation—despite its limitations—promotes more accurate evaluation when conclusive evidence is not available and profit performance is not completely indicative.[13] It is especially useful in identifying individual potentialities among the younger generation of managers within the organization.

> We look through the organization for young men who give promise of management ability, who some day may develop into top executives. Then we make a chart with lines indicating sixty years, fifty, forty, thirty, twenty years. On it we plot the ages of these young men. This shows whether we have distribution of management potential in each age bracket. It is amazing how few names qualify for this chart. Though we employ twenty-five thousand workers, less than forty men appear on our chart.[14]

Development

Although judgment is not always subject to change because of its relation to personality, frequently improvement is possible. It may be self-engendered or encouraged by deliberate procedures. The common prerequisite is motivation. Organizations cannot motivate unless the individual responds, but they can make clear the value they attach to sound judgment by reiteration in management statements and by specific identification in decision-making procedures, position descriptions, performance evaluation, and personal communication.

Methods of developing general judgment naturally relate to its attributes. First and foremost is breadth of awareness and knowledge. In the comprehensive appraisal applied in corporate planning, the full range of elements and considerations is involved: people, money, equipment, structures, time, and environment in a complex of forms and interrelationships. The mental scan must be inclusive, not only with respect to the range of pertinent factors at any given time, but also with reference to their development over time. Recognition of past history, present trends, and future probabilities supplies this additional dimension of comprehension. Superior judgment reflects "basic" knowledge in such fields as socio-economics, politics, science, psychology, and history, as well as the "applied" skills most commonly associated with business analysis. The consequence of blind spots is impaired understanding at the very first stage in the formulation of judgment.

Perception of interrelationships is an essential part of the mental picture of a comprehensive planning situation. It is acquired through direct experience, observation, and study. Some interrelationships are established by scientific method. Others represent the logical conclusion or intuitive opinion of the individual. This comprehension of how elements interact is extended into a sense of specific correlation. Relative weights are associated with different elements, and a concept is developed of the network of interaction as they change separately and together. As a single illustration, the importance of the personnel factor varies with difficulties of replacement, salary or wage rate, training costs, situation with respect to organized labor, possible effect on customer or public relations, legal obligations, considerations of morale, moral commitment, or personal preference.

Ideally, several forms of conscious review or mental monitoring operate throughout the formation of subjective judgments. The source, intent, derivation, and reliability of informational inputs are noted as they are pigeonholed in the mind. Throughout the process of analysis, a critical attitude is applied to foster a mental image of reality and reduce progressive distortion and wishful thinking. Recognized gaps in knowledge are filled by others, and known areas of emotional inaccuracy are compensated by appropriate self-adjustment. Realization of the necessity of simplifying complex, open-ended comprehensive planning questions to mentally manageable proportions is reflected in a continuous choice, elimination, and combination of information and deduction. Awareness of when a conclusion must be reached to be useful establishes the time and conceptual restrictions within which the evaluative effort is made. Understanding the nature of intuition helps in recognizing the value and limitations of this insight, whether intentionally applied in conscious analysis or immediately responsive as demanded by circumstance.

Even this cursory review of subjective judgment supports deliberate effort toward its development. The scope of awareness in key personnel is broadened by exposure to the diverse elements of corporate planning problems and decision. This is accomplished in several ways: opportunities to listen and learn at sessions which deal with unfamiliar aspects; a routing of operational documents and distribution of information which emphasize the range of relevant factors; the requirement that periodic reporting be comprehensive in its coverage; and supervisorial stimulation and guidance in personal contact. Educational activities—formal or informal, inside or outside the company—are suggested, related to performance evaluation, made a condition of eligibility for certain positions, or required for advancement. Programs of executive rotation diversify experience. Some companies rotate many line managers through the corporate planning unit as a broadening experience, and transfer those recruited as central staff personnel to operating positions after five or six years.[15] In appropriate ways, the importance of general judgment as a basic ability of management is disseminated throughout the organization to stimulate the many individual responses which result from positive leadership or even expressed opinion at the top.[16]

Ordinarily, the judgments of subordinates and associates are restricted to their areas of responsibility. Under adverse circumstances familiar to business men, they may be expressed reluctantly or not at all. In some positions, they are requested infrequently. It may therefore be desirable to encourage or request statements of opinion on a variety of subjects and typical corporate situations. Experience and responsibility are simulated in this way, and either an impression of competence or a record of judgment is accumulated for discriminating review as part of periodic evaluations of executive capability.[17]

Subjective analysis is improved if several requisite conditions are met. These are deceptively simple, so reasonable from the viewpoints of common sense and experience that they are sometimes underestimated.

Time and concentration are required. Some people produce best by continuous application, others by coming back to the problem several times. The executive who maintains he has no time for cogitation is begging the basic question. If he believes that his role is fulfilled without careful analysis on his own part, or that he can accomplish all that is necessary in a few minutes, this at least is his real claim. Of course, this disclaimer fails to fit the nature of business organizations, the consensus of management opinion, or evaluations of executive efficiency which report that insufficient time is set aside "to think and plan."[18] Increasingly, management creates the conditions favorable to longer-range appraisal and decision. ". . . Each year a Great Lakes ore boat leaves Chicago for Duluth. . . . On board are six to eight top executives of Emerson Electric Manufacturing Co. . . . They spend the week-long trip in daily meetings that last from just after breakfast until midnight. Their purpose: to chart the company's course firmly for the next year, tentatively for a year or two more. . . . 'If there's anything in which we excel . . . it's perhaps in long-range planning, to foresee problems before they lead us to the brink of disaster.' "[19]

Equally important is a constructive attitude toward the analytical task. Fruitful results are unlikely if there is conscious or unconscious antipathy to sitting down and undertaking intellectual effort, as opposed to getting up and performing more active operational duties involving greater motor energy. In marked contrast with the bustle and gregarious contact of operations, individual intellectual effort is comparatively solitary as well as difficult. Unlike the automatic generation of operational activity by the demands and communications of the moment, subjective analysis requires both self-starting and self-sustaining interest. Any personal reluctance to apply the time and effort necessary normally yields to recognition of the importance of the corporate problem and the responsibility of executive solution or confirmation. Any intellectual disinclination lessens with continued application. Managers who recognize within themselves a strong preference for effectuation rely to a large extent on planning analysis developed by others in whom they have confidence.

As suggested in the previous chapter, intuition is part of general judgment. The executive who postpones decision until he can "think the matter over for a day or two" is providing time for intuitive reaction. During this interval, an initial "hunch" or mental "warning bell" crystallizes into further questions which should be asked. An insight discloses a fatal flaw. A favorable impression is upheld because no qualms emerge during the period of mulling it over, or it is reinforced by further thoughts which come to mind without deliberate reflection. The full implications of the impending decision may dawn to the point where supplementary opinions are sought, or the manager may accept the judgment of an executive with greater experience in the matter at hand. Both courage and caution are involved in the constructive application of intuition.

> ... "Development of high-level personnel and the appointment of the right people to the right top places is my principal preoccupation." And regardless of the details of a company's system of management development "the important thing is to have some system in proper operation."[20]

SYNTHESIS

Conceptualization

To identify the elements of a complicated business problem and establish salient facts and judgments concerning these parts and their interactions, some form of visual or graphical exposition is helpful. Organization charts are a familiar example. To conceptualize numerous components in both vertical and horizontal interrelationships, it is necessary to resort to paper or blackboard. The operations of the organization cannot be conceived and studied without this charting which makes possible the expression of refinements of comparative position and size, line and staff relationships, and grouping. Similarly, in plant layout, production planning, and distribution-marketing, picturization on paper is common practice.

Verbal discussion is valuable for general orientation and preliminary exploration, but until ideas and words are transformed into more tangible form, the problem at hand remains nebulous and analytical progress is delayed. A point can be identified when further verbal discussion and internalized mental effort produce diminishing returns. Some visual, "written" pictograph is necessary to externalize the matter in mind. Protracted verbal discussion is often in reality an avoidance of this step. Not only is there sometimes a reluctance to undertake this task, for reasons mentioned previously, but surprisingly few people have developed the facility to structure problems in this way. As a consequence, we sometimes tend to make the easier decisions first, postponing those which require exposition and graphical study.

Visual conceptualization is more than a listing of items on paper. It involves their grouping into categories, an indication of interactions and priorities, the incorporation of quantification, progressions, comparative weighting, identification of important unknowns —whatever will in the simplest notation express most clearly the situation as it is conceived initially. There are, of course, graphic notations widely used and understood: solid and broken lines for different interconnections, the arrow as a directional relationship, the underline or asterisk for emphasis, indentation for subgrouping, the wheel for circular interdependence, and numbers or order for relative importance. Familiar graphical forms are available: tables, bar charts, growth curves, balance sheets, organization charts. There are numerical indicators such as the simple ratio, equality, differential, percentage, unit cost, return on investment, or turnover of capital. And the types of calculative conclusion derived by the mathematic-statistical techniques outlined in the first part of this chapter are used increasingly.

The problem at hand is most usefully depicted if the form of conceptualization evolves from the nature of the analytical problem itself, rather than being made to conform to a certain kind of statement. Ordinarily, analysis of cash flow and production-assembly operations is best accomplished with flow lines as the central graphical expression. In anticipating facilities expansion, the principal elements are represented by a combination of forecast lines depicting employee-population growth with different sales assumptions, and the capacities of existing and new buildings under different densities of occupancy (Figure 5). As mentioned earlier, a new geometric construction has been proposed to better conceptualize the important financial interactions within a business. It incorporates on a single page

> . . . three standard accounting presentations: the Balance Sheet, Operating Statement, and Application of Funds. These are combined to represent quantitatively: (*a*) what has occurred in the recent past, (*b*) the dynamics of the current situation, (*c*) present trends and (*d*) the readjustments of assets and liabilities required to accomplish a given end. The model is intended to simplify the accounting task and give management, after familiarization with its different form, a readily understandable and more complete concept of the financial interrelations within the business.[21]

FACILITIES PROGRAM

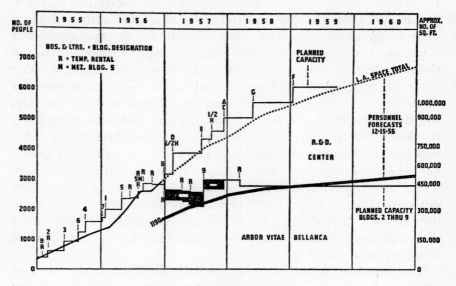

FIGURE 5

This facilities program and the portrayal of capital funds in Figure 6 are photographic reproductions of planning charts, approximately four by six feet in size, maintained in the type of corporate representation shown in Plate I (following page 128). Since "stick-on" materials are used throughout, the chart itself is easily modified or reformulated. Drafting and redrafting are not required. Alternative plans are developed directly on the display surface.

Verbalization is probably the best possible expression of value judgments which represent intuitive insight rather than consciously conclusive deduction: the prediction of consumer attitudes, an impression of inefficiency from a quick inspection, or strong opinions concerning people on brief acquaintance, to cite a few familiar examples.

The blackboard is one means of achieving the flexibility fundamental to this process of notation and initial formulation. Since erasure is easy, the conceptualization can be shaped in a few moments with each new awareness, thought, or conclusion. Equal flexibility cannot be attained on paper. After several erasures, there is an unrecognized reluctance to rub out and change; and, after several successive reformulations on fresh sheets of paper, the expression becomes sufficiently complicated to create the same resistance to starting all over again. These practical difficulties subtly but surely restrict the extent to which the early stages of analysis—the basis for further study—are developed on paper. This is the reason why blackboards are a characteristic of professional offices in many businesses producing scientific products or services, and will likely be found in many more executive-administrative offices in the future. Any problems of office decor and sartorial cleanliness will, it is hoped, yield to hidden blackboards, dustless chalk, and improved erasers. Until some new highly flexible, inexpensive means of conceptualization is available to perform the same function, the blackboard is the best mechanism of personal, informal visual analysis.

By such visualization, worthwhile analytical objectives are achieved. The problem at hand is transposed from the mind or thin air of verbal discussion into a form in which it can be seen, structured, and studied further. In this transposition, significant clarification is effected. Continued analysis is facilitated by the ease of progressive development which is possible with a flexible means of portrayal. The results of thought and discussion are advanced. The formulation on the blackboard can be photographed with a fast camera and passed on to others for further work or information. When an executive in a position of over-all knowledge and responsibility has structured a problem in this way as a basis for his own thinking and action, it may be most useful as a guide for staff study or follow-up planning by line managers.

Since the blackboard is primarily an informal, ever-ready, personal tool of analysis, the forms of expression employed are those which enhance the thinking of a single individual or several. Most people conceptualize in accordance with the ancient Chinese proverb: "A picture is worth a thousand words." Graphical images are most easily remembered and manipulated mentally, since they are accumulated in our conscious and unconscious mind from birth. Because our direct experience in life has included comparatively few abstractions, we comprehend the visually descriptive more readily than symbolic abstractions. Analytical thinking is therefore mainly in terms of objects, forces, and relationships reflecting the physical world and our experiences in three dimensions.

Some people possess an exceptional facility for conceptualizing in abstractions. Mathematicians, certain scientist-engineers, composers, musicians, and other specialists such as chess masters conduct most of their professional thinking in the mental language or abstraction of their field of concentration. For them, the mathematical-statistical statement, the musical score, or the chessboard expresses most clearly the elements and interrelationships with which they are concerned. The mathematician "sees" interactions in a formula most of us, without his predisposition and training, comprehend only by description more representative of three-dimensional experience. We remember an automobile license plate by visual memory or association with the physical world. The mathematician is likely to remember it as twice π to the fourth decimal place or some abstract associative recall. Examining a score, the composer "hears" the music as clearly and audibly as we do only if it is performed. A chess master mentally projects checkmate many moves in advance, whereas the intelligent layman cannot discern the inevitable outcome without extensive explanation. Some business men are recognized and respected by colleagues because of their exceptional ability to derive information from balance sheet and operating statements. Such forms of abstraction relate to human experience each in its own way, hence directly or indirectly to planning.

There is ample evidence that abstract thought is becoming more important in our thinking. Mathematical-statistical methods are increasingly necessary and widely employed in human affairs. In business, some executives are called upon today to choose among inventory policies derived by linear programing, adopt sales projections developed from multiple-probability assumptions, or approve new product research recommended because of estimates of the state of a technical art and market analysis based on a scientific sampling of opinion with definite confidence limits. Evaluation employing quantification, mathematics, statistics, probability, and other scientific methods will be more prevalent in the future.

Thinking in terms of a single kind of analytical expression is restrictive. If this is recognized, the executive enhances his potentialities of subjective judgment by acquiring a sufficient understanding of unfamiliar means of analysis to permit their incorporation into his conceptual framework—even though he may not comprehend the techniques in detail. Naturally, the use of familiar abstractions facilitates participation by others, but the primary purpose is personal elucidation. However extensive the quantitative data available, the final resolution of most corporate planning matters is by subjective judgment. Techniques which advance its quality and effective application increase the likelihood of favorable results at this level of decision.[22]

Institutional Mechanisms of Conceptualization

The accumulation and presentation of information to executive management have always been an essential part of business. Many methods have come into common usage over the years: status reports, operating-financial statements, descriptive memoranda, time schedules, forecasts, and special-project or functional analyses of various kinds. The decision maker must mentally accept, reject, or modify this material as to its factual and analytical validity. He must integrate it in his mind, since it is interrelated in one way or another—directly or indirectly, importantly or unimportantly, as the case may be. To select and remember significant information and correlate it within the mind is the manager's most difficult task—one which is never accomplished in a complete sense. As business management has become more complicated in the ways outlined in the introductory chapter, correlation and conceptualization require improved mechanisms of memory and analysis. These are now being applied to production control and data processing, but their direct application to corporate planning is just beginning.

In the military services, command control centers have been developed to a high degree. During World War II, war plans and operations rooms were expanded in scope, and the techniques of gathering, correlating, and displaying information greatly improved. Specialized centers were created for combat information, fighter direction, convoy-antisubmarine operations, and air defense command.

Subsequent developments in both the weapons performance and systems complexity of aircraft, ballistic missiles, submarines, and mobile ground forces have given rise to improved control centers with high-speed communications, automatic data processesing, and advanced display of both the tactical situation in being and underlying strategic considerations. A system ". . . at NORAD (North American Air Defense Command) headquarters . . . provides

NORAD's Commander-in-Chief and his staff with total visual information available on which to base decisions for the aerospace defense of Canada and the United States against enemy air spatial attack, . . . a data processing and display system which records the movements of multiple airborne objects and projects their paths on a graphic display to help in vital judgments."[23] Because of the diminishing time span within which critical decisions must be made, these mechanisms incorporate a background of past intelligence which is projected to provide, insofar as possible, an early warning of impending events and a check on the correct interpretation of current information.

Similar centers are employed by some business enterprises to direct operations. The Operations Briefing Room of United Air Lines in Denver, Colorado, is "primarily utilized to give Management a daily and continuous picture of what is going on all over the airline. . . ."[24] Process control centers have been developed for refineries, chemical plants, and utility generation-distribution systems which continuously monitor operations, anticipate difficulties or breakdown, and direct the system in the most profitable manner with respect to its functional requirements, fluctuating demand, price changes, and other external conditions. "Monsanto's ammonia unit at the Barton Plant is now [1960] under complete full-time control of [a] digital computing-control system and has been operating successfully for several months."[25] The control room for the business management by private enterprise of the research, development, and production of the U.S. Air Force Ballistic Missiles Program has been described as "an information center organized to promote coordination, planning, and analysis of effort of top management, . . . a meeting place where all channels of information relating to a given enterprise can conveniently be brought into focus."[26]

The Corporate Representation [27]

For the most part, these control centers are used by business to direct current operations. They are operating rather than planning devices. In military terms, they are intended for tactical purposes rather than longer-range strategic planning, with important but limited objectives. They relate to functional, rather than over-all, corporate management. By extending the concept and fundamental features of such centers, a mechanism of business planning—or *corporate representation*—is available to conceptualize the past, present, and projected future of the enterprise as a whole. An instrument of analysis and decision is at hand to serve as a better bridge between men and machines: to assist management in synthesizing the quantifiable and unquantifiable, objective data and subjective judgment, scientific method and human insight.

Characteristics. Information selected to meet the requirements of corporate management is received, classified, and stored. It is processed in accordance with criteria and assumptions supplied by the chief executives. It is as comprehensive in its scope as practicable. All significant considerations are incorporated as meaningfully as possible. It is an integrated formulation in that each element is consistent with every other element. The portrayal of a construction program, for example, correlates with information concerning the availability of capital, anticipated sales volume, profits, depreciation and taxes, production, manpower, and the other primary concerns of executive management depicted in the representation. Not only is this correlation an obvious requisite of coordinated planning, but it discloses "new" interrelationships useful as ratios or planning factors in considering the present and future of the business.

The corporate representation is flexible. Information is assimilated fast enough to permit efficient management and implementation. When one element is changed, other elements are revised in time to maintain the entire analytical array in consistent adjustment. By expedious feedback and feedforward, the representation embodies the repeated modifications prompted by circumstances and judgments. The time lag which can be tolerated depends on the nature of the business and the specific use of the representation. If the permissible delay is sufficiently short, special communication, data processing, or high-speed computing equipment may be necessary.

The corporate representation shows past trends and is projected into successive stages in future time. It is used to simulate the results of alternative courses of action, project the cumulative effects of present commitments and trends, and identify the probable consequences of a major decision or event. It is therefore integrated, not only "horizontally" at any given time, but "vertically" over a period of years, since successive extrapolations are also mutually consistent. From this projective dimension are derived additional correlations for forecasting elements individually, and collectively as a comprehensive plan.

The information is organized and portrayed in as simple and unequivocal a manner as practicable. Any feasible means is employed to make complicated material more readily understandable. New methods of conceptualization are devised to depict data and interrelationships which do not lend themselves to the usual kinds of portrayal. They evolve from the nature of the material, the clearest expression of its significance for planning purposes, and a form of display which facilitates its assimilation in the minds of those who perform corporate analysis, decide, and take action (Figure 6).

To achieve these characteristics of scope, integration, flexibility, timeliness, projection, and clarity, the corporate representation comprises a careful *distillation* of the mass of information available.

CAPITAL FUNDS—AVAILABILITY AND REQUIREMENTS

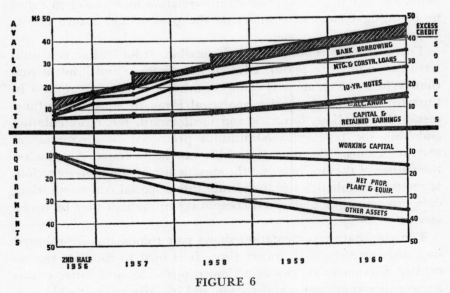

FIGURE 6

This portrayal of financial data is the same type of photographic reproduction explained in Figure 5 (page 156).

Otherwise, it would become so large, complex, and slow that its basic purpose could not be realized. Its installation and operation would also be most expensive. Executive managers want to view the over-all situation clearly, quickly, and continually. Their primary concern is the conduct of the business as a whole. Accordingly, they concentrate on the essential elements which enable them, at least initially, to view the forest rather than the trees.

It is crucial that the key elements selected for regular display be those that are most indicative of the business organism and are consistent with its details. These "control" elements are checked regularly to determine whether they can be refined, or whether they should be supplemented or replaced with others as conditions change. In effect, the corporate conceptualization is a simplified but truly representative model or analogue. It is an instrument of planning analysis, not a business gaming device. ". . . As a problem solving device, gaming in any of its numerous forms has severe limitations. Many of these stem from the fact that gaming is not analytic."[28] Factual statement and deductive objectivity are emphasized, to the end that the implications of the information may be debated and opinions differ concerning the conclusions to be derived, but the relevance and established limits of accuracy of the representation itself are accepted.

Function. The function of the corporate representation strongly favors its establishment as a room (Plate I, following page 128). Within this space, different ways of maintaining information can be employed, ranging from manual posting to the type of mechanical recording used in automatic stock-quotation boards. Various materials, graphical methods, and devices are available for flexible display (Plate II).[29] We are concerned here with function and use rather than details of construction and operation which will vary widely between companies and budget allocations. Basically, there are two ways in which the mechanism can be utilized. Combinations of these two purposes are possible, and the mechanism can be refocused from one to the other.

In one, the portrayal of the business is maintained week by week, or even day by day. It is used regularly for both shorter-range operations and longer-range planning. It is therefore fast-acting. Except for smaller businesses and special situations, electronic data-processing equipment may be required for rapid reformulation and simulation. As a consequence, costs are higher. To provide a steady flow of operating data and environmental information, internal reporting within the business must be efficient. Since vital facts, problems, and intentions are shown, the representation may be restricted in whole or in part to top management as a precaution against disclosure to competitors, premature revelation within the company, or the misinformation and disruptive rumor which can arise among employees when they interpret tentative analyses as final conclusions.

The alternative use of the corporate representation depicts the approved plan of achievement, conceptualizing the company at a future point in time. It presents the over-all target toward which the company is working. It shows not only what the business expects to accomplish and "look like" in the future but, generally, how this will be realized. It is revised periodically, and does not change during the interim unless circumstances call for immediate revision. It does not function directly as a mechanism of analysis and planning, although it serves as the necessary backdrop or starting point for such investigations. These are conducted by the planning staff, who will employ means and methods other than the corporate representation itself. Electronic data processing is probably not needed as an integral part of the mechanism. Internal reporting and external fact finding are not as immediate. Since a primary purpose is to portray agreed-upon objectives and specific accomplishments at successive mileposts in future time, it is available as a constant reference to those with a legitimate interest. Certain studies preliminary to reformulation, internally sensitive material, and significant competitive disclosures are protected from casual view.

In general, the mechanism advances the corporate ability to formulate a succession of sound comprehensive plans within the time limits ordinarily desirable, and to replan quickly when necessary. One which can service the minimum time lag crucial for some businesses permits a degree of organized forethought otherwise impossible. The mechanism does not, of course, operate in a vacuum. It is one part of a process which threads throughout the business. Its effectiveness is in large part dependent on the quality and timeliness of its informational input. If the information needed from within the business is not forthcoming promptly, the representation is correspondingly out of date or must be developed from estimates derived centrally. If executive analysis and decision are slow, its usefulness is impaired.

Corporate representations perform several corollary functions. The comprehensive planning purpose and process assume effective intercommunication among line executives, among staff personnel, and between top management and the owner or board of directors. All concerned must be "talking the same language," comprehending factual materials in the same way, and visualizing in their mind's eye the same over-all business situation and planning considerations. Although the extensive research being conducted today in the field of communication reflects the fundamental complexity of this crucial aspect of business activity, practical success depends on technique, organization, operating procedures, and personalities.[30] Because it provides a common denominator of understanding and a base reference for factual comparison, the corporate representation promotes constructive intercommunication relative to a wide range of operational-planning matters. Besides this function for the executive group directly responsible, it assists departmental managers, staff specialists, and others not directly concerned with company-wide planning in keeping themselves fully informed about the rest of the company and their relation to it.

It functions as a mental reminder for top management, although this may not be recognized at the time. The limitations of our memories and awareness are well known. Often, we recall an important fact or thought after we have completed consideration of the particular matter and are engaged in other affairs. The juxtaposition of diverse information in the corporate representation within a single visual sweep reduces such delayed reaction and enhances the comprehension applied during periods of analytical appraisal.

Since the idea and physical form of the representation impress people favorably, it is an effective means of introducing selected visitors and certain new employees to the activities of the company. It is an excellent mechanism for formal briefing purposes. The emphasis on factual and deductive objectivity helps to keep working conferences held within the room on the track, increasing their positive output and tending to highlight unrealistic, personally opportunistic, or unconstructive reactions. The room can also be a place for quiet contemplation by a single occupant. Its displays can be reproduced photographically and combined as convenient references for desk and brief case.

Clearly, the corporate representation is no magical device. Although it has its own substantive features, its success as a mechanism relates to preferences on the part of the executives it is intended to serve. For those with compatible management concepts and work habits, it functions effectively and uniquely. With executives who choose to work exclusively on their desk tops with traditional materials, or limit planning to what they can accomplish within their own heads, it serves little or no purpose. If the initial attitude of top management toward the mechanism is unfavorable but not prohibitive, it should be undertaken only in a limited form or postponed. If the management climate is one of moderate interest, qualified acceptance, or constructive experimentation, the mechanism should prove itself.

The establishment of a corporate representation in room form takes time; realization of its full potentialities normally requires several years. Installation-operating costs bear constant watching. There are inexpensive and expensive ways of achieving its objectives of conceptualization and analysis. Since it is a *working* tool of management impressive in its own content, elaborate design and "gold-plated" installation are unnecessary and often inappropriate. Without constant control, it is easy to accumulate more and more data until the complexity of analysis and display defeats the basic purpose. The incorporation of additional information found necessary for management purposes can usually be matched by the elimination of data no longer essential or by some other simplification.

A corporate representation can be constructed in transportable form, but size limitations restrict the information-analysis which can be included, impair its visual portrayal and cross-comparison, and reduce flexibility. It is possible to prepare material in notebook form, but unique advantages of comprehension are lost when correlation requires an awkward referring back and forth between pages in different sections of a book. Change is made more difficult by retyping, reproduction, and substitution of pages. Because by their nature they cannot incorporate the fundamental features previously described, transportable forms of corporation representation hardly merit the special designation. Occasionally, they are worthwhile as a temporary means toward the mechanism of analysis which in reality represents a different end.

Performance of People

Individual. In formulating a subjective judgment preparatory to executive decision, the individual applies as many of the principles of constructive mental attitude, analytic approach, and personal behavior as he can. He employs whatever practicable representation most thoroughly conceptualizes the business for his mind and eye. He uses the best combination of men and machines to prepare the quantifications he wishes for his appraisal, to simulate the probable consequences of alternative courses of action, and to resolve particular problems which he can postulate but which require special professional skills for analytical solution. He seeks the opinion of others in areas of human judgment in which he is not well informed. On blackboard or desk he performs such personal analysis as will assist him in reaching a conclusion.

To the extent possible, he subordinates self to the analytical problem at hand. His mind is receptive to the conclusions of scientific method and informed opinion, but he has the courage to proceed on his own convictions in the face of widespread disagreement. Admittedly, this approach is not always easy to achieve, but corporate planning decisions in the longer-range interests of a business institution merit a maximum effort toward objectivity. By this approach implicitly and explicitly applied, the executive increases his own managerial effectiveness and sets a desirable precedent for the performance of subordinates.

A balance of introspection and extroversion is involved. As previously mentioned, self-perception underlies many of the personal qualities contributing to sound subjective judgment. At the same time, the environment external to the individual embodies the end objective of most decisions and the informational context of all business analysis. Realistic understanding of this external component of judgment requires powers of observation which spring from an extrovertive interest in people and the march of events.

"The fine art of executive decision consists in not deciding questions that are not now pertinent, in not deciding prematurely, in not making decisions that cannot be made effective, and in not making decisions others should make."[31] The executive ". . . decides; sometimes he decides right, but always he decides."[32] Of course, this is more easily said than done. Successful performance reflects experience, broad awareness and knowledge, emotional maturity and inner security, the ability to delegate, perceptive interest in the managerial process itself, and the capacity to weather the stresses and strains of executive responsibility.[33]

Since in business the manager can seldom encompass all the fields of knowledge which relate to his decisions, he functions in considerable measure as a catalytic agent in corporate planning analysis. He must comprehend, evaluate, interrelate, and judge the work and thoughts of others without being able to absorb them in detail. Frequently, the nature and validity of analysis and opinion must be sensed through the person responsible, rather than by precise discussion of substantive material and prolonged logical argument. The chief executive untrained in law cannot debate with his corporate counsel the chances of success in a legal action. Yet he must decide whether a suit, appeal, or settlement is preferable from such corporate viewpoints as cost, internal policy, and customer and public relations. The recommendation of corporate counsel may be influenced by professional pride, desire for new experience, fascination with legal subtleties, or—occasionally—organizational "empire building." Normally, the manager identifies the weight of such factors in each case through the person involved: by perceptive questioning derived from understanding people in general and the individual in particular, which unearths additional information; and by prior experience, indirect indicators, or constructive intuition. Outside consultant advice is also available, but there are practical limitations to the frequency of this managerial resort, as well as its additional cost and delay.

Half the task of corporate planning analysis is the evaluation, management, and development of other people's logical conclusion and opinion. The successful executive knows when and how to act in this respect. He discerns unexpressed motivations as well as stated purposes. He exercises analytical as well as operational leadership, in ways which fit the problem, situation, and people concerned. In establishing planning objectives, he has "the serenity to accept the things [he] cannot change, the courage to change the things [he] can, and the wisdom to know the difference."[34] Because such qualities are in large part personal attributes, characteristics of personality and psychological understanding of oneself and others are as essential as substantive knowledge in comprehensive planning; ". . . the human element must be the most important part of scientific management or it will be a complete loss."[35]

Much remains to be accomplished before general guides to individual analytical thought and behavior for planning purposes are replaced by specific technique. It remains to be seen how the knowledge of individual and social psychology which will have accumulated in a few years will translate itself into reliable method. For the present, psychological generalization and psychoanalytic insight must be applied by each individual to the extent of his knowledge and emotional capability.[36]

There are many occasions when an individual is asked to look into a particular matter, analyze it, and report his conclusions. Of course, he is not expected to do this by himself. He confers with those concerned, obtains necessary background material, and may ask for special studies to fulfill his assignment. He is an intermediary agent for both the requestor and those involved within the company. In effect, he is the responsible head of a team or the chairman of a "committee" which is not formally established. The approach and method of operation are therefore up to him. He is not obligated to convene a group and develop a consensus, but he is obligated to identify all significant problems and consider different views in his analysis. The purpose in delegating the project task to an individual is to utilize his special ability and employ a procedure which avoids the time and difficulties incident to formal committee action. Sometimes, basically conflictive interests may exist to the point where a solution accepted by all members of a committee would be no solution at all from the viewpoint of the corporation or other higher management level.

Planning a new multi-divisional facility is illustrative. Operational requirements must be developed by those who will use the establishment. Each has special problems and desires. The many different specifications relating to location, space, equipment, and people must be integrated to meet the limitations of the project budget, financing, architectural-engineering and construction requirements, maintenance costs, and future rearrangement and expansion. Conflicts and inconsistencies must be resolved. Corporate interests and objectives must be represented and the efficient functioning of the total establishment insured, since the whole is more than the sum of its parts. Such project planning is a management task of *representation* in the fullest sense of the word. Either a "prima donna" approach by the executive in charge of master planning, or his acceptance of all declared requirements in an effort to make everybody entirely happy, of course results in an unsuccessful facility.

This role of management synthesis and representation calls for additional qualities in the individual.

> . . . If the task force captain behaves as if the solution came exclusively from him, he will not continue to get answers long. Hence the kind of men who can get results tend to be magnanimous in giving credit to others.

> . . . Teamwork isn't something that happens; it is a state of mind of the man who is responsible for handling a problem. It is an attitude of accepting the fact that he doesn't know all the answers, and can't do the job by himself.

> [He] must have an especially broad view of the problem itself and of the types of people who can contribute to the answers. Only then can he reach out for appropriate interdepartmental assistance and collaboration.

> This leader must be able to resolve differences. They inevitably exist in any human organization, and he has to work them out in a timely and friendly fashion. Furthermore, he ought to be able to state any that remain for the benefit of a superior who may be involved in subsequent review. He must be expeditious in coming to grips with a problem or recommendation, though he ought to respect minority views and in the interest of fair play and cooperation should state such views courteously and reasonably when presenting the majority solution.

> Unfortunately, minority views are not often treated with respect, and few executives state them with emphasis especially when they are being reviewed by higher echelons. . . . If you treat the minority with respect, if you understand its position, if you give it proper emphasis when presenting the problem to other people, you will often find the minority going along with the majority. . . . Not only the leader but also the various members of the group should be able to listen understandingly and respectfully to the positions of others, evaluate them, and modify their own preconceptions accordingly. . . .

. . . The thing to remember is that the type of problem you face constitutes one of the conditions which help to determine whether a task force concept, or any other teamwork practice, will work out successfully. . . .[37]

Group. At the apex of the organization in medium- and large-size companies there is usually an advisory committee reporting to the chief executive. It spreads the load of corporate analysis and planning. The different competences represented on the committee provide a breadth and depth of knowledge seldom found in one person. It comprises a team effort, mutually supportive among its membership as well as to the chief executive. Since it is the final instrument of *group* appraisal prior to decision and implementation, its performance is vital in corporate planning. When its functions are divided among several committees each reporting to the chief officer, the procedure of synthesis is different but operational requirements for effective group action are the same.

The purpose of such a group is to provide the ranking executive with collective analysis and opinion useful to him in making decisions. The end objective is to enlighten his choice among alternatives and to develop coordinated plans for consideration and action. It is a working rather than a discursive committee. It performs the tasks it can handle best, relying on others for work accomplished as well or better elsewhere. The intent is not analytical exploration for its own sake, nor the advancement of functional programs separately, but constructive accomplishment in the over-all corporate interest. Even if based only on brief study or pure judgment unsupported by specific data, a recommendation in time to meet the needs of management is more helpful than an analytical exposition of unresolved problems. As Prime Minister Winston Churchill said in a memorandum to the Chief of Combined Operations during World War II: ". . . Let me have the best solution worked out. Don't argue the matter. The difficulties will argue for themselves."[38]

The group operates as a unit, each member deferring his prejudices to business realities, his personal preferences to the corporate purpose, his predilections to group action. Since the committee functions within operating limits of time and expense, discussion is controlled by formal procedure or informal agreement. It is constructive and additive, rather than negative, argumentative, and self-justifying. *Interpersonal compatibility is as important as aggregate brainpower.* Overreaction to the opinions or mannerisms of others slows progress. Undue aggression, rivalry, or unconscious clash of personalities can destroy group effectiveness. Dissenting opinion is neither sacrificed to a lowest common denominator of concurrence nor allowed to become so pervasive that useful agreement and solution are impossible. "Where all think alike, no one thinks very much."[39] Individuality is not subdued but controlled. Any tendency to defer irresolutely to majority opinion is discouraged.[40]

There are desirable as well as inherent limits to the intentional organization of human behavior in the interest of rational appraisal. It is never easy to assemble from eligible executives a small group of individuals who can work together compatibly in close and continuing interrelationship. Ordinarily, membership is from four to six persons at the most. The chairman is often the key to success. In large measure, he sets the tone, guides, and motivates group activity. He establishes the procedural framework of accomplishment. Dependent on circumstances and the membership, his direction may be formal, or subtle and inconspicuous. More than the rest of the committee, the chairman subordinates self and assumes the role required for the group to function most effectively. "In the absence of overt coercion, the appropriate leader is signaled by the *members'* needs and is evaluated by the *members.*"[41] He represents the corporation in his responsibility of achieving the objectives it sets for the committee. At the same time, he represents the committee as the agent of its composite action.

The chairman devotes himself to the analytic end and the best means of its achievement through the human instruments at hand. He focuses on purpose and the contribution of others. He maintains in his mind's eye a picture of the group's stage of development in its analytical resolution, and what remains to be accomplished to serve the corporate purpose. As occasion demands, he postulates the collective position for clarification, acceptance, or modification before proceeding. He acts for the group in continuously identifying factual information and its reliability, and contrives its acceptance as a basis of inference. His own ideas and conclusions are offered without expectation that they will be accorded extra weight because of his position.

The chairman is sensitive to the personalities and mood of the membership. He draws out the retiring person and finds ways of keeping overassertiveness within bounds. He is a constructive listener, providing each member with an opportunity to express himself during or between meetings. The respective interests and strengths of each member are discovered and utilized to the full. Awareness of an unfamiliar element or interrelationship is stimulated by relating it to an active interest. In devising his own pattern of performance, he identifies insofar as possible the other person's situation, point of view, and way of thinking and acting. He accepts him as he is and not as he may think he should be. He is sensitive to the strong feelings and overreaction to be expected occasionally in others and within himself, since this recognition promotes procedural harmony.

Some type of corporate representation, as discussed earlier in this chapter, is maintained by the chairman for the committee. It serves as a factual referent which reduces wasteful digression because of lack of information, misunderstanding, or avoidance of matters of fact. It assists the group in conceptualizing the analytical problem and thereby advances its work. It embodies the consequences and current stage of analysis, available at all times to both membership and corporate management. It emphasizes the objective end to which personal interests are subordinated and related. It permits a structuring and expression of individual contributions otherwise more difficult. It reduces the need for minutes and recapitulation between meetings. It facilitates continuity of effort and more rapid indoctrination as membership changes.

The attitude of the executive to whom the group reports influences its operation. If he demands a near-perfect record of analysis and recommendation, he not only is unrealistic, of course, but restricts the scope of committee consideration to certainties and safe generalizations, stifles the courage to explore, and inhibits its activities in general. "Mistakes are the very soil of progress. Mistakes are experience. Experience develops judgment. And judgment is necessary to good management."[42] Supportive groups necessarily reflect this executive's instructions and reactions. He cannot expect objective analysis if he imposes a strait jacket of foregone conclusion, premature opinion, or prejudice. Nor will he achieve an effective relationship if he himself is subject to repeated overreaction and cannot motivate the committee by the appropriate blend of authority, understanding, encouragement, and critical review.

By careful selection of the committee chairman and consultation with him concerning the membership, the chief executive contributes to the performance of the group and thereby its value to him. To the extent practicable, title and other hierarchial matters are secondary as a qualification for membership to the requirements of a productive team. The chief executive upholds his end of the clear and regular intercommunication which not only is essential to the successful functioning of the committee but keeps him informed of what is going on and avoids disconcerting surprises. "Good leadership implies consideration of those who follow. It requires a communication system that works both ways—from the bottom up, as well as from the top down."[43]

The chief executive observes the committee's operation from a distance and exerts his influence, if needed, to support the chairman in improving the performance of the group. Occasionally, he may sit in unobtrusively to observe the functioning of the committee at first hand; he may identify a desirable change in membership or the chairman. "Except perhaps during an enterprise's very first stage of growth, one-man management by an intuitive genius has little place in the modern world of management. . . . For the accent has shifted from solitary leadership to teamwork. . . ."[44]

The ideal situation is rarely achieved. By no means are all human motivations constructive. Only to a point can we subordinate personal ambitions and emotional drives to analytical objectivity and the institutional interest. But the best performance within our capabilities does not occur by happenstance. It demands intentional effort. To the extent each of us is aware of the desirable ends and preferable methods of applying this effort, group achievement is advanced.[45] Naturally, the company's attitude toward the individual must be consonant with the attitude required of him for his best achievement in its behalf. If its policy is unduly selfish or opportunistic, it cannot expect better from its planning personnel.

SUMMARY

Techniques of analysis in comprehensive planning divide into two broad categories: scientific and judgmental. There is, of course, no precise demarcation between the two. Human judgment enters into the premises, criteria, and methods of scientific analysis; quantifications, experimental approaches, and logical procedures are incorporated in subjective judgment. Nevertheless, for practical planning purposes, analysis is scientific and factual in nature or judgmental in that it is not supported by a systematic structure of logic, mathematics, or experiment.

Techniques described in the first section of this chapter have been established for the category of scientific analysis. Except for questions of premise and procedural detail, the results derived by these techniques are accepted within their limits of accuracy. Ordinarily, we do not challenge the validity of careful counts of unit production per unit of time. With a quick check for significant error, we accept internal statements of financial condition prepared in the approved manner and consistent with previous reporting. And more sophisticated mathematical analysis and experiment, such as actuarial calculation and optimum machine loading, are accepted as they are proved in practice.

The other "half" of comprehensive planning is concerned with matters composed of so many different elements, intangibles, and variables that scientific method cannot be applied. A system of quantification or experimental method embracing all relevant factors does not exist to solve such crucial management decisions as the most profitable use-distribution of corporate resources or the best direction and strategy of growth. Individual and collective judgments must be employed without benefit of a consistent framework of conclusive analysis. The emphasis is therefore on people and methods of applying human judgment, rather than efforts toward a means of calculation, complete chain of deduction, or further refinement of available facts. Psychological improvements in human performance are as important at present as attempts to expand the scope of scientific method.

The synthesis of these categories of information, analysis, and decision requires both types of processing and conclusion. Factual-scientific materials are developed and used to the extent possible and practicable. Executives are selected and procedural methods adopted which improve the quality of subjective judgments. Whereas there are accepted techniques of scientific analysis, the ground rules so far established for promoting judgment are broadly behavioral in nature. Important instruments for their synthesis are the corporate representation and effective group appraisal.

REFERENCES CITED

[1] National Industrial Conference Board, reported in Management Section, *Business Week,* September 16, 1961 (No. 1672), p. 112.

[2] P. F. S. Otten (President of the Board, N. V. Philips' Gloeilampenfabreiken, Netherlands), *ibid.,* p. 116.

[3] John Cohen, "Subjective Probability," *Scientific American,* November 1957 (Vol. 197, No. 5), pp. 128–138.

Horace C. Levinson, *The Science of Chance—From Probability to Statistics,* 1950 (Rinehart & Co.), 348 pp.

Irwin D. J. Bross, *Design for Decision,* 1953 (The Macmillan Company), pp. 33–84, 183–254.

[4] Richard Austin Smith, "How a Great Corporation Got Out of Control," *Fortune,* January 1962 (Vol. LXV, No. 1), p. 66.

[5] Irwin D. J. Bross, *supra,* pp. 161–182.

E. F. Beach, *Economic Models: An Introduction,* New York (John Wiley & Sons), 1957.

Frank M. Bass (Editor), *Mathematical Models and Methods in Marketing,* (Richard D. Irwin, Homewood, Illinois), 545 pp.

[6] Norbert Wiener, *Cybernetics, or Control and Communication in the Animal and Machine,* Second Edition, 1961 (MIT Press–John Wiley & Sons), 202 pp.

[7] George A. E. Boehm, "Next, the Solid State Vice President," *Fortune,* December 1960 (Vol. LXII, No. 6), pp. 161–165ff.

Ernest F. Johnson, "Automatic Process Control," *Science,* 9 February 1962 (Vol. 135, No. 3502), pp. 403–408. "Automatic Control," *Scientific American,* September 1952 (Vol. 187, No. 3), pp. 44–160 (entire issue).

[8] Oskar Morgenstern, "The Theory of Games," *Scientific American,* May 1949 (Vol. 180, No. 5), pp. 22–25.

Leonid Hurwiez, "Game Theory and Decisions," *ibid.,* February 1955 (Vol. 192, No. 2), pp. 78–83.

John McDonald, *Strategy in Poker, Business, and War,* 1950 (W.W. Norton & Co.), 129 pp.

J. D. Williams, *The Compleat Strategyst, Being a Primer on the Theory of Games of Strategy,* 1954 (McGraw-Hill Book Company), 234 pp.

[9] Francis Bello, "The Information Theory," *Fortune,* December 1953 (Vol. 48, No. 6), pp. 136–158.

Gilbert W. King, "Information," *Scientific American,* September 1952 (Vol. 187, No. 3), pp. 132–148.

W. Wesley Peterson, "Error-Correcting Codes," *ibid.*, February 1962 (Vol. 206, No. 2), pp. 96–108.

George A. Miller, "Information and Memory," *Scientific American*, August 1956 (Vol. 195, No. 2), pp. 42–46.

[10] W. Allen Spivy, "Linear Programming," *Science*, 5 January 1962 (Vol. 135, No. 3497), p. 23.

[11] *Ibid.*, p. 27.

William W. Cooper and Abraham Charnes, "Linear Programming," *Scientific American*, August 1954 (Vol. 191, No. 2), pp. 21–23.

Part Three: "Some Industrial Applications," *Operations Research Reconsidered*, Management Report No. 10, 1958 (American Management Association), pp. 83–143.

[12] Simon Ramo (Vice Chairman of the Board, Thompson Ramo Wooldridge Inc.), "The Guided Missile as a Systems Engineering Problem," *Canadian Aeronautical Journal*, January–February 1957 (Vol. 3, Nos. 1, 2), pp. 3–9, 38–43.

[13] John Dearden, "Problem in Decentralized Profit Responsibility," *Harvard Business Review*, May–June 1960 (Vol. 38, No. 3), pp. 79–86.

Robert N. Anthony, "The Trouble with Profit Maximization," *ibid.*, November–December 1960 (Vol. 38, No. 6), pp. 126–134.

[14] Frederick C. Crawford (Chairman of the Board, Thompson Products, Inc.), "How to Increase Executive Effectiveness by Creating the Proper Climate and Incentives Within a Company," address (typescript) at the Harvard Business School, 13 June 1953, p. 7.

[15] John G. McLean (Vice President, Coordinating and Planning, Continental Oil Company), "The Development, Operation, and Organization of Central Research Staffs in Industry," address (mimeo) before the Annual Meeting of the Business Research Section of the Southwestern Social Science Association, Galveston, Texas, 27 March 1959.

[16] Perrin Stryker and the Editors of *Fortune, A Guide to Modern Management Methods* (Chapter Three, "Can Executives Be Taught to Think?"), 1954 (McGraw-Hill Book Company), pp. 34–53.

[17] Arch Patton, "How to Appraise Executive Performance," *Harvard Business Review*, January–February 1960 (Vol. 38, No. 1), pp. 63–70.

[18] Chester L. Brisley, "Executive Inefficiency," *Industrial Research*, February–March 1960, pp. 59–62.

[19] Wallace R. Persons (President, Emerson Electric Manufacturing Co.), "Slow Boat to Success," *Forbes Business and Finance*, 1 March 1961 (Vol. 87, No. 5), p. 32.

[20] Thomas J. Bata (President, Bata Ltd.), Management Section, *Business Week*, 16 September 1961 (No. 1672), p. 116.

[21] Bernard Whitney and Marion S. Israel, "A Working Model of the Financial Dynamics of a Business," *Operations Research*, July–August 1958 (Vol. 6, No. 4), p. 573.

James W. Culliton, "Diagram of Management Control," *Harvard Business Review,* March–April 1960 (Vol. 38, No. 2), pp. 144–145.

Lee Adler, Exhibit I, "Factors and People Influencing Media Selection," *ibid.,* May–June (Vol. 38, No. 3), p. 117.

[22] Several points included in this discussion are made briefly in M. C. Branch, "Logical Analysis and Executive Performance," *Journal of the American Academy of Management,* April 1961 (Vol. 4, No. 1), pp. 27–31.

[23] Advertisement, *Forbes Business and Finance,* 15 May 1961 (Vol. 87, No. 10), pp. 34–35.

[24] Warren E. Alberts (Vice President and Assistant to the President, United Air Lines), personal communication, 12 December 1950.

[25] R. D. Eisenhardt and T. J. Williams, "Closed-Loop Computer Control at LULING," *Control Engineering,* November 1960 (Vol. 7, No. 11), p. 103.

[26] Control Room Presentation (*Management Control–Air Force Ballistic Missiles Program*), Air Research and Development Command (Ballistic Missiles Office), Ramo-Wooldridge Corporation (Guided Missile Research Division), Los Angeles, undated, 10 pp. and illus.

[27] Melville C. Branch, Jr., "Conceptualization in Business Planning and Decision Making," *Journal of the American Institute of Planners,* Winter 1957 (Vol. XXIII, No. 1), pp. 13–22, illus.

[28] Charles Hitch, "Uncertainties in Operations Research," *Operations Research,* July–August 1960 (Vol. 8, No. 4), p. 443.

John McDonald and Franc Ricciardi, "The Business Decision Game," *Fortune,* March 1958 (Vol. LVII, No. 3), pp. 140ff.

[29] Melville C. Branch, Jr., *supra,* pp. 18–22.

[30] Henry H. Albers, *Organized Executive Action* (Part Four: "Planning and Control Information Systems"), 1961 (John Wiley & Sons), pp. 327–433.

[31] Chester I. Barnard (President, New Jersey Bell Telephone Company, 1927–1948), in *Forbes Business and Finance,* 1 July 1959 (Vol. 84, No. 1), p. 54.

[32] John Patterson, *ibid.,* 15 July 1959 (Vol. 84, No. 1), p. 46.

[33] Editors of *Fortune, The Executive Life* (Chapter 5, "How Executives Crack Up"), 1956 (Doubleday & Co.), pp. 79–93.

[34] Reinhold Niebuhr.

[35] Arthur K. Watson (President, IBM World Trade Corporation), in *Business Week,* 12 March 1960 (No. 1593), p. 74.

Stahrl Edmunds, "The Reach of an Executive," *Harvard Business Review,* January–February 1959 (Vol. 37, No. 1), pp. 87–96.

[36] James C. Coleman, *Personality, Dynamics, and Effective Behavior* (Part 3: "Resources for Effective Living"), 1960 (Scott, Foresman, & Co.), pp. 289–422.

[37] Edward C. Bursk and Dan H. Fenn, Jr., *Planning the Future Strategy of*

Your Business (Edmund P. Learned, "Getting the Organization to Work Effectively as a Team"), 1956 (McGraw-Hill Book Company), pp. 77, 79.

[38] *Evidence in Camera,* Special Edition [Air Ministry ACAS (1)], 27 November 1944 (Vol. 8, No. 9), p. 165.

[39] Walter Lippmann.

[40] Dorwin Cartwright and Alvin Zander (Editors), *Group Dynamics* (Chapter 12, S. E. Asch, "Effects of Group Pressure upon the Modification and Distortion of Judgments), 1956 (Row, Peterson), pp. 151–176.

[41] Robert L. Katz, "Toward a More Effective Enterprise," *Harvard Business Review,* September–October 1960 (Vol. 38, No. 5), p. 95.

[42] Frederick C. Crawford, *op. cit.,* p. 11.

[43] William Menninger, M. D.

[44] P. F. S. Otten (President of the Board, N. V. Philips' Gloeilampenfabreiken, Netherlands), Management Section, *Business Week,* 16 September 1961 (No. 1672), p. 116.

[45] Victor M. Longstreet, "Management R&D," *Harvard Business Review,* July–August 1961 (Vol. 39, No. 4), pp. 125–134.

Robert F. Bales, "How People Interact in Conferences," *Scientific American,* March 1955 (Vol. 192, No. 3), pp. 31–35.

Warren H. Schmidt and Robert Tannenbaum, "Management of Differences," *Harvard Business Review,* November–December 1960 (Vol. 38, No. 6), pp. 107–115.

James C. Coleman, *op. cit.* (Chapter 8, "The Social Setting of Behavior"), pp. 249–287.

Henry H. Albers, *op. cit.* (Part Five: "Leadership and Motivation"), pp. 437–586.

CHAPTER VI

Implementation

Companies interested in comprehensive planning indicate that they are most concerned at the present time with implementation. "The best-laid plans of mice and men" do not produce results until they are translated into action by the different units of the business. Effectuation poses its own requirements of organization, procedure, and technique. These are shaped by important considerations relating to the people who will carry them out. Inasmuch as the current intensification of interest in corporate planning is comparatively recent, less has been written and reported on implementation than other phases of this activity.

ORGANIZATION

Since it is a primary responsibility of line executives, planning affects the organization of a company to the extent that it functions more effectively in one formal arrangement than in another. The line manager can plan only those activities with which he is directly charged. If information concerning the activities and intentions of another segment of the business is necessary for his own planning but is unavailable, either organizational clarification is needed or the other component is not communicating satisfactorily.

The formal organization of a company expresses both longer-range planning and current operating responsibilities. "Planning and doing are separate parts of the same job, they are not separate jobs."[1] Traditional staff units are organized as much with reference to their function of assisting in planning ahead as their activities in support of current operations. Units specifically established for planning purposes are of course so designated and located. Since the formal organization chart rarely denotes all administrative interconnections, special arrangements are made for such situations as a sales department which is outstanding in the persuasive techniques of selling but weak in longer-range planning. Professional assistance in planning sales is provided elsewhere within the company or obtained from an outside service.

> Organization Planning [is] an activity having as its purpose the preparation for those changes which will be necessary to keep the organization at top efficiency. . . . Forty years ago, a most intensive bout of "organization planning" completely changed the structure of Du Pont. . . . The general structure then adopted has withstood the intervening decades. . . .

> There was first of all an appraisal of performance, which was found to be unsatisfactory. There was a period of fact-finding to identify the causes of the difficulty. There was the formulation of a basic organizational plan—which in this instance more sharply defined areas of responsibility and authority, and provided better concentration and coordination of effort. There followed a considerable period during which the basic plan was worked out in detail before it was put into operation.[2]

When the company is organized functionally, coordination is effected and comprehensive plans are drawn at the *single profit center* which controls at least production and sales (Figure 7*A*). When management is conducted through multiple profit centers, comprehensive planning of the activities controlled at each center is the responsibility of its line manager (Figure 7*B*). Depending on the degree of decentralization or autonomy, each of these managers relates his plans to those of the other major subdivisions of the enterprise, and to the objectives and limitations established by corporate management. A sound principle in either single or multiple profit centers is that only those planning activities are conducted at the corporate level which cannot be delegated, or for valid reasons are better performed centrally. In turn, each line executive delegates to the heads of units under him all planning accomplished as successfully at lower levels. He retains for his own personal analysis, supervision, and decision comprehensive planning for the organi-

CORPORATE ORGANIZATION

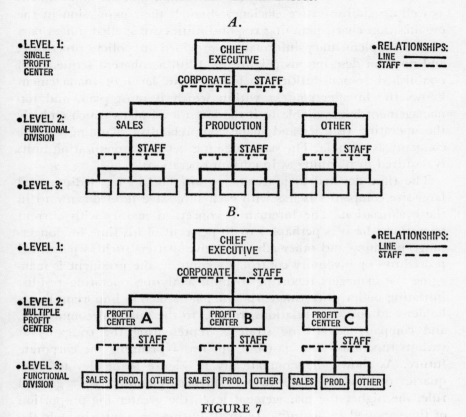

FIGURE 7

zational units he controls, and functional planning which requires or needs his attention.

The primary motivation of managers is success in their job.

> . . . Perhaps one can accurately talk about "management" as a meaningful, cohesive class sharing common motivations re what they want from their work, if their responsibilities are defined in terms of job rather than organizational effectiveness. . . . [The only possible exceptions are those] at the level of plant managers and higher, or perhaps men who are primarily integrators and policy makers, having a broad perspective and a criterion of personal success based on organizational rather than job effectiveness.[3]

Clear definition of planning responsibilities is therefore doubly important, for it relates to personal motivation and accomplishment as well as administrative efficiency. Besides their expression in the organization chart, planning responsibilities are spelled out as part of the supplementary information provided in policy, procedure, and position descriptions (Figure 8). With a coherent sequence of established responsibilities, each successive level of management knows the broader context within which it must plan, and top management has available to it the lower-level plans which embody the operating realities and shape comprehensive planning for the company as a whole. The same meshing between organization units is required in planning as in current operations.

The time devoted to longer-range forethought in medium- and large-size companies is less with each successive level downward in the organization. The foreman is concerned mainly with current operations; he uses perhaps 5 to 10 per cent of his time for longer-range planning and other administrative matters such as personnel procedures or inventory control. By contrast, the president is managing the managers reporting to him; analyzing operating results; initiating policy; directing corporate affairs such as important stockholder and customer relations, reports to the financial community, and company advertising strategy; representing the company at various functions; and—last but not least—planning the corporate future. As shown diagrammatically in Figure 9, he devotes one-quarter to one-half of his time to advance planning. As a general rule, the higher the management level, the greater the proportion of time applied to planning. In small businesses, approximately the same distribution of activity maintains between organizational levels, but the proportion of the chief executive's time spent in administering current operations is naturally much greater. In the smallest enterprises, the manager may have to work overtime to find time for planning beyond the immediate future.[4]

A procedure for plan processing is prepared and distributed. The scope and content of plans at different levels are described to prevent duplication and omission. A schedule of preparation, review, and approval is adopted which permits periodic re-examination and rapid reformulation when called for. The organizational pathways along which plans progress up, down, and across are designated; and informal channels of communication which will supplement

(Text continued on page 188)

Position Description

VICE PRESIDENT, LONG RANGE PLANNING

Autonetics (A Division of North American Aviation Inc.)
1962

I. FUNCTION

Plans and directs the operations and activities of the Long Range Planning Office in accordance with corporate and Autonetics policies for the purpose of developing long range plans which will achieve optimum growth, stability, and profitability for the Autonetics Division.

II. COMPANY RELATIONSHIPS

A. Autonetics

1. *Executive Office*—Reports to the Executive Office; assists in the development of Autonetics' policies, plans, and objectives; advises on Long Range Planning performance and other matters affecting the future of Autonetics.

2. *Divisions and Other Staff Offices*—Coordinates and integrates the Long Range Planning activities in the various divisions and staff offices.

B. Other NAA Operating Divisions

Confers and coordinates with management of other operating divisions on matters of mutual interest.

C. General Offices

Coordinates Long Range Planning activities with General Offices executives; obtains their policy guidance and assistance. Furnishes to them reports and information required for their purposes.

III. RESPONSIBILITIES AND AUTHORITY

Within the framework of established policy and approved plans and programs has the responsibility and authority to:

A. Formulate and submit proposals for long range objectives, programs, and plans to the Executive Office for approval.

B. Apply corporate policy as adapted in terms of Autonetics requirements, and establish and administer implementing policy and procedures for the development of Autonetics' long range plans.

C. Direct the activities of Long Range Planning within the framework of established policy and approved plans and programs as follows:

1. Determine what data and analysis are needed as a basis for planning; coordinate efforts to obtain such data.

FIGURE 8*A* (page 1)

2. Analyze domestic and international politico-economic trends and evaluate their effect on the growth and development of Autonetics.

3. Maintain close familiarity with military planning and research efforts and evaluate their probable effect on Autonetics operations.

4. Review commercial market research studies and all proposals for entrance to non-defense markets, and take appropriate action.

5. Coordinate efforts to assess technological trends and imminent technological developments within NAA and Autonetics and by competitors, suppliers, and customers.

6. Coordinate activities to analyze Autonetics' capabilities and limitations and alternative uses of Autonetics' resources, including facilities, personnel, production techniques, organization structure, and finances.

7. Review proposals for investment of NAA capital by Autonetics in relation to risk, estimated earnings, cash flow, returns on investment, and Autonetics' long range goals and objectives.

8. Direct efforts to determine the trend of competitors' policies and behavior.

9. Review and approve all long range forecasts prepared by Autonetics division and staff offices.

10. Correlate and interpret all data and analyses received, forecast the future competitive environment; propose goals and objectives; and prepare proposed plans to achieve approved Autonetics goals and objectives.

11. Integrate, through coordination, Autonetics divisions' plans to ensure that they are in accord with approved long range plans and objectives.

12. Review all proposals by Autonetics personnel for company mergers, acquisitions, and joint ventures; and recommend such proposals to the appropriate General Offices executives.

13. Control the hiring, developing, evaluating, promoting, and disciplining of employees of the Long Range Planning Office.

14. Direct all other managerial functions necessary to the operations of the Long Range Planning Office, such as: assign responsibilities and authority; determine standards and goals; budget and control departmental operating funds; and advance operational efficiency.

D. Provide Long Range Planning assistance to all Autonetics divisions and staff offices.

E. Represent the Long Range Planning Office in contacts and meetings with customers, representatives of government, industry, and the public.

F. Serve on the following Autonetics committees:

Long Range Planning Committee—Chairman
Executive Committee
Management Council
Proposal Policy Board

FIGURE 8A (page 2)

Position Description

DIRECTOR OF PLANNING

Continental-EMSCO Company
(A Division of the Youngstown Sheet and Tube Company)
November 1960

[Reports to Vice President–Special Projects]

Basic Responsibilities

Provide information to assist Management in formulating long- and short-range goals and plans of the Company. Also assist in the updating of these goals plus general monitoring of attainment.

Coordinate activities and prepare special studies centering on acquisition, disposals, joint endeavors, manufacturing rights, and patents.

Serve as resource for determining the acquisition, disposal, and movement of physical properties.

Encourage the stimulation of ideas from Management toward broadening Company operations; extract these ideas and follow up on possibilities.

Develop, recommend, and obtain Management approval of plans, procedures, and policies to be followed in implementing diversification program.

Perform basic research on diversification, using such sources as American Management Association, National Industrial Conference Board, Research Institute of America, and other points of information.

Perform internal and external economic studies to secure necessary information for over-all planning.

Utilize staff service personnel plus line and committee persons in accumulating and evaluating data.

Analyze the Company's physical properties and personnel capabilities to determine our production span.

In conjunction with staff services, periodically survey performance capabilities of sales, engineering, manufacturing, and service components of the Company.

Conduct an initial survey of the manufacturing organization's physical properties (facilities, equipment, and tools) and keep information current.

Investigate and determine possibilities of other significant use for our basic products.

Assist in communicating and implementing the diversification decisions of Management during transition periods.

Prepare necessary reports to keep Management informed.

FIGURE 8B

(Text continued from page 184)

the formal procedure are identified. Responsibility for each plan is assigned to an *individual,* not a committee. He may use a committee and work with many people, but he is personally and directly accountable for the completion and quality of the plan. In essence, a system is organized for the accumulation and coordination of unit

DIVISION OF EXECUTIVE RESPONSIBILITIES

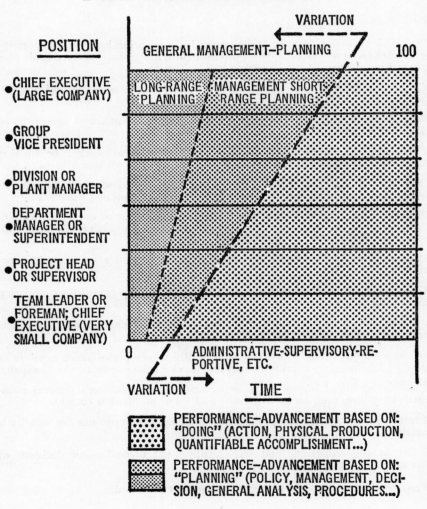

FIGURE 9

ORGANIZATION FOR CORPORATE PLANNING

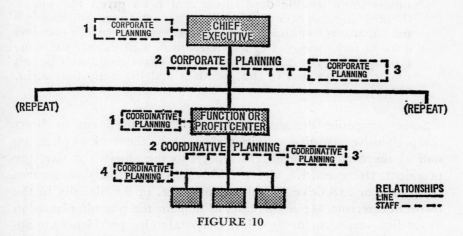

FIGURE 10

plans into larger groupings, their synthesis and modification at the top, implementation, subsequent review for variances, and regular revision. "People cannot plan adequately unless they are provided with tools, procedures, techniques, and know-how. Planning is as dependent on good organization, specific training, and good administration as any other phase of work."[5]

Besides time, concentration, and the functional knowledge available in larger institutions from staff as well as line managers, comprehensive planning requires special skill in coordinative analysis, conceptualization, and over-all deductive conclusion. The small group selected to perform this synthesis is shown separately on the organization chart. When the company is big enough, full-time positions are established on the corporate staff to assist in this integration of component plans. Several organizational locations for the function are shown in Figure 10. It is this unit through which divisional executives are sometimes rotated to broaden their managerial perspective and provide experience in comprehensive planning analysis. As shown in Figure 10, such units may operate also within groups and divisions.

In discussing what part of the organization should be the polarizing point for long-range planning, it is important to realize that it is dangerous to talk about a given company pattern of organization without knowing anything about the people in the company. . . . I can remember many instances where no long-range planning would have been accomplished at all unless some specific department had been given the job of shepherding the over-all planning effort. In one company, the president was too impatient; . . . he considered such a program a lot of nonsense. Yet in another business of exactly the same type and size, the long-range planning effort could well be left under the direction of the president and his immediate assistant.[6]

Some companies designate a corporate vice president to direct comprehensive planning activity and supervise the work of planning staff at the corporate level. He reports to the chief executive, the president, the executive vice president, an executive management committee or executive planning committee, or occasionally to the board of directors. He acts as *chief of staff* for the planning function to his line management superior. Corporate vice presidents are appearing in organization charts with such descriptive subtitles as "coordinating and planning," "long-range planning," "plans and programs," "plans," "advanced technical planning," and "marketing and planning." Alternatively, executives performing these functions are designated "corporate director." Directors of planning are also appearing with increasing frequency at group, divisional, and even departmental levels.[7]

Occasions arise when the regular procedure of plan preparation and processing is modified temporarily. For example, two or more divisions may be equally concerned in planning and producing a single product or complex system. Or, as discussed in an earlier chapter in a different connection, master-planning a new facility for several divisions is usually more successful if special provision is made for its planning. When the expenditure is large, coordination difficult, and time limited, it may be desirable to set up a temporary position—sometimes with supporting committee and staff—to meet the special requirements of project planning. This is arranged to supplement and not conflict with existing lines of authority and established corporate planning. The temporary position is discontinued after the project is completed, unless there is further work of the same nature and permanent reorganization is contemplated. In this case, the special unit may be incorporated into the permanent planning staff of the new grouping, if one exists, or become the nucleus for such a staff, if none exists.

Long-range planning should have the objectivity to cut across established functions and procedures, to stimulate a change in direction and where necessary suggest changes of policy, procedure, and methods. The [long-range planning] task force recommended a reorganization of manufacturing, a reorganization of distribution that developed from their study, a reorganization of the customer service and quality assurance development to complement distribution, and a reorganization of the International Division.[8]

PROCEDURAL CONSIDERATIONS

Companies embarking upon more extensive planning conduct considerable preparatory investigation to determine what they will seek to achieve and how they will go about it. Not all executives are familiar with the fundamental characteristics of the comprehensive planning process. The best method of introducing or extending planning within the existing organization must be carefully thought out. A "plan for planning" is developed by a small group of high officers within the company.

The first step toward adequate planning is the establishment of a planning climate. Best results are achieved when this begins with top management—the very top—the chairman of the board, the president, the executive vice president, and the important vice presidents. They must buy the proposition that planning *per se* and as such is an identifiable, controllable function essential to the health of the enterprise. And they will be completely convinced only if they do a little work on the subject. They must study some of the pertinent literature to familiarize themselves with planning techniques that have been successfully applied in other companies, attend some high-level conferences, take a little time to think and talk about the subject. And they ought to write down their conclusions for everyone to see and improve. Somebody has said, "If you haven't written it out, you haven't thought it out." That is as true of planning as it is of any other fundamental principle.[9]

An experienced consultant can sometimes assist in this initial formulation by bringing to bear a diversity of experience and a disinterested reaction to preliminary proposals. But it is essential that corporate management perform its own analysis and reach its own best conclusions concerning a process so fundamental to the conduct of the business and so intimately a part of its management responsibility.

Corporate planning must then be explained to the rest of management and subsequently throughout the organization.

> As a basic aid, we organized a committee on planning, consisting of the president, the executive vice president, and all the vice presidents, plus a secretary. The committee meets once a week for an hour and a half, and attempts to encourage widespread establishment of objectives, stimulation of plans to meet these objectives, and promote the principle that planning is primarily a line responsibility. It recommends projects, and points out areas where planning is needed. Members discuss the policies and perimeters within which plans should be formulated, foster organization for planning, and discover and promote the best methods used in modern, successful business enterprise. . . .

> People must be made aware of the importance, the necessity, the techniques, and the pay-off, of planning. This is not a simple thing to achieve. Top management belief in planning is not enough. Supervisors and specialists at all levels . . . must accept the fact that planning is part of their job. And the best way of convincing them is to have them do some actual planning on specific assignment. The subject must be kept alive, also, by the usual techniques of communications and by training techniques.

> The principal conclusion has been that planning does not just happen. It must be planned. This is true whether we are talking about short-term planning or long-term planning. In fact, the skills are the same in both cases; only the objectives are different. People who have not first learned to develop good short-term plans are unlikely to produce good long-term plans.[10]

Clearly, comprehensive planning is not established quickly by directive or executive desire. Not only is time needed for organizational preparation, general familiarization, and preparatory experience, but employee reactions described in the next section can prolong the period of implementation. Executives and supervisory personnel must become accustomed to the demands and consequences of intensified planning. A cardinal principle of successful comprehensive planning is therefore a deliberate policy of *gradual implementation*—step by step as carefully thought out in advance.

Almost invariably, haste means waste; objections are accentuated, and acceptance is slower than would otherwise be the case. If a corporate plan, when completed and announced, comes as a surprise and harbinger of unexpected events, it will compound problems of communication between management levels which it should mitigate. Sufficient time is of the essence, and patience a necessary virtue if the frustration frequently experienced by active proponents of planning is to be avoided.

Careful scheduling is as important in the regular conduct of planning as it is in its introduction. At the corporate center of comprehensive planning and at primary subcenters within the company, master schedules are maintained covering the various stages of preparation, processing, and implementation. Without this information and control, confusion would be the order of the day and successful integration impossible. Scheduling can become sufficiently intricate in larger companies to occupy the full time of one or more persons, but like many management operations of this type, such coordination is more than repaid by the improvements in production performance brought about by increased supervisory efficiency, and the clarification of operational interrelationships provided each participating unit. Important "milestone" events are identified, useful correlations and conflicts are noted, and procedure is studied continually for simplification, improvement, and adjustment to meet new conditions.

Improved scheduling techniques, developed in recent years by the military services, are expanding into industry. By the use of computers, programs of implementation are studied in much greater detail in advance, and more closely monitored throughout production to determine progress and identify the critical points of productive interdependence where failure to meet any one of several commitments on time will cause disproportionate delay in the completion of the entire project.

> Technical management continuously faces the problem of coordinating the diverse activities found in the large-scale project. The accuracy of management's estimates for schedules, cost, and manpower often spells the difference between success or failure of a project. . . . Existing management-control systems are based upon gross estimates of total requirements obtained from past experience. Furthermore, these estimates are arrived at independently by individuals responsible for their own

increment of work, and there is scant coordination (if any) among individuals. The sheer complexity of many large-scale projects limits the use of existing . . . management-control systems such as bar (or Gantt) charts. . . .

During the past decade, large-scale computers have become generally available and opened the way for more sophisticated . . . systems. Existing management-control systems are essentially manual systems even though machine-processed. Upon installation of a computer, many firms programed their existing systems of obtaining reports but did nothing to increase the quality of the information. The advent of the high-speed computer permits . . . approaches that express relationships not previously considered feasible because of the time and labor necessary for data processing.

One means of expressing relationships visibly and mathematically is the network. A network model depicts the ordered sequence of events and their interrelationships in reaching a goal and . . . detailed estimates of elapsed time required between events. The technique utilizes time, money, and manpower as variables reflecting planned resource applications and performance specifications. It takes into account alternative options involved in the projection of both physical and intellectual activities. The system detects the expected completion of each event, both singularly and collectively, and determines the paths of critical events. . . .

The network concept was first applied to a large-scale system in the Navy Special Project Office (SPO) for the Fleet Ballistic Missile (FBM) program. The system was called Program Evaluation Review Technique (PERT). . . . The original concept has proved extremely valuable within the framework for which it was designed, the single dimension of scheduling over time. PERT has been credited with helping to reduce the time required to develop the Polaris FBM program from 10 years to 5.

The Du Pont Corporation has developed a network system used for the construction of new facilities. This technique is named Critical-Path Planning and Scheduling. The General Electric Corporation, too, is experimenting with the network concept to schedule the more complicated manufacturing processes. Other firms such as Aerojet and Lockheed Aircraft are using versions of the PERT system to aid in scheduling.[11]

Although primarily instruments of project implementation, such systems are also used for planning purposes.[12] Alternative methods of effectuating production and other programs of accomplishment are simulated in advance, and the solution is chosen which best meets project needs and the over-all corporate situation. Because of the cost of computer installation and the expensive technical man-power required for its operation, these scheduling systems are restricted at present to larger corporations with production pro-grams big enough to justify the investment. Much remains to be accomplished in their further development to encompass the full range of consideration in business operations and make them com-patible with the methods of general management, other company activities, and traditional procedures.

> Such techniques as PERT are having an increasing influence on management methods. Yet it should be clear that merely having the computer to do the calculating isn't the main objective. Gathering information, setting up the systematic production and accounting procedures, estimating costs and times realistically, and deciding which system to use remain very much of a job for intelligent management men.[13]

In time, certain key elements will be simplified to the point where they can be calculated without highly specialized knowledge and incorporated as useful approximations in the inexpensive mechan-isms of planning and control which small business can afford. In the meantime, significant management improvement is possible by the more widespread use of existing methods and the development of general-purpose corporate representations as described in the pre-vious chapter.

Budgets are closely related instruments of planning implementa-tion and control. They establish comparative levels of activity be-tween different units beforehand, they limit autonomous expendi-ture, and they measure performance in part. They elicit the accurate and continuous data needed for control purposes, and often reveal trends before they reach the serious proportions which make their correction more difficult. Associated with budgets are other tools of administration such as cost accounting, quality and inventory con-trol, or the management of cash and receivables. Although flexible to the extent determined by higher authority, all things considered, budgets are the basic referents of planning implementation for the fixed, shorter-term periods of accountability.

When electronic data processing is employed, a centralization of information is the consequence of its cost, speed, and capacity. Data accumulated traditionally within separate organizational units are maintained within a common facility. Not only is the center a service organization to operating units in this way, but it provides each level of coordination and review with comparative analyses otherwise unavailable. Since data must be translated into the special language of machine processing, operating-planning information is expressed to the extent practicable to facilitate this transformation. A balance is struck between the requirements of efficient mechanization and conditions contributing to the development and use of information by human beings. Formal organization, scheduling, and budgeting are adjusted to fit central data processing, but never in such a way as to impair the crucial function and unique contribution of people.

Like other endeavors, planning contains within itself procedural dangers to be watched and avoided. Because plans are measures of performance as well as expressions of intent, they can become havens of conservatism and insufficient achievement. Realizing he will be judged on whether he attains the objectives stated in his plan, and concerned that adverse circumstances beyond his control will not be taken into account, the manager may set the lowest goals acceptable to his superior. Without this downgrading to protect himself against unsatisfactory performance, his goals and attainment would be higher. When this attitude is widespread, comprehensive planning represents the lowest common denominator of individual expediences, rather than the true potential of improvement and growth.

If corporate planning is applied completely and effectively, the use of plans for protective purposes is prevented by the process itself. The analysis performed at each management level for its own coordinative planning makes it relatively easy to identify the general level of attainment appropriate for each of its components. Facts and figures concerning past performance and current capability are available, and frequently the achievements of competitors can be compared. In this way, the managers of profit centers can substantiate their questioning or rejection of inadequate objectives on the part of subordinates, and upgrade the goals of component units to represent reasonable attainment. The ultimate instigator or monitor of company effort is top management. It evaluates current performance continually and, in reviewing the corporate plan and its extensions into the future, discerns when objectives are too ambitious or too low. It is responsible for setting the tempo of the institution and devising ways of accomplishing what it considers necessary and desirable.

> The general managers themselves [of a holding company] were not happy with their new arrangements [under decentralization]. They had not been given objectives, policy statements, performance standards for their divisions, or any training for their revised responsibilities. They did not know how far they could or should go on their own, for they were not told how much authority they had. They felt a decreased sense of security.[14]

Conversely, excessive interference in the planning of subordinate units is equally to be avoided. The autonomous manager cannot be held accountable for the profits of his unit over time if he cannot substantially plan its future.

> Sales responsibility was being returned to the general managers. They certainly welcomed the news, for all during the period [when the executive vice president for industrial products] had taken over sales, nobody had relieved the general managers of the companion responsibility of turning in the profit demanded. Now, with power over sales restored, they could strike a better balance between the irreconcilables of getting more market and getting more profit.[15]

If a new product is imposed by corporate management, the divisional manager is not as responsible for its success as for that of one which is developed as part of his own internal program. He is not accountable for the consequences of a temporary level of production directed from above, since it may leave him with excess capacity and unit costs both higher and uncompetitive. Nor can he be expected to increase short-term profits, if he must include in his accounting a heavy overload of unprofitable items, or development expenses which are not the consequence of his own actions and do not benefit him directly or indirectly. Most profit centers support a share of the general and administrative expense of company management, corporate research, special development costs, temporary divisional losses, and other charges which should not or cannot be borne by a single profit center. But any excess above a general average accepted throughout the company should not be included in the profit performance of a particular unit without specific justification.

No executive nor supervisor pursues a plan for his own jurisdiction, imposed from above, as wholeheartedly as one which he has in large part formulated himself. Certainly, each component plan incorporates elements which are the consequence of decisions properly made elsewhere within the company. But the manager will not be as effective in implementing directives which he considers are unrealistic and mistaken or require means and methods he believes vitiate his best effort. A plan without predominant responsibility and acceptance will not stand. By identifying requirements beyond his control and accounting separately for exceptional cost burden, a consistent record and reasonable measure of profit performance can be maintained. In this way, managers are not disheartened by a method of appraisal they consider unfair. Their energies are not dissipated in self-defense, but are applied to the task and responsibility they acknowledge.

Of course, profit performance is never resolved to everyone's complete satisfaction. There are inevitable differences of interest, attention, and responsibility. The divisional manager cannot embrace the corporate view, nor can the corporation fully appreciate the pressing problems of operating units. In the final analysis, success depends on achieving as much mutual understanding and cooperation as possible. In corporate planning, this is facilitated if the genesis of programs and expenses is clearly identified and remembered. A basis for appraising management capability and calculating bonus rewards is worked out which takes into account relevant considerations in addition to immediate profit. Each level of management imposes on those below the fewest restrictions and "external" costs consistent with its own responsibilities.

How to work an incentive plan is a matter of opinion. . . . It should promote teamwork among the management group; and it should reward individual effort, taking into account the desired objectives.

Here is one I think works pretty well. It is based upon return on investment. We create a pot from earnings. Part of it, say forty per cent, we pay in proper proportion to each manager for the over-all effort of management. This promotes teamwork —it keeps the different division managers helping one another.

The other part of the pot, sixty per cent, is then paid to the managers in amounts based upon their individual performance within their respective divisions.

In measuring this performance, goals are set for each division. The goals are weighted to take into account return on investment, percentage of profit on sales, size of earnings in dollars. This takes account of the larger as compared with the smaller divisions. Weight is also given to improvement in performance, product and, finally, marketing.

This program gives great flexibility. To promote growth in a new division you can weight the goal for research and growth, etc. In an old division you weight for performance or for profit and efficiency.[16]

Because they go beyond profit record, sales growth, share of the market, and other operating data subject to accurate quantification, management performance standards are an important instrument of planning effectuation.[17] Since they encompass a broader range of significant management activities, they are more descriptive of the scope of achievement required in comprehensive planning. Prompt administrative reorganization or a revised system of distribution may be as crucial for the future as sales expansion. Although it may not be reflected in the profit statement for some years, recruiting several key persons may be a paramount need. Formulating longer-range objectives or developing a new product may be equally essential. Or perhaps some legal ambiguity must be clarified before necessary advances can be made. These kinds of managerial achievement cannot be quantified in the usual meaning of the word. But they can be identified and spelled out in advance, and their accomplishment enumerated and evaluated at regular intervals. In this way, profit performance is extended to include other vital elements of management performance. To rely on profit alone is to run the risk of discovering inadequate performance after the general management activities which might have prevented the unsatisfactory situation are long overdue. Despite the extension of administrative paperwork, management performance standards provide a delineation of comprehensive planning requirements and a basis for the evaluation of achievement otherwise impossible.

Certain information derived in corporate planning must be withheld from internal circulation or external revelation. Untimely disclosure of plans for reorganization can seriously disrupt current operations, as people react and begin to jockey for new positions. And the intention to relocate a component of the company is best kept under tight wraps until a fully developed plan is announced.

> [The company] picked a dozen tentative sites—then ran a survey among its employees to see how many would move with it. So few would that it abandoned plans to move, after paying considerable sums to seek sites and survey employees. But it was too late. Key professional workers, able to get a job by asking for one, had begun quitting in droves, each eager to get the best available job before the company moved and threw a lot of competition on the market.[18]

Policy changes involve enough difficulties of realignment without the confusion of premature rumor and uncertainty. Matters relating to position and security of personnel are most sensitive. With respect to the external environment, especially revealing financial-cost information, new product plans, anticipated acquisitions, proprietary production processes, and the like must be guarded against disclosure to competitors. The passing of a dividend or a reduction in workforce should be announced only after careful preparation, since clear explanation in the first instance and a well-thought-out plan of effectuation in the second are the best means of alleviating such disturbing news.

First and foremost for the security of sensitive information is its limitation to those with the "need to know." It is their responsibility to exercise whatever form or degree of reticence is required. If the sensitive information is needed to complete the descriptive material portrayed by the corporate representation, it is kept out of general sight and locked at night. Information reported throughout the company is organized to exclude restricted data, which can be supplied separately, expressed indirectly, or even referenced to some code. In critically competitive situations, deliberate camouflage or false leads may be worthwhile, provided they are not equally confusing to friend and competitive foe alike. Certainly, planning procedures are complicated when many materials are company-confidential or subject to military classification.

It is no secret that business secrets are hard to maintain. The number of people concerned in business operations and transactions, the necessity of widespread communication and contact, and the human preference for unrestricted discussion present internal difficulties. Externally, the commercial intelligence activities of financial institutions, investment houses, government agencies, newspapers, periodicals, and competitors are designed to discover the real situation, prospects, and plans for the future. At the same time, business as well as government tends to accumulate classified information needlessly. Sometimes the material is no longer sensitive; sometimes it can readily be deduced from published data, or unavoidable follow-up actions are revealing. Some originators classify material to protect themselves against possible criticism, without regard for the impairment of efficient operations and additional costs of handling. Since information is the substance of corporate planning, careful attention is devoted to limiting company-confidential material to that which is truly sensitive. Procedures are drawn which prevent overcautious restriction by units throughout the company and provide for its declassification as soon as possible, as well as insure its protection in transmission and storage. Usually, this means some form of central review, policy formulation, and standard procedure. Except for a relatively small body of information which must be guarded carefully, successful performance and a dynamic program of remaining in the business vanguard are the best corporate security.

HUMAN FACTORS [19]

There are natural human reactions to be taken into account in developing specific programs of implementation. Many people prefer as little planning as possible. Life at work is simpler and easier if the added analytical effort and schedule of performance implicit in planning are avoided. Energy and enthusiasm for improvement are as much the exception as the rule. Comprehensive planning requires a capacity not only for wrestling with indeterminates but for deciding and acting with incomplete information. People resist uncertainty. They would rather wait until a situation is clarified or adopt a deceptive positiveness unjustified by the facts. "Life is too short" to worry any more than necessary about uncertainties. Forecasting is "sticking one's neck out"—an invitation to possible challenge for not making good.

Since corporate planning means reducing present return to advance institutional accomplishment over time, longer-range benefits may accrue to different individuals from those who instigate and carry out the first phases of the plan. The necessary subordination of immediate self-interest does not come easily. Because progressive improvement is its basic objective, planning means change. But people at large do not welcome change as a matter of course. They may believe it will impose further demands upon them, threaten personal security, or necessitate the assimilation of new ideas and ways of doing things. Many persons pay lip service to change, but underneath—perhaps unknowingly—resist it as actively as is safe. Maintaining the *status quo* is the path of least resistance.

Looking beyond one's own jurisdiction, recognizing and accepting the interdependence of different activities, is a requisite of comprehensive planning. Unit plans must fit the needs of other components and the corporate entity. Emotionally, however, our natural attachment is to the area of our greatest concern. Self-interest and self-preservation are modified by the rational precepts of society and the environmental situation, but they are never eliminated. As mentioned earlier in this chapter, objectivity in favor of a collective interest is a quality which is far rarer in people than we like to think.

Planning emphasizes balanced reason, all things considered. But emotional man exists just below the surface. Only with intentional effort do we recognize within ourselves and others the strength and pervasiveness of emotional likes, dislikes, prejudices, fears, aggression, and ambition. Society demands their containment, morality their mollification. Individually and collectively, the application of reason involves an awareness of the constant presence and power of emotional factors on the one hand, and of the requirements for their constructive subordination to institutional purposes on the other hand.

Only when business management has a realistic understanding of human attitudes and reactions can it formulate procedures of implementation which reduce natural resistances and evoke potentially positive responses.[20] These procedures are designed to achieve two basic purposes: creating or maintaining favorable employee attitudes toward executive management; and making planning an acceptable and desirable activity from the employee's personal point of view.

The Image of Management Within the Company

There is an inevitable difference between the viewpoints of the manager looking down and the subordinate looking up. Each sees the organization through the lens of his particular endeavor and personal interest. Executive management is sometimes surprised to find that the corporate situation is not understood by employees generally, pronouncements are not accepted at face value, the intent of policies and procedures is misinterpreted, or a lack of confidence has developed through poor communication or mistaken inference.

> One of the interesting developments of the past year was the formulation by the Executive Committee of "A Statement of Policies and Objectives" for the guidance of supervisors. It is an attempt to express some of the many things which top management is likely to take for granted as being understood by all—yet, when we came to reduce these allegedly well-known matters to writing, an extended period of drafting and redrafting was required.[21]

Most executives assume they have the confidence and loyalty of their employees; a few consider this unnecessary. But, more often than supposed, employees view management direction with a jaundiced eye. They question the wisdom of those in control, their understanding of problems at the working level, their willingness and capacity to communicate, and sometimes their motives. In our society today more than ever before, the soundness of management and a reasonable subordination of executive self-interest in the best interests of the business as a whole must be demonstrated to those who are expected to respond. When personnel doubt the ability and question the motives of their bosses, efficiency is reduced. Response is slow rather than prompt. The quality of solution and execution is lowered. When relations break down, employees can delay action in many subtle ways: exaggerated difficulties appear, excuses are manufactured, political maneuvers are undertaken in active opposition, or a reactive apathy sets the slower pace of involuntary acquiescence.

By positive procedures, management minimizes negative reactions. It explains the importance of comprehensive planning to each major category of personnel from their point of view in language which they understand. Examples are chosen with which they are familiar. Since unforeseen reactions can develop which call for further clarification or changes in policy and procedure, time is allowed for the emergence of significant questions, misunderstanding, or disagreement. To confirm that management knows what it is doing, the exposition represents careful analysis and conclusion. It cannot be carelessly drawn, with omissions or failure to resolve outstanding difficulties apparent to everyone. It must make sense not only to those who compose it but to those for whom it is intended. The relationship between the advancement of the individual within the organization and his contribution to the development and effectuation of its plans is emphasized. By expressing the importance it attaches to corporate planning, management engenders more positive response. Employees do not assume that all management desires are equally serious and vital. Coincident with the thorough explanation which precedes the inauguration of corporate planning and accompanies subsequent directives, it is of course made clear that executive decisions are binding regardless of individual concurrence.

When planning is fully operative, employee confidence depends on management's record of sound conclusion, continued explanation of its directive actions, and frank acknowledgment of mistakes made and lessons learned from error. Probably the most common cause of loss of confidence is executive reluctance to formulate the longer-range objectives which are needed for the preparation of sound component plans throughout the company. Almost equally destructive of confidence is failure to announce these goals within the organization, and to modify them promptly when it is clear that circumstances have changed. Executive reluctance to cut the Gordian knot implicit in the open-ended context of planning, to cope with its built-in uncertainties, or to face inevitable change and percentage error quickly transmits itself throughout the company.

Some managements are unduly secretive, minimizing explanatory contact with employees and maintaining executive aloofness. From an inner circle, pronouncements emerge without preparatory notice —sometimes as a complete surprise. When the main reason for such an atmosphere is executive irresolution or a need to underline who is boss, this may be personally satisfying to the ranking managers who make policies and decisions, but it prevents the free flow of intercommunication necessary for comprehensive planning. Plotting the destiny of the company or component is best accomplished as cooperatively and openly as possible by all concerned. Since the unexpected is frequent enough in business, needless administrative surprises produce confusion, resentment, and occasionally active opposition. Employees often interpret such surprises as symptoms of executive indecision, precipitate action, or unwillingness or fearfulness to work closely with subordinates and utilize their capabilities to the full by a reasonable sharing of confidence.

The image of leadership is fully tested in corporate planning. The required combination of action and analysis, projection into the future, coordinative-cooperative management, good judgment, and positive but flexible direction is not only demanding but revealing. The true extent of executive capability is exposed to view. Managerial inadequacies are more difficult to camouflage. Morale and constructive effort are more closely responsive to the realities of executive competence and wise leadership.

Employees

Within the framework set by alternative job opportunities, labor-employment contracts, and legislation relating to individual rights, employees must comply with management directives. But compliance and constructive acceptance are significantly different. The company concerned exclusively with the immediate present can tolerate the limited performance standards of passive compliance, but planning requires positive participation. Each person is expected to look ahead, accept an approved goal for his area of activity, and perform his part of the adopted program of action.

Since employees respond most positively to these expectations if they understand the precise part they are to perform, plans are expressed simply in a form which is clear and meaningful. The emphasis and form of expression are different for people in accounting, public relations, manufacturing, sales, or maintenance. If necessary, programs are restated in the language of a particular group to insure comprehension. At the same time widespread participation in the formulation of plans promotes a constructive identification of personnel with planning, it contributes to their understanding of the process and the specific programs they must interpret and carry out. Unless individual roles and responsibilities are spelled out clearly, plans have little real meaning. Equally important, employees must understand how planning can benefit them personally by improving their performance, progress, or rewards. Implementation will be half-hearted at best if they believe planning will help the company and enhance the record of others, but will not advance their own self-interest and self-realization. This means relating specific plans to the individual, and evaluating personal performance with reference to longer-range planning as well as immediate profits.

Constructive identification is as subtle as it is vital. Most people want to be an accepted part of an organization or group, to feel they are in on things rather than informationally or operationally excluded. Often, this feeling of involvement spells the difference between a willing acceptance of direction and the reluctant taking of orders. It encourages us to discover through experience, to exercise initiative, to look beyond immediate concerns. It increases the flow of ideas, suggestions, and cooperative energy at the operating levels. And, in so doing, it provides executive management with a better sounding board for determining the nature and extent of the organizational capabilities with which it must work. An employee spirit of identification and participation allows significantly higher goals than are possible otherwise. The larger the company and the more detailed its plans, the greater the need for efficient procedures which extend the practical limits of employee participation. Oftentimes, a working group can suggest alternative ways of accomplishing the component plan which it is given to put into effect. Or a subordinate unit of the company can be asked to devise its own component plan which meets corporate objectives and comprehensive planning requirements.

The desire to participate is self-generated in some employees; another group cooperate only to the extent they must. For example, the "organization man" so strongly identified with the company he accepts any and all directives on faith belongs to the first category, along with those so insecure they dare not question or those too unimaginative to see beyond the current task. There are a few rugged individualists and congenital recalcitrants who resist any plan because it means collective action and represents higher authority. Such types are excluded from directly active roles in planning, but not from participation in the planning program if their special capabilities can be utilized without disrupting the process itself. Of course, procedures designed to promote involvement generally throughout the company cannot cater to minority attitudes which are emotionally predetermined and subject to little or no change.

Employee participation involves a few limitations as well as numerous benefits. When opinion and specific suggestions have been engendered throughout the organization, a consensus cannot be ignored even if coordinative analysis discloses its weaknesses. Programs of effectuation are always modifications of the analytical ideal to fit particular people and the existing situation. Part of this adjustment may be for the purpose of retaining the support or even enthusiasm stimulated by participation. In both instances, more is achieved within these limitations than by trying to impose analytically superior plans from above. By explaining clearly beforehand the conditions within which component plans must be composed, and by carefully reviewing the reasons why reformulation is necessary from a corporate viewpoint, management can in most instances generate plans which combine analytical soundness and participative support.

Line Executives

On those matters of particular concern to him, the line manager is in a position to react more forcibly than the average employee. He has attained his position because he is exceptionally able, aggressive, strong, competitive, ambitious, and single-minded. Since his personal success is usually dependent on the performance of the organizational unit he directs, he is ready, willing, and able to fight for the results which enable him to retain and enhance his authority. He is protectively alert against developments he believes might challenge his present position and anticipated future. For the occasional executive, staff assistance in planning represents a potential danger or an acknowledgment of personal inadequacy. He prefers not to depend on others for information and analysis relating to his own managerial function. The more material unique to his own head, the stronger his personal situation. Since he has no one to protect him in the sense that he can shield many of his own employees, he is sometimes self-reliant to the point where he finds close confidence in staff associates difficult or competitively questionable.

There are executives who need more than the authority of their positions in order to feel personally secure. Additional status may take many forms: privileges and perquisites of rank, reluctance to delegate responsibility, inability to accept disagreement from below, disinterest in the ideas of others, difficulties of constructive listening, excessive expectations of loyalty, uncommunicativeness, or unrealistic demands upon subordinates.

In larger organizations, more managers than we would like to admit are less interested in planning for improvement than in maintaining acceptable performance. The road up was long and hard, possibly fiercely competitive. The time at the top is relatively short. "Let's not get too fancy, Dan, and upset the applecart." Bonuses, stock options, approaching retirement, company politics, social relations between executives, and personal public relations are important elements of executive behavior. As mentioned previously in a different connection, some executives prefer to be perpetually on the go; they resist the intellective demands of comprehensive planning.

These latent tendencies on the part of line executives are mentioned here because they are not often discussed in management literature. Since they compound the difficulties of planning, they must be recognized and handled realistically when they exist. Fortunately, they are neither characteristic nor immutable. Most managers accept the planning function wholeheartedly, and apply it in an organized manner to the extent they believe practical and desirable. Doubts and adverse reactions are dissipated as experience establishes the association between planning and the personal satisfactions derived from improved performance, constructive support, and a reduction of uncertainty, possible refutation, and disruptive surprises.

As their job becomes more demanding, difficult, and complex, line executives are examining their own role to better understand its diverse requirements, find ways of improving performance, and maintain a sense of personal satisfaction.

> As manager of a [company manufacturing chemicals in Europe] he was more and more in a position where he merely administered. . . . He was always acting on the basis of knowledge of other people, never his own since he did not have the time to study matters for himself even though they were of the utmost

importance to his company. . . . He reached the point where he realized that he was no longer really capable of studying problems for himself, indeed of really working. Instead, he was for several hours each day weighing what one employee presented versus what another presented without really contributing anything of significance other than making a decision by guessing who was right.[22]

. . . The role of a public manager is very similar to the role of a private manager. . . . He can either act as a judge or a leader. In the former case, he sits and waits until subordinates bring to him problems for solution, or alternatives for choice. In the latter case, he immerses himself in the operation of the business or the governmental activity, examines the problems, the objectives, the alternative courses of action, chooses among them, and leads the organization to their accomplishment. In the one case it's a passive role; in the other case, an active role.[23]

As pointed out in the previous chapter, there is growing recognition among executives that greater use of existing quantitative techniques contributes to successful general management. And, slowly but surely, knowledge is being extended to meet the needs of modern business, with its requirements for a more scientific and professional direction of activities.[24] Unless this technique and this knowledge are applied in an organized manner, the manager cannot make the substantive contribution expected of him in his position. Nor can he derive the satisfaction of solving general management problems himself, rather than acting merely as a "mixing valve" of thinking by others. As a corollary, professionalism in management calls for enhanced qualities of executive personality. Increasing emphasis is placed on a proper balance between constructive individuality and institutional interest, between subjective insight and objective analysis, between scientific method and entrepreneurial acumen, between emotional maturity and idiosyncrasy.

As the significance of improved analysis is established in the mind and experience of general managers, the function of staff planning support is more apparent. It is seen to be more important than ever in times of adversity, rather than subject to elimination as a dispensable luxury when profits fall and costs are under rigorous scrutiny.

It is surprising how often what appear to be very desirable

long-range objectives and very attractive long-range plans are dumped in the wastebasket at the first sign of stormy weather. If long-range plans are any good, they should be sustained through such periods and kept in the proper relationship to short-range matters. Perhaps the most constructive viewpoint to take is that periods of temporary difficulty or stringency are good for a long-range planning program in that they cause everyone to stop, look, and listen, and to reappraise the real worth of the long-range planning effort.[25]

There are periods when staff activity in corporate planning must be curtailed to meet conditions of crisis. Longer-range planning is postponed while everyone concentrates on the critical problems at hand, which must be solved immediately to insure survival. But the abolition of the function entirely is in effect to deny the validity of its establishment in the first place. And it is unrealistic to expect that such a management function can be reactivated *de novo* without great wastage of time, money, and experience. However, by the nature of their responsibilities as well as their personalities, line managers evaluate organized planning and any other new or expanded management activity on the basis of its tangible contribution to efficiency, profits, and their own personal success. Rarely will they accept a long interval before there is either a demonstrable return or a personal conviction of its worth.

Staff Planning Personnel

Since education in planning *per se* is recent, most staff planners within business today have acquired their special skills through experience. Their interest in planning, or their assignment to the task, led them to apply their specialization to this end and acquire knowledge and technique wherever they could to help solve the coordinative and projective problems at hand. Year by year, there are more men and women professionally trained in one of the several educational approaches to planning, or in the planning aspects of a traditional academic discipline.

The attributes of the staff planner are second in importance only to those of the executive decision maker. His personality must be compatible with the operating requirements of his position. He must be alive to the human factors in planning, which are as important as its financial, statistical, technical, and other quantitative aspects. He must understand, accept, and incorporate in his work all of the realities of the business operation. He cannot be Utopian or ivory-tower in his approach, or otherwise disassociate himself from the management he serves. He is obligated to produce results of demonstrable worth. It is his responsibility to synthesize different materials and points of view toward the comparative analysis most useful to his line superior. Most certainly, one such form of appraisal is the combination of balance sheet and operating statements. Without complete familiarity with these financial instruments of management expression and evaluation, the staff planner is handicapped indeed.

He understands that successful planning only starts on paper. Because the best solutions derived from dispassionate study must be adjusted to fit the realities of ingrained attitudes, traditional practices, and the many problems of actual accomplishment, plans are conceived from their analytical beginning through feasible implementation. The staff planner must possess the *strategic* ability to develop the best analytical solutions which meet the tactical requirements of adoption and execution. This includes the critical capacity to perceive those interests and predilections of different individuals to which other matters may have to be related, if these matters are to be considered carefully or perhaps receive any attention at all. It is one of the reasons he listens constructively far more than he talks. Great flexibility is required of him in his coordinative work with line managers, staff associates, and the various teams formed for comprehensive planning purposes. This flexibility—as well as the inclusiveness of his thinking, his deductive ability, his intuitive perception, and his capacity to learn—depends as much on emotional maturity as on professional training and specific business experience.

Besides these positive attributes, the successful staff planner possesses his share of troublesome tendencies which management bears in mind in using him most effectively. Like many other professionals, he may tend to overemphasize his specialty and overplan. As discussed in an earlier chapter, there are times and situations when limited planning is the best solution. Too strong a belief in the virtue of complete plans can sometimes obscure the greater significance of the planning process itself when it is applied gradually, continuously, realistically, and flexibly. Because he is in a position to accumulate a more comprehensive and objective picture of what "ought to be" or "could be" than those preoccupied with specific operational responsibilities, the staff planner may tend to be impatient. Occasionally, he has an unconscious attachment to his own analytical contribution. When he does not fully appreciate the practical problems posed by people, organization, past history, and present business environment, his concept of the desirable and achievable may exaggerate the potentialities of planning and the speed with which it can be accomplished.

Most professional planners today are better grounded in the traditional quantification associated separately with finance, sales, engineering, and physical facilities than in comprehensive or "systems" analysis. Not only have the former been studied and reported more thoroughly, but the latter is still in its infancy. In addition, many line executives do not take staff planning personnel sufficiently into their confidence to enable these associates to understand and share the full range of managerial considerations. The professional planner is not inclined to be aggressive or overtly competitive. A large part of his contribution is reflective, analytical, and coordinative, and he may have to adjust himself to the operating pressures imposed upon the decision maker and indirectly upon his staff.

A productive relationship between line manager and planning staff depends on compatibility of personalities as well as of general attitude and respective capabilities. The decision maker cannot be so individualistic or insecure he resists or neglects staff support. He must understand its value and want it for the better fulfillment of his numerous tasks and crucial responsibilities. By wise direction, he derives great benefit from this assistance, maintaining his staff associates' interest and sense of achievement. In appropriate ways, he compensates for any limitations and frustrations they experience from having such close contact with management information and its conclusive analysis—yet having no power of decision. When line executives are incapable of making the most of staff support, the reason is almost invariably rooted in their personalities.

For his part, the staff planner must be content with his more passive function of assistance and representation. He must earn the confidence of his line superior. If he has an overt or hidden urge to be the line executive and make operational decisions himself, if he is overassertive or overcritical, difficulties are certain to arise. A basic and irreconcilable conflict can develop which will not only reduce the value of supportive planning activity but ultimately necessitate the replacement of the staff planner or his transfer to a line position. The line manager plans in his managing, deciding, and doing; his staff associates integrate and extend the analytical background required for this organized forethought. Working in harmony, they can produce a quality of business planning which cannot be attained separately. When line managers are rotated through corporate planning as part of their executive development, they too must temporarily transform their predelictions toward active direction into constructive support. This direct experience in staff work serves them in good stead when they return to line positions.

* * *

Some readers would undoubtedly prefer more precise prescriptions than are provided in this chapter: exact procedures, categorical do's and don'ts, or administrative recipes guaranteeing results. The literature of management is filled with case histories and specific experience, but every company is unique in significant respects. The essential prerequisites are an awareness of these unique conditions coupled with a thorough understanding of the general criteria of effective implementation. This managerial discernment precludes precise prescription, for it responds differently to each organization, its environment, and resultant conditions of change. The best procedures are variations on a general theme which reflect the particular characteristics of each company. It is a "do it yourself" task, with basic objectives and broad specifications the most meaningful guides.

REFERENCES CITED

[1] Peter F. Drucker.

[2] Robert L. Hershey (Vice President, E. I. du Pont de Nemours and Company), in "Company Growth Through Profit Planning," *The Controller,* September 1961 (Vol. XXIX, No. 9), p. 450.

[3] Hjalmar Rosen and Charles G. Weaver, "Motivation in Management: A Study at Four Managerial Levels," *Journal of Applied Psychology,* December 1960 (Vol. 44, No. 6), p. 392.

[4] Acknowledgment is made of the confirmation of conclusions and illustrative expression contained in: C. A. Efferson (Manager, Organization Planning, Kaiser Aluminum and Chemical Corporation), "Organization of the Planning Process," a paper (mimeo) presented to an AMA seminar on "Planning to Meet Corporate Growth," San Francisco, 25 April 1960, 35 pp., illus.

[5] Ralph M. Besse (Executive Vice President, Cleveland Electric Illuminating Company), "Company Planning Must Be Planned!" *Dun's Review and Modern Industry*, April 1957 (Vol. 69, No. 6), p. 46.

[6] Mason Smith (Vice President and Treasurer, Whirlpool Corporation), "How to Initiate Effective Long-Range Planning," *The Dynamics of Management*, Management Report No. 14, 1958 (American Management Association), p. 75.

[7] Edmund K. Faltermayer, "Corporate Horizons—More Companies Peer into Distant Future, Try to Prepare for It," *The Wall Street Journal* (Pacific Coast Edition), Wednesday, 25 October 1961 (Vol. LXV, No. 81), pp. 1, 17.

[8] Robert E. Brooker (President, Whirlpool Corporation), Long Range Planning," *Business Topics* (Graduate School of Business Administration, Michigan State University), Summer 1961 (Vol. 9, No. 3), p. 35.

[9] Ralph M. Besse, *supra*, p. 47.

[10] *Ibid.*

[11] H. Grossman, "The Development of Scans—A Network System for Management Control," *FN-4556-1* (System Development Corporation, Santa Monica, California), 14 February 1961, pp. 2–4.

[12] Office of Naval Material, Department of the Navy, *Line of Balance Technology—A Graphic Method of Industrial Programming* (Navexos P 1851), 24 February 1958, 19 pp.

A. C. Gehringer, "In the making of missiles management uses a tool called LINE OF BALANCE," *Naval Reserve Information Bulletin* (The Bureau of Ordnance), Fall 1958 (Vol. 12, No. 3), pp. 16–21.

Norman C. Miller, Jr., " 'Maps' for Managers Show Problem Areas of Big Defense Jobs," *The Wall Street Journal* (Pacific Coast Edition), 16 August 1961 (Vol. LXV, No. 22), pp. 1, 19.

Philip J. Klass, "PERT/PEP Management Tool Use Grows," *Aviation Week*, 28 November 1960 (Vol. 73, No. 22), pp. 85–91.

J. Taul, "Spectrol—A Management Control System for Research and Development Applications," *SD-3340* (System Development Corporation, Santa Monica, California), 26 February 1960, 26 pp.

R. W. Haine and W. Lob (Eclipse-Pioneer Division, The Bendix Corporation, Teterboro, N. J.), "The Application of Closed-Loop Techniques to Engineering Project Planning, *IRE Transactions on Engineering Management*, September 1960, pp. 29–103.

[13] "Packaged Logic for Computers," *Business Week,* 23 September 1961 (No. 1673), pp. 70–78.

[14] A. V. MacCullough, "Why Decentralization Fails," *The Management Review,* August 1960 (Vol. XLIX, No. 8), p. 53.

[15] Richard Austin Smith, "The Incredible Electrical Conspiracy" (Part I), *Fortune,* April 1961 (Vol. LXIII, No. 4), p. 172.

[16] Frederick C. Crawford (Chairman of the Board, Thompson Products, Inc.), "How to Increase Executive Effectiveness by Creating the Proper Climate and Incentives Within a Company," address (typescript) at the Harvard Business School, 13 June 1953, p. 15.

[17] John W. Enell and George H. Haas, *Setting Standards for Executive Performance,* Research Study No. 42, 1960 (American Management Association), 120 pp.

[18] Alfred G. Larke and James K. Blake, "Location Analysis, How to Plan a Fiasco—It's Easy If You Overlook People," *Dun's Review and Modern Industry,* April 1956 (Vol. 67, No. 4), p. 92.

[19] Grateful acknowledgment is made to Karl R. Kunze (Manager of Personnel, Lockheed Aircraft Corporation, Burbank, California) for the contributions from his thoughts and experience expressed in a personal communication of July 1961 and reflected in this section.

[20] Robert N. McMurry, "Empathy: Management's Greatest Need," *Advanced Management,* July 1953 (Vol. 18, No. 7), pp. 6–11, 34.

[21] Frank B. Cliffe (Vice President and Chief Financial Officer, H. J. Heinz Co.), *How H. J. Heinz Manages Its Financial Planning and Controls,* Financial Management Series No. 106, 1953 (American Management Association), pp. 7–8.

[22] Robert J. Leaver (International Counsel, Thompson Ramo Wooldridge Inc.), personal communication, 23 August 1961.

[23] Robert S. McNamara (U.S. Secretary of Defense; formerly, President, Ford Motor Car Company), quoted in *The News* (Mexico, D.F.), 3 October 1961 (Vol. XII, No. 91), p. Three B (George Sokolsky, "Public Managers: Judges Or Leaders?").

[24] Harold F. Smiddy (Vice President, General Electric Co.), "Management as a Profession," *Journal of Engineering for Industry* (Transactions of the ASME), American Society of Mechanical Engineers, August 1961 (Vol. 83, Series B, No. 3), pp. 261–277.

[25] Mason Smith, *supra,* p. 75.

CHAPTER VII

Cost and Return

Confronted with the necessity of keeping overhead within bounds and allocating men and money as wisely as possible, chief executives want to know the costs and contributions of staff functions. What evidence is there to justify the establishment, continuation, or expansion of specific management activities? They know from experience that such activities can proliferate to the point where Parkinson's Law of governmental bureaucracy is temporarily descriptive of competitive enterprise. Whether he is specifically harassed by rising costs and declining profits, or is performing a periodic review of management efficiency, each manager must reach a decision for the administrative functions within his jurisdiction. Limitations of available funds always require a choice among alternative expenditures.

Difficulties of Measurement

Since corporate planning is an aspect of general management, it shares the same difficulties of precise measurement. The dollar value of a company president or divisional manager cannot be calculated numerically. Although profit performance is certainly the vital measure, it is impossible to isolate specifically how much of this

217

record is attributable to the executive manager himself, how much to associates and subordinates for whom he may or may not be entirely responsible, how much to environmental developments beyond anyone's control, and how much to unanticipated events. The best practical measure of management competence is the composite evaluation of the operating record by board of directors, owners, business community, executive associates, and employees; and even this composite judgment is mistaken part of the time. It is fortunate for the vitality of competitive enterprise that inadequate profit performance—or failure to reduce losses in exceptional situations—results sooner or later in the replacement of general managers, regardless of their personal responsibility.

The benefits to the company of many general management functions cannot be demonstrated upon demand. Either they are broadly directive, with cumulative results over an extended period of time —so intermixed with related activities that separate identification is impractical—or they are not directly quantifiable by nature. Normally, the benefits of business diversification, administrative reorganization, or improved methods of forecasting are not realized for several years. So many other factors, both within and outside the business, are influential during this interval that many relationships of cause and effect cannot be traced—much less specifically quantified.

> The nature of the petroleum industry is such that there is a very considerable time lag between entrance into a project and realization of profits from it. Our Coordinating and Planning Department was established in its present form in 1956, and our staffing was not completed until 1957. Consequently, many of the projects in which we have participated do not yet have identifiable results [in late 1961].[1]

The wisdom of investment in foreign manufacturing may not be resolved for years, because of such interdependent variables as earnings reinvested abroad, tariffs and quotas, labor costs and productivity, market peculiarities, availability of competent managers, nationalistic restrictions, or different business customs and practices.

It is usually impossible to establish *post facto*, let alone in advance, a numeral relationship between corporate legal decisions and profits. The value of "corporate image" advertising and its relationship to different product sales cannot be calculated definitely. Normally, expenses for patent protection are justified by average experience or management judgment, rather than specific quantification. The return on investment of research and development can only be approximated, because of the many repercussive effects throughout a company which are neither identified nor credited. A profitable improvement in a manufacturing method or machine by a production engineer may be the consequence of his conversation with a research scientist on another matter, but such connections are rarely established among the multitude of business interactions. The point here is neither to decry the necessity nor to depreciate the value of subjective judgment, but to emphasize the impracticality or impossibility of quantifying many important decisions of executive management. "In general . . . the higher the level of a corporate planning group, the less likelihood that its activities can be measured in terms of specific savings."[2]

It is relatively easy to identify and to make a rough evaluation of errors committed in the past that have been due in a large part to inadequate planning. It is difficult to get agreement as to how much of this loss could have been eliminated through planning, and it is particularly difficult to claim such savings on current or future operations. The problem is very much the same as though you were to ask for precise information regarding the savings that are effected through improved management. In the long run these savings will show up on the balance sheet, . . . but in the short run it is difficult to make precise allocation.[3]

. . . I do not believe that one can usefully come up with dollar earnings or dollar savings attributable to the Long Range Planning function. This is because usually the function is a necessity to the conduct of a business which survives and the real question is whether it is formally recognized as a separate and distinct function or one which is joined with other functions and does not get clearly demarcated.[4]

Of the many difficulties of measurement, *time lag* and *differentiation* are most significant. Since many of the benefits of comprehensive planning do not manifest themselves for some time, today's operating record reflects planning analysis and decision several or many years ago.

On our Northwest tree farms we harvest the timber crop periodically, but some sixty to eighty years may pass from the time of planting to the time of final harvesting. As a result our Timber Department typically thinks in terms of decades rather than years, and the timber-cutting schedules range from next year to eighty years hence. . . . Most people in Crown Zeller-bach are not shocked by a discussion involving 1975.[5]

More usually, there is a time lag of two to four years between major management decisions and the returns which permit an evaluation of their soundness. Since the fiscal period is one year, and there is a strong tendency to "let bygones be bygones" and concentrate on the present and future, the connection between past analysis and decision and the current situation and prospects is rarely established. When the logical and accounting difficulties of differentiating the consequences of specific planning decisions from the many other factors involved are added to the problems of historical backtracking, it is not surprising that a quantification of cause and effect is seldom feasible.

As shown schematically in Figure 11, identification of the specific results of comprehensive planning varies with the length of the planning period and the nature and situation of the company. When, by choice or circumstance, planning is projected only a year or two into the future, the consequences of actions for which it is mainly responsible are more easily noted. Not enough time elapses and there are not enough changes of environmental situation to obscure cause and effect. Furthermore, since under these circumstances planning is a limited extension of operating decisions, its contributions can be judged to a greater extent by operating results. When the nature of the company or its particular situation limits both the breadth and the projective depth of its corporate planning, results are less difficult to quantify than when it is longer-range and more inclusive, and judgmental certainty of its value is much more likely.

The results of comprehensive planning are also more easily identified in certain functional areas of application. The internal operating efficiency of a new distribution facility, and its profitable performance in response to a regional need established through corporate planning, are more precisely demonstrable than the effects of company advertising. Evaluating the consequences of refinancing is more conclusive than estimating the impact of new personnel policies on increased productivity. Parenthetically, staff planning personnel should bear these differences in mind when justifying their activity.

Because in its present intensified form it is quite new, corporate planning sometimes is subjected to overcritical review. Once it is better understood and established, it will not be expected to justify itself more specifically than the office of the corporate counsel, the public relations director, or other staff support. It will be accepted as an essential aspect of corporate management and judged generally as to its effectiveness and mode of operation, rather than by excessively time-consuming or unrealistic attempts at precise measurement.

Conceptualization

VARIATION IN SPECIFIC IDENTIFICATION OF COST AND RETURN OF CORPORATE PLANNING

[by length of planning period]

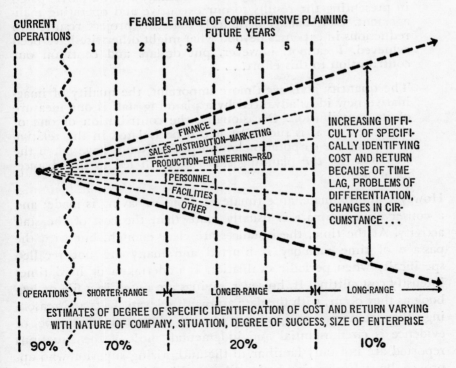

FIGURE 11

Means of Evaluation

There are several ways of appraising the benefits of comprehensive staff planning. The first is so apparent it is surprising how seldom it is used. A record is kept by the director of each staff planning unit within the company of specific instances when, in his opinion, the work performed or suggested by his department contributed to profits by identification of a business opportunity, improvement in management anticipation, more reliable forecasting, increased procedural efficiency, reduction of duplication and conflict, or prevention of costly mistakes.

> . . . In 1960 our President appointed a committee of executives to study and review the overhead and operating expenses of all functional departments in an effort to reduce these expenses where possible. [The coordinating and planning department] helped structure and carry out this study, and we participated in presenting the results to our executive and operating management. Our management feels that this project resulted in reductions in expenses beyond what might otherwise have been achieved. I cannot, however, put dollars and cents on our contribution to this effort. . . .
>
> The quantity and, even more important, the quality of imaginative new ideas advanced by a planning staff is one measure of its contribution. Occasionally, the contribution of one of these new ideas is such that it can be isolated in the relative sense that the corporation would probably not have taken the step had not the planning staff's research led to its advancement.[6]

However approximate, an estimate of profit or saving is made; and a conservative estimate is usually more than the cost of the staff activity. At the time, the instances are clear enough, but with the passage of time memory is blurred and many are not recalled specifically when periodic evaluation is undertaken or hard times intensify cost cutting. If, however, savings are noted in a file or logbook as they occur, with the date and with relevant facts and reasoning, they comprise a significant record. Although this type of evidence is circumstantial and judgmental, most of the situations reported are not only familiar to the authorizing superior who approves the staff planning budget, but so like his own areas of management decision that they are meaningful to him despite the absence of precise quantification.

A second instrument of appraising comprehensive planning activity is the *ad hoc* committee. Several executives are selected on the basis of experience, knowledge of planning in general, and limited involvement or vested interest. They report their collective or separate opinions with a clear explanation of the reasoning behind each judgment. The total framework of premise, inference, deduction, and conclusion is logically consistent and clearly stated. This kind of evaluation is also subjective. Its merits lie in plural manpower, the possibility that three or four well-selected heads may be better than one, and the advisory assistance provided the decision maker by preliminary fact finding and opinion.

When the responsible manager evaluates the worth of corporate planning personally and privately, presumably he incorporates in his appraisal the intent of each of the previous approaches. He recalls all the circumstantial evidence he can, takes an unbiased view, and performs his own analysis. It is another of the difficult general management decisions which he faces constantly and which require certain personal prerequisites of background information and reflective environment conducive to his best appraisal. At the least, he avoids the hurry, distractions, and lack of personal preparation which impair sound mental resolution; he seeks his own means of attaining objectivity.

The best evaluation of corporate planning involves a combination of these three approaches. Records of circumstantial evidence are available, together with the observations and opinions of the committee, and the final decision is made by the individual who is responsible for the planning function and for whom it is principally intended. Figure 12 lists illustrative areas of corporate activity to which comprehensive planning makes a positive contribution; rarely is it possible to treat all of them simultaneously. In some areas, the contribution is vital, in others less significant; in some direct, in others indirect. The larger the company, as a rule, the more different areas of activity to which corporate planning contributes substantially and recognizably; and the extent to which significant quantification is possible varies with different management functions.

Of the various things we [coordinator of long-range planning] did at Crown Zellerbach I would sort out two as of paramount

Illustrative

AREAS OF CONTRIBUTION BY CORPORATE PLANNING
AS AN ORGANIZED STAFF ACTIVITY

SIZE OF BUSINESS ANNUAL SALES (*Millions $*)	LARGE 500	MEDIUM 50	MODERATE 5	METHOD OF EVALUATION
	ORDER OF SIGNIFICANCE*			
Employee Morale-Productivity	1	2	2	
Explicit Objectives	1	1	1	
Executive-Supervisory Training	1	1	2	Non-
Management Information	1	2	2	Quantifiable
Allocation of Corporate Resources	1	1	1	(Judgment)
Managerial Performance Criteria	1	2	2	
Coordination of Operations	1	1	1	
Consistent Policies-Procedures	1	2	2	
Product-Process Research	1	2	3	
Prevention of Legal Difficulties	2	3	3	
Consistent Advertising	2	3	3	
Improved Forecasting	1	1	1	
Patent Utilization	1	2	2	
Tax Policies and Management	1	2	3	Quantifiable
Volume Purchasing	1	2	3	(Cost Analysis
Financing-Banking-Leasing	1	2	3	&
Facilities-Equipment Utilization	2	2	1	Specific Costs)
Retirement-Insurance Coordination	1	2	3	

* 1 = highly important; 2 = important; 3 = moderately important. These comparative numbers refer only to organized staff planning as a distinct activity. A lower number does not indicate that this aspect of planning is of lesser importance; it means only that it can be carried out satisfactorily by regular personnel as part of accepted assignments of duties. Special staff is not necessary.

NOTE: Each illustrative area of application is not of equal significance to a company. Also, these subjective judgments of relative importance are not cumulative. For example, the large number of 3's ("moderately important") listed for the moderate-size company does not suggest that organized planning is unimportant; its contribution to those areas marked "1" ("highly important") justifies deliberate effort.

FIGURE 12

and "survival" importance. The first was to establish the size of the market for Crown Zellerbach's products and the share that would flow to Crown under alternative circumstances. . . .

"As do many corporations, Crown Zellerbach develops annually a capital budget, which includes a financial forecast, applicable to the next and several succeeding years. Ideally, the capital budget functions as the vehicle by which priority ranking—based upon the anticipated rate of return or other policy considerations—is established for the alternative or competing projects requiring new dollars of capital investment. Since there is no other corporate activity which surpasses in importance the major capital decisions of the corporation, the capital budget should be treated as the focal point where future sources of development are considered, compared, and decided. As a closely related tool for the capital budget, we are working toward a long-range projection of new dollar investment needs that will be based upon our long-range economic, market and production projections. . . ." We did in fact in the long-range planning function coordinate the capital budget and we did administer it in terms of alternatives and priorities.[7]

One of the first projects . . . the [coordinating and planning] department undertook was the development of a uniform method of utilizing present worth concepts in the valuation of proposed capital investment. . . . We are certain that our selection of investments has been improved over prior conditions where the different departments used different criteria. . . .

* * *

Through studies of crude oil surpluses in the Free World, the increasing costs of finding and developing reserves in the United States, the economics of finding and developing crude reserves abroad, and the rapidly growing petroleum markets in many foreign areas, our [coordinating and planning] department concluded that it would be highly desirable for a domestic integrated oil company to secure crude reserves overseas. We are, therefore, part of the group that influenced Continental's recent substantial moves into foreign petroleum operations. . . . [We believe] these developments will contribute substantially to Continental's profits in the future.[8]

As electronic data processing becomes widely utilized and mathematical analogues or "models" of companies are developed which represent the full scope of business activity, the accounting difficulties of time lag and differentiation will diminish. With high-speed computation, it will be possible to trace many more of the effects of general management decisions, as well as simulate or precalculate the probable outcome of alternative actions. It will be feasible to employ regularly more complicated methods of investment appraisal, such as the discounted cash flow rate of return or profitability index, and more sophisticated techniques of business analysis which undoubtedly will be forthcoming.[9] This will not only increase the reliability of general management decisions but, coincidentally,

ORGANIZED CORPORATE PLANNING

Hypothetical Annual Budgets

Size Category Annual Sales	Large $500 Million		Medium $50 Million		Moderate $5 Million	
Vice President, Corporate Planning[1]	(1)	30,000				
Secretary to Vice President	(1)	6,000				
Director, Corporate Planning[2]	(1)	20,000	(1)	20,000	(½)[3]	6,000
Secretary to Director	(1)	5,000	(1)	5,000	(½)	2,000
Planning Analysts[4]	(3)	30,000	(1)	10,000		
Secretaries[5]	(2)	9,000	(1)	4,500		
Overhead[5]		70,000		27,500		4,000
	(9)	170,000	(4)	67,000	(1)	12,000
Corporate Representation:						
Graphical-Statistical Technician[6]	(1)	5,000	(½)	2,500	(8)	1,000
Operating Cost[7]		5,000		2,500		
Total	$	180,000	$	72,000	$	13,000
Per Cent of Sales		.035%		.14%		.26%

[1] General management of corporate planning staff activities; direction of staff analysis, policy, and procedure; liaison with chief executive, corporate officers, and group or divisional general managers.

[2] Immediate supervision of personnel and staff analysis; liaison for divisional or departmental implementation, review, and detailed contact; supervision of corporate representation.

[3] Fractions indicate approximate portion of time at work applied to corporate planning.

[4] Preparation of special financial, mathematical-statistical, and other analytical studies as directed; informational liaison with divisions or departments.

[5] In companies of large and medium size, overhead is estimated at 70%. In companies of moderate size, it is reduced to 50%.

[6] Maintains and posts past, present, and projected data of corporate representation.

[7] One-half of operating cost represents 5-year amortization of installation cost.

[8] Director and his secretary maintain corporate representation.

FIGURE 13

facilitate the quantification of costs and returns. By this time, however, justification of the corporate planning function *per se* will hardly be necessary, since its techniques will have become an integral and accepted part of general management.

Because by accounting definition and tradition they are limited to expenditures which can be quantified in dollars, costs are easier to determine than benefits. The salaries and overhead costs of staff personnel engaged in whole or in part in comprehensive planning are readily available. Line executives can designate the percentage of their time and other expenses related directly to this activity. The operating expenses of special mechanisms of corporate planning, such as the corporate representation or data processing and calculation, can be established. And any reimbursable costs for specific studies or services performed for other profit centers are taken into account.

Several hypothetical budgets for organized staff planning are formulated in Figure 13. They are based on the limited information available concerning existing experience, and the author's opinion of the manpower and related expenditures believed necessary to perform comprehensive planning as described in this book. They will vary not only according to the size of the company but also with differences in growth situation, type of business, organizational complexity, and other particular characteristics. If systems engineering and electronic data processing are undertaken in addition to the corporate representation, this expense is added; occasionally, the expenditure estimated for the representation might be used instead for computer time. These budgets apply to comprehensive planning both at the corporate level and within autonomous or decentralized divisions with equivalent annual sales.

Accurate accounting of the time and money represented in the actions stimulated by comprehensive planning throughout the company would of course be difficult, impractical, and prohibitive in cost. The distinction between general management and corporate planning is never simple and clear-cut. To obtain total cost, it is sufficient to add to the budget of the corporate planning staff the expenditures for planning of different operating units which are specifically responsive to a corporate request for a corporate purpose, which are not a normal part of the efficient management of these units, and which are over and above the organized planning expected in line operations throughout the company as an established policy.

In general and administrative activities, costs are a source of more continuous concern than contributions. One reason, of course, is that cost control *is* essential. Past expenditures and current commitments are hard fact, whereas benefits necessarily follow costs and profits are indefinite until earned. We accept the traditional accounting of administrative dollar costs which is practical because it does not purport to be inclusive. Rarely, for example, is the executive time expended in a general management activity completely recorded. We cannot quantify the comparative value of time spent in different managerial endeavors. We do not determine the dollar cost to a company of using administrative personnel in ways which fit neither their capabilities nor their interests. Certainly we do not calculate the costs of operating pressures on key persons in time lost through shortened careers and increased expenses of training and recruitment; there are no standard costs for managerial ulcers or professional discontent. By contrast, we are keenly aware that meaningful measures are hard to find for general methods and particular procedures of executive management relating to such matters as coordination, efficient intercommunication, morale, corporate reputation, or the numerous longer-range decisions which cannot be proved out for years—and in some instances cannot be specifically validated at all.

In considering the costs and returns of corporate planning, we accept expenditures at face value because "real" numbers are used, but we tend to challenge benefits unduly because they are forecast, estimated, and largely subjective. In reality, both sides of the cost-benefit picture are inconclusive. Both involve the critical element of general judgment. The appraisal of benefits is less tangible and more difficult in degree rather than in kind. In justifying comprehensive planning, a burden of numerical proof which is unrealistic or impossible defeats its purpose. If returns could be quantified as closely as costs, corporate planning would not represent the crucial category of general management decision which is inherently and inevitably less precise—precisely because it incorporates intangibles and projections into the uncertain future.

The concept of general and administrative expenses has been accepted as representing those costs which cannot be identified directly with particular revenue-producing operations and the profits they generate. The most meaningful measures of these expenses are, first, their proportionate relationships to costs and gross profit; and, second, general comparison with the experience of similar companies. In the final analysis, the proportion of gross profits which can be devoted beneficially to general management is a matter of judgment, involving time, sales, costs, and various aspects of the particular situation such as dividend policy and expectation, growth prospects and plans, and type of business. The numerical "reality" of cost data must be matched by subjective conviction relating to benefits. At the present, there are no analytical proofs to dispel the personal worry associated with such general management decisions. For better or worse, management judgment transcends as well as shapes and reflects quantitative data.

REFERENCES CITED

[1] Jarvis B. Cecil (Manager, Coordinating and Planning Department, Continental Oil Company), personal communication, 11 October 1961.

[2] John G. McLean (Financial Vice President, Continental Oil Company), personal communication, 11 September 1961.

[3] Edward J. Green (Vice President–Planning and Marketing, Westinghouse Air Brake Company), personal communication, 5 September 1961.

[4] Dean O. Bowman (Vice President, Long Range Planning, Autonetics, A Division of North American Aviation, Inc.), personal communication, 27 September 1961.

[5] Dean O. Bowman (Co-ordinator of Long-Range Planning, Crown Zellerbach Corporation), "Elements of Corporation Planning," paper (typescript) presented at the Industrial Economics Conference, sponsored by Stanford Research Institute, Los Angeles, 30–31 January 1956, p. 11.

[6] Jarvis B. Cecil, *supra,* 27 November 1961.

[7] Dean O. Bowman, *supra.*

[8] Jarvis B. Cecil, *supra.*

[9] William D. McEachron [Manager, Long-Range Planning Department, Standard Oil Company (Indiana)], "The Role of P. I. in Investment Evaluation," *Chemical Engineering,* 12 June 1961 (Vol. 68, No. 12), pp. 239–242.

CHAPTER VIII

Probable Future Developments

Unless we have a concept of trends, each tomorrow must be evaluated anew. What is worse, we are likely to be surprised at many situations which should have been anticipated, and chagrined at developments which could have been avoided. One of the fundamental characteristics of any operating program or longer-range plan is that it must be conceived in terms of the future—whether tomorrow or years hence—as well as the past and present. Unless it fits expected developments during at least a minimum period of time, it is outdated before it is put into practice. Even when plans incorporate sound projection, unforeseen developments would often justify their constant modification were it not for the practical limits of continuous change. Assumptions concerning the future are imperative in any plan and almost all human activities.

It is important to anticipate the probable course of *corporate planning itself*. The intensification of organized comprehensive planning by business is relatively recent. We can therefore expect more rapid advances during the next decade than are likely to occur irregularly over a longer time as major breakthroughs in technique or great changes of environmental circumstance occur. It is necessary to speculate imaginatively about the future, arrive at our own judgment of what can be expected, and orient corporate planning accordingly. In particular, the younger man embarked on a career of staff planning in business must set his sights and keep pace

231

with developments in anticipation of the time 15 to 20 years hence when, at the peak of his career, he must produce successfully within the advanced environment *of that future time.*

MECHANICAL-ELECTRONIC

Information Processing

We can anticipate continued progress in the discrete expression and manipulation of information. With more and more information produced as the number and knowledge of men increase, ways will be found of handling this mass of material expeditiously. Otherwise, we are in danger of retarding institutional achievements by the sheer involvement of overelaborate paperwork. Since further advancements in data processing will encourage the gathering of more information, there is continuing pressure toward improving our methods of formulating and using information. This is one of the reasons, of course, why there has been such an expansion in the development and use of electronic and mechanical data-processing equipment in recent years.

One implication of these unmistakable trends is that information must be gathered and expressed in ways which simplify its intermediate classification or reformulation, preliminary to final analysis and conclusion. If this is not done, the time and expense required for its utilization are excessive or prohibitive. This simplification means many things. It means maximum practical uniformity in the collection and recording of information, to the extent that some exactness may be sacrificed in the interests of timely and frequent processing. Sales, cost, and profit data pertaining to different divisions engaged in different activities will be formulated to provide either direct comparison or rapid adjustment to some meaningful basis of measuring each with respect to the other. For example, uniform methods of expressing return on investment, profit on sales, and inventory valuation, or of denoting the obligation represented by leases as contrasted with capital investment, will be worked out to extend performance evaluation and comparison. If a computer is programed to calculate inventory requirements successfully, as confirmed by operating experience, inventory management can be largely by exception. Developments which exceed established limits or display unexpected characteristics are flagged for special examination and executive decision.

We can anticipate continued expansion in the use and usefulness of computers: as manufacturing costs are reduced by the amortization of research and development expenditures, further technical advances, greater standardization, and increased volume; as generalized computer programs are written which many enterprises can employ with minor modification; and as more people are trained in this area of professional specialization. With information collected in forms facilitating its electronic processing and even faster computer speeds, a greatly extended and more up-to-date picture of the company situation will be available. Offices and plants at different locations will be interconnected with a corporate computing center, and a considerably larger proportion of data will be collected semi-automatically from operator-controlled office machines such as those employed in accounting and purchasing, or automatically from divisional process-control computers, mechanical and electronic sensors, and television monitoring devices. Rarely will corporate planning in larger companies be restricted for lack of quantitative data; its boundaries will be set by limitations of data-processing procedure, analytical comprehension, mathematical-statistical technique, and human performance.

Analysis

Coincidentally, the computer will expand the range and depth of analysis. Its speed permits calculations otherwise impractical; already its application in inventory control, accounting and internal auditing, purchasing, billing, and machine maintenance permits an extension of operating and projective analysis. For example, in continuously processing data concerning many machines of different age and type, significant facts are revealed which would otherwise go unnoticed. Higher maintenance requirements and costs may be disclosed over time in a particular service area. Further processing of stored information may suggest the cause is poor supervision, a characteristic of certain equipment, differences in maintenance methods, or special conditions such as plant vibration, local environmental peculiarities of above-average dust or moisture, or seismic disturbances affecting precision. The case histories of all machines together and subclassifications by location, type, maintenance record, or environment can be scanned electronically to identify statistically significant uniformities and exceptions. Once identified, these are investigated by management and their significance decided by direct observation, operating experiment, subjective judgment, or further corroborative data processing. In this mechanically exploratory way, the computer extends the range of human analysis by making possible a more complete search and statistical formulation of large quantities of information. Some of the relationships it uncovers by such broadly directed examination would not be known otherwise for some time, or perhaps not at all if management time and attention are directed elsewhere.

For comparative purposes, it will be feasible to recall from electronic storage more complete data pertaining to business operations in the past. These can be re-expressed quickly to take into account differences in labor rates, monetary value, cost of money, sales volume, and other significant changes of situation. With such correlation of data from past periods, historical analogies will be more meaningful than they are often considered today. It will be possible to resolve to a greater extent the contradiction implicit in the acknowledged value of experience on the one hand and, on the other, the uniqueness of each particular situation as expressed in the adage that "history never repeats itself."

Similarly, as mentioned by Dr. Wooldridge in his introduction to this book, the probable results of different decisions management is currently considering can be examined more thoroughly. As well as a better interrelationship of past and present, the complex sequence of consequences throughout the company of alternative courses of action confronting management today can be calculated. For example, what are the associated costs and profits to be expected over the next few years from a decision to increase sales by expanding the sales force and distribution outlets, as compared with a rigorous campaign of cost reduction and price competition? In deciding whether to make or buy a manufactured item, the choice between these alternatives usually depends on such related considerations as manufacturing capacity and efficiency, existing plant and equipment, capital funds available, cash flow, supervisory-labor requirements, employment stability, and the effect on product price and profits. If the analysis of consequences is to be employed regularly in conjunction with important decisions, such interrelationships involve enough calculations to require a computer. Once a method is developed which allows modification to fit current circumstances, it can be used repeatedly to provide quickly the type of informational analysis helpful for recurrent classes of decision.

Electronic computers will also be employed more extensively and intensively in projection and simulation. Frequently, the extrapolation of trends is no simple matter. Especially when the phenomenon is neither straight-line nor uniform in its behavior, calculations may be needed which take many man-hours with ordinary office machines. When, in addition, the projection into the future combines two or more component projections, their repeated reformulation under different assumptions or conditions for study purposes is feasible only with electronic computation. Of course, such extrapolations are no better than the data on which they are based, the accuracy of the analytic method employed in their derivation, the validity of underlying assumptions, and the soundness of judgments incorporated in any part of the process. But their value as elements of decision making, and their predictive corroboration and improvement with experience, are enhanced with the habitual use which is practical with a computer.

Past experience, present situation, and projection into the future can be combined into a single formulation which is analytically representative of the company as a whole. This simulation can be used to determine more completely and reliably the network of interconnection between different elements of the business, to estimate the effects of crucial corporate decisions, to identify the most important areas of need and points of control, and generally to maintain a continuing portrayal of the past, present, and probable future of the company as an improved analytical referent and mechanism of decision making. The balance sheet and financial operating statements have been employed traditionally for this purpose. With the electronic computer, many more factors can be incorporated in the simulation, in greater detail, and with many more interrelationships included in the quantification. For example, separate estimates of the likelihood of consummating many different sales can be combined into a composite probability which is readily translated into the expected total sales volume needed for many corporate planning purposes. If the estimates of success for specific sales can be expressed realistically, not as a single percentage, but only between two limits of likelihood, these ranges are combined into an anticipated sales volume with upper and lower limits.

It would be a mistake either to regard such simulation as an analytical panacea or to discount its potential value. If approached carefully and constructively, a quantitative representation of the dynamics of the company and its environmental situation can be developed over time which improves the batting average of sound corporate decision. The crucial requirement is to proceed slowly and carefully. The first formulation is as simple as it can be and still provide useful information for executive management. A good point of departure is translation of the balance sheet and operating statements into a quantitative model which expresses their dynamic interrelationships. Comparison of this initial formulation with more detailed operating facts and figures will undoubtedly reveal improvements which make the model more precisely and accurately descriptive. Step by step, by constantly checking with actual experience, additional factors are introduced into the simulation. If, in so doing, its representative reliability is reduced, the extended form is rejected until a way is found of including these added elements without loss of simulative accuracy.

Naturally, the company must be willing and able to make the initial investment of developing the simulation through the first stages of formulation, trial and error, and comparison with operating experience. Thereafter, its continued improvement is possible with little additional expense. As discussed in the previous chapter, the size of the general and administrative budget allocated for this analytic mechanism depends on how much it is used by corporate executives in decision making and their judgment of its worth. Since the intellectual curiosity of the operations research personnel who quantify the model and program its data processing will lead them to explore its development well beyond the point of present practical usage, supervisory restraint is advisable.

Two areas of current research may extend analysis with the aid of computers even further: heuristic problem solving and game theory. Heuristic programing proposes to accelerate the range and depth of analysis by utilizing computers to produce valid interrelationships or "equations" which are new in that they were not foreseen in the general instructions to the machine and might not have occurred to the human mind for some time if at all. Once again, speed of computation is the key. By directing the computer to examine very large quantities of data for relationships which meet criteria of mathematical validity—or to process smaller quantities of data over and over again with progressive advancement toward these criteria each time around—combinations are discovered which were unknown before. Somewhat like Sir Arthur Eddington's postulate that a sufficiently long-lived monkey would in time type out all the works of Shakespeare, by semi-random programing the computer comes up with quantitative expressions, meeting necessary requirements for their own validity, which so far exceed the instructions of the human operator that considering them as produced by the machine itself is defensible.[1]

Also still in its infancy, game theory is of potential significance in corporate planning. As discussed in Chapter V, its purpose of logicizing and quantifying *strategy* is highly relevant to competitive private enterprise. Game theory is frequently explained by reference to the game of poker, and business men often describe situations with such analogies as: "He holds all the cards," "He's bluffing," or, "Never draw to an inside straight." At present, game theory has been structured with analytical validity only for simple situations involving a few opponents, within highly limited alternatives of participant behavior and external environmental change. Since business involves a great many variables both within and external to a company, and normally there are numerous competitors to be taken into account in connection with different activities, it will be some time before game theory is incorporated mathematically in corporate planning.

It is not the intent to expand further on the mathematical-statistical techniques described in an earlier chapter; for each of these areas of investigation, Dr. Nelson has given an indication of future developments. They are mentioned here because they are likely to extend corporate analysis in the future; as they advance in calculative scope and reliability, corporate planning will follow suit. For practicing and potential managers today, awareness of these efforts and their possible practical contribution may preclude arbitrary dismissal of any staff proposal at some future date which is a consequence of accelerated accomplishment in either field.

Although undoubtedly electronic data processing and analysis will be employed more and more in corporate planning with each passing year, non-technical advancements must be made which are of even greater import to its continued development and successful application. The hard facts of the matter are that we are not now utilizing, in corporate affairs and in the conduct of our society in general, many simple but effective techniques. To greatly expand the employment of analysis, reason, and structured judgment in business, we need new techniques less than the motivation and behavioral capacity to apply those at hand.

Display

In recent years, remarkable advances have been made in the visual presentation of information. The cathode ray tube in particular has advanced the translation of electrical impulses into visual images, culminating in the new technology of television. Over a longer period of time, display has also advanced in such applications as automatic stock-quotation boards in brokerage offices and recording instruments such as the barograph or cardiograph. In general, these devices have been oriented and used to present information in visual forms which are comprehensible to many people, or more easily studied by fewer users. For the most part, they are characterized by continuous automaticity and conceptual clarity. They are the crucial links between electrical and mechanical transmitters and manipulators of information, and the human mind and sensory system.

Lately, electronic-tube visual displays have been linked experimentally with computers in a more directly reciprocal relationship. Not only are data stored and processed by the computer translated into trend lines, bar charts, scatter diagrams, matrices, and other graphic forms, but the computer can be instructed to modify or re-express these displays in accordance with changes desired by the human viewer. Several highly important advantages for the user are achieved in this way. He can request presentation of the information and its analysis in the visual form most meaningful to him. He can modify this form within limits to increase his comprehension and deduction by requesting a different scale, more or less refinement, or a change in proportionate relationship between ordinate and abscissa. He can ask for comparative displays, in succession or side by side, which portray a different set of assumptions or alternative situations. Because of the speed of the electronic process, he can obtain these visual displays without the usual delay which taxes the conscious memory or prevents comparative conceptualization and assimilation. In effect, he achieves a kind of symbiotic relationship with a machine which comprises a vastly expanded reservoir and analyzer of information.

The implications of this research and development for management and corporate planning are quite clear. A tool will be available which can greatly extend the process of rational management. The mind of the executive will be able to function more effectively without the present constraints embodied in the many delays of securing and revising information, the restricted quantity and scope of data immediately available, and the limitations of the unaided human mind in performing rapid computation and analysis. He will be able to employ his mental capabilities to a greater extent at the higher levels of perception, exploration, and deductive analysis —and less in connection with the obtainment, organization, and recall of intermittent and often unrelated information. It is not farfetched to envisage the chief executives of a larger company some day in the future with display consoles at their deskside. As data and their analysis are needed for decision, managers will call on the computing center for the display and progressive processing of the material—all within a few minutes (Plate III, facing page 129).[2]

Corporate planning staffs will make use of this display-computing equipment for their own purposes, and will arrange computer programing which provides principal executives with the information and analysis they desire for their personal planning and decision. In time, the corporate representation described in Chapter V will be composed for the most part of electronic display equipment which can retain informational picturizations indefinitely, be modified quickly by direct communication with the computer, present alternative outcomes and comparative simulations, or portray operating records and projections continually adjusted by automatic updating from the data-processing and -storage center.

As yet unanswered are important questions relating to the matching of electronic data processing and the human user. In its present state, and without new ways of constructive thinking, how much information can the human mind absorb how often without mental confusion? How much supportive analytical equipment can we afford, if existing capabilities with simpler methods are not being employed efficiently? What limitations are imposed on the usefulness of higher-speed corporate decision-making devices, if the system of implementation operates on a much slower time schedule inherent in the productive process itself or set by environmental factors outside and beyond the control of the company? Since there are operational limits to continuous change, how fast and often should comprehensive corporate plans be reviewed and revised? What is the point of diminishing informational return? Among the many competing demands upon the surplus resources or "disposable income" of a company, how much is wisely expended on improved decision making by electronic processing and display versus other procedural means or the replacement of certain people in the system?

PEOPLE

The Mind of Man

It is difficult to predict future developments involving the human mind and sensory system. Not only is this the continuing area of our greatest ignorance, but the world today is torn between conflicting political ideologies which are both cause and consequence of very different ways of thinking and feeling. The following expectations assume the environment of a democratic society, with continued extension in freedom of thought and its expression.

That we are now in the midst of an age of science there can be little doubt. Its impact on our minds and methods is unquestionable. Each succeeding generation will incorporate more readily into its thinking the point of view and techniques of thought carried forward by its predecessor. The concept of the theory of relativity, for example, difficult for one generation to grasp, is more easily understood and taken for granted by succeeding generations. Mathematical methods of thought associated with the use of the electronic computer, difficult for many managers to understand today, will be easier for their executive successors tomorrow. Most certainly, one continuing consequence of scientific advancement will be new knowledge and improved methods of rational analysis. We can hope the outcome will be greater awareness and application of rational thought *vis à vis* unconstructive emotional reaction. But, if this extended rationality is to improve the conduct of our societal and business affairs, it must be developed and applied within the limits of a healthy balance of mind and emotion.

While science is advancing rapidly, the era of psychology is commencing. A general recognition of matters psychological which did not exist 75 years ago has diffused far and wide. Although much of this awareness is popular and understandably superficial, usable knowledge has accumulated. Even more important, the substantive bases for a new realm of knowledge have been established and the wheels set in motion for more significant achievements in the future. We can anticipate major breakthroughs in psychological understanding and its blending with knowledge in the physical, mathematical, and medical-physiological sciences to provide more precise information concerning the working of the human brain and nervous system. Whereas we cannot now describe—much less define scientifically—the nature of human thought, emotion, or memory, we can reasonably expect more accurately descriptive, experimentally valid, and practically useful knowledge of these basic psychological "particles" of the mind within perhaps the next 20 to 50 years. With this knowledge will come a clearer picture of human judgment: the working of the individual mental-emotional process of observing, remembering, reasoning, concluding. By knowing more about how we think, we will be able not only to develop more effective procedures and mechanical aids for our analytical reasoning but, in time, to expand our capacities of *internalized* thought by new mental techniques difficult or impossible to imagine at present.

By learning more about our emotions, we will understand enough of how they relate to logical thought to identify more clearly their constructive and disruptive effects. In this way, the processes of subjective perception, thinking, and feeling will be advanced and translated into the many benefits to be derived from the more effective application of human judgment and analytical conclusion. Except in the field of analytical psychiatry, the emotional and deliberative aspects of mental activity have in the main been considered separate and distinguishable. It will probably be proved that the spontaneously perceptive, intuitive, emotional elements of thinking are in fact inseparable from deliberately rational mental effort, and that the soundest analytical thinking by each individual results when there is an appropriate balance between the two. With this confirmation, attention will be focused on greater awareness and increased understanding of emotional factors both within the individual and in his environment. The limitations of purely rational constructs such as those of mathematics, which exclude the undefinable, unpredictable, and emotional, will be clarified. And perhaps finally, in time, an analytical formulation will be devised which integrates logical-quantitative statement and emotional-intuitive values in a single expression encompassing them both. In the meanwhile, analytically helpful mechanisms such as the corporate representation discussed in Chapter V or the display devices described earlier in this chapter will be modified to fit increased understanding of the operating characteristics of the human mind.

Besides the absorption of new psychological knowledge through the written and spoken word, more managers will experience direct contact with psychiatry. The thought of clinical help in personal psychological problems is still rejected by most business men, but many more than announce the fact have benefited from such assistance. From this experience, they have acquired a keener sensitivity to emotional factors within themselves and in their relations with others than is attained by academic study alone. As psychiatric consultation and therapy lose their present implication of inadequacy or failure, and are regarded in the same light as organic medicine, more executives will accept psychotherapy without personal shame or automatic blemish to their corporate record. The day is fast approaching when psychotherapy will be considered as sensible as treatment for any organic condition such as eyestrain or palpitating heart. Younger employees will be encouraged to seek help when needed, since by so doing they will strengthen their capabilities, expand their comprehension, and improve their performance within the company. As more employees have direct contact with clinical psychology, they will pass on to others some of the sensitivities thus acquired and apply their new understanding in management actions. In these ways, psychological knowledge and experience will have a cumulative impact on general management and corporate planning in the future.

One highly probable outcome of future developments, therefore, is more attention to psychological considerations in business management. The prevalent contention today that "there is no account-ing for taste," or "for what people will do," will be replaced by considerable comprehension and capacity to project human re-actions. Better indicators will be found of individual capabilities, limitations, and motivations. Since management is the most im-portant single ingredient of business success, and the crucial de-cisions are made by a comparatively small group of managers, any improvement in the appraisal of individual capacities and the pre-diction of performance in different positions is clearly important in corporate operations and planning.

Human Interaction

Intimately related to individual psychology is the psychology of groups. Equal in importance to the dynamics of the individual are those between people. Not only are these group interactions the most vital element in the functioning of any organization, but of course they have a great deal to do with the performance of indi-viduals. The personnel of a company coexist and conduct its activ-ities in a symbiotic interrelationship in which the individual influences the group and the group affects the individual. The first of these interactions is widely recognized in the significance attrib-uted by management to individual qualities of leadership and initiative and their acceptability to others. The impact of the group on the individual is less well documented in history and experi-mental study. One recent illustrative disclosure is the extent to which individual judgment is molded by majority opinion. Experi-ments indicate that, to a surprising extent in a group of equals, conclusions which are firm and even obvious to the individual by himself can be reversed by the pressure of unanimous opinion to the contrary by the rest. Dependent on such factors as personal security, the importance of agreeing with the others, concern about the consequences of rugged individualism, or excessive self-doubt, the individual may literally deny to himself a clear-cut fact or obvious truth.[3]

That likes and dislikes are important considerations in business operations is generally acknowledged. Sometimes these interpersonal reactions are realized by those involved; sometimes they are rational-ized by explanations which camouflage the real or unknown reasons.

There are people who can accomplish a regrettable reduction in workforce or unwanted reorganization with the minimum uncooperativeness or antagonistic reaction. Others magnify the same difficulties, by their personality and handling of the situation, to the point where they may have to be replaced. Some persons communicate effectively and often; others are known for their inability or unwillingness to receive and impart information. A particular combination of people work together in a productive harmony which yields results unattainable by a different group comparable in experience and professional knowledge. By personality and position, some employees are prone to accept wild rumor and retransmit it in exaggerated form.

Human interaction comprises two interdependent aspects equally important to the most successful conduct of the business enterprise: substantive communication and interpersonal reaction. Their linkage is shown by our natural tendency to avoid communication with those we do not like and—whether we recognize it or not—either to absorb less information from them or to distort it in some degree to fit the image of our personal dislike. Substantive communication and group or social psychology are bound together in the "real life" of business activities. Stimulated by advancements in individual psychology and the needs arising from the increasingly interdependent nature of the business community and company operations, we can expect rapid development of knowledge concerning many aspects of interaction between people.

We will extend our understanding of the attitudinal differences between such professional-occupational groups as accountants, engineers, scientists, sales personnel, and corporate staff planners. More will be known about the roots of labor attitudes which we now comprehend mainly as symptoms. We will have a clearer concept of the subtle emotional factors which generally influence job satisfaction, performance, and collective morale. The psychology of human intercommunication, different forms of organization, and methods of administration will be advanced. The requirements and techniques of constructive leadership will be clarified, and more reliable measurement of consumer and public attitudes and response will be possible. Ultimately, limitations may have to be established on the deliberate manipulation of people—made possible by greater knowledge of group psychology—in order to provide time for that maturation of understanding on the part of the body politic and company employees which is necessary to preserve the essential elements of a free society in the first instance and to maintain a consciously responsive organization in the second.

This expanded knowledge will be incorporated in comprehensive plans. General objectives and specific programs for making human interaction within the company more effective will be thought out as carefully as financial goals and budgets. The psychological implications of management actions and formal procedures will be considered an integral part of their administrative feasibility. The impact of corporate advertising and other public relations will be more accurately reviewed and forecast. Most important, the performance of management groups in determining the longer-range direction of corporate effort, formulating and appraising plans, and reaching decisions will be improved with better understanding of the psychological factors involved in collective action and analysis by small working groups. Selection of members, methods of operation, and techniques of collaborative investigation will all be affected. Within limits, the personal and attitudinal compatibility of an executive team will prove as important a productive resource as their combined brain power.

Motivation

Since effective management will depend increasingly on comprehensive appraisal and cooperative action *in the institutional interest,* further understanding of human motivation is especially important for business planning. Personal desires and ambitions shape everyone's actions, but planning and managing the modern corporate enterprise call for objective appraisal and mutually supportive effort. Successful general managers must modify purely personal goals to fit the needs of the organization. Corporate staff planning personnel, in particular, must work to achieve the analytical objectivity which is their primary responsibility. And, because the formulation and implementation of plans involve the entire company, performance will not measure up to plan unless employees in general are also cooperatively inclined.

Besides the accepted desires for personal profit, security, status, recognition, or power, there are others—such as appreciation, acceptance, a sense of belonging, or courtesy and consideration— which comprise another level of response and motivation. The deepest level consists of psychological drives unrecognized by the individual but occasionally apparent to close associates. The three categories are, of course, closely interrelated. A direct interconnection may exist between a forgotten hurt and a current oversensitivity. An urge for power may be rooted in unconscious desires derived from logically unrelated experiences which have long since been repressed beyond intentional recognition. It is these instigating forces which psychological tests seek to illuminate. As more is learned about human motivations generated by the complex interaction of thinking and feeling at these different levels, plans and operations will be shaped accordingly.

Once the nature of the common wish for security is more fully demonstrated, job stability will share importance with wage and salary levels. The subtler aspects of job contentment, more a matter of supervisory attitude and administrative method than extra expense, will receive greater attention. Motivational differences between occupational and professional groups will be reflected in company plans. For example, the importance attached to intellectual advancement by engineers and industrial scientists will be represented in policies promoting individual publication, attendance at technical conferences and special courses, after-hours teaching, and in-plant training. On the other hand, plans will be made for the separation of research and product engineering before this same intellectual curiosity on the part of research personnel is carried beyond the point of practicality and profitability. The untapped potential of certain supervisory personnel such as facilities maintenance and security people, who are sometimes treated as second-class administrative citizens, will be stimulated by improved status, management recognition, and encouragement to themselves expand the content and performance of their jobs. Motivational differences between men and women will be reflected to a greater extent in the modifications of supervisory policy, working environment, and performance appropriate to each.

The confusion which sometimes results from an oversimplification of motivation is illustrated by decentralization. The basic justification advanced for this organizational concept is the motivation provided the manager by independence. By formal assignment of profit responsibility and decision-making authority, the manager employs his potentialities to the full and improves the performance of the unit. But the fact that the matter is not so simple is evidenced in recent discussion in the management literature.

Unless the controlling management is a holding company, a decentralized unit is in fact anything but autonomous. Normally, it cannot borrow money, commit capital expenditures beyond a limit, maintain wage and salary levels very different from those prevailing in the rest of the company, or engage in unrestricted competition with another division. Its longer-range objectives cannot be in conflict with those of the corporation as a whole. It must pay its share of corporate general and administrative expense, various legal and tax matters are handled or correlated at corporate headquarters, and central services are often used until they can be supported separately. The decentralized manager is in fact only half-free. And, since profit margins are usually narrow, corporate costs and restrictions can make the difference between his successful performance and frustrating failure. Yet complete uncoordinated independence would not only operate to the over-all company disadvantage, it would deny the function of corporate management.

Irresolution concerning decentralization is a consequence of this unrealistic assumption concerning motivation, rather than organizational invalidity. The successful decentralized manager cannot be so strongly motivated toward autonomy that he is frustrated by necessary controls and desirable coordinated effort; nor can he rely on direction from above to the point where he does not apply the freedom of action which is his. He must combine the motivations of independent responsibility and corporate participation in a realistic balance which utilizes and molds the corporate context to advance his own achievements. By the same token, a top management which denies the restrictions and directions it imposes on decentralized managers not only is itself unrealistic but transforms the intended encouragement of independence into self-protective maneuvering which extends sometimes to illegal acts.

The real reason for decentralization is the growing complexity of management. Chief executives of larger companies and corporate staffs have found it next to impossible to keep pace with all that is going on and planned. It remains to be seen whether new techniques will not re-establish the feasibility and desirability of the central cognizance and control common in the past. At least in this way, the extent of corporate direction will be determined by the combination of management responsibilities at different organizational levels which produces the best results, rather than a necessary relinquishment of functions because of informational and analytical difficulties.

Executive motivation is deeply involved in corporate planning. Stock options, liberal expense allowances, perquisites of many kinds, and increasing retirement income and benefits paid by the company are temptations toward performance in the interest of purely personal security and the accumulation of a moderate fortune rather than in the interests of the institution. Executive positions can become a means to personal gain rather than a corporate trust which provides reasonable reward for successful or at least effortful performance in the corporate behalf. Comprehensive planning presumes the subordination of personal goals and gains which is necessary to determine the objectives best for the company. What will be the future course of the conflicting motivations present in our culture today?

One hopeful trend is the rise of management as a profession. The more knowledge and special capability required in management, the greater the intellectual stimulation, pride, and satisfaction derived from the experience. There is also a sense of purpose and achievement in making a substantive contribution to a professional discipline: a new technique, a useful formulation of principles, or an improved method. The gratifications of monetary and material accumulation are shared with those derived from professional ability and accomplishment. Professionalism also establishes standards of performance and a code of responsible behavior.[4]

There is some evidence that the satisfactions of working in collaborative harmony, of acceptance and responsive appreciation within an organizational endeavor, of contributing as well as receiving, have been underestimated. Certainly, their stimulation in both management and labor will require a heightened sense of responsibility upward and downward within the management chain. And a continued rise in the educational level and in the information available to stockholders and the body politic should shape the performance of management and labor increasingly in the corporate and public interest.

Corporate Planners

For medium-sized companies, there will probably be more generalist planning positions established. These may combine all top management planning, both "short-range" and "long-range," and may have titles such as "assistant to the president" or "vice president, administration."

For the large corporations, there will probably be more staff positions created which are specifically devoted to long-range planning and given titles accordingly.

. . . Planners must have been exposed . . . to a wide variety of company operations. Only men with . . . broad experience in the company will have the random pieces of knowledge of internal variables . . . which are necessary to make sense out of the abstract summary information they must receive from all parts of the system.

The men who fill the planning positions will also need a wide variety of knowledge about the structure of U.S. society. Not [that they will need] a detailed knowledge of business cycle theory—or population statistics or labor union tactics—but [they] should at least be acquainted with the structure of society and some of its many sub-parts and processes. This . . . suggests a fairly good grounding in macroeconomics, sociology, history, and the philosophy of culture.

Generalist-type planners must also communicate with many different . . . departments, in rapid-fire succession, and inspire trust on the part of other executives. Since communication with other humans is one of their principal research methods, this means . . . a gregarious type of individual . . . who has a degree of social skill, a degree of "other directedness," and a trusting, rather than a suspicious or fearful, view of the world. It also means selecting a person who . . . can sustain himself in a wide variety of social contacts, with high frequency and long duration, without losing his interest or propensity to communicate.

. . . Planners in the lower [levels of organization] will . . . have a bent for empirical investigation and detail, . . . [be] men who prefer to be thorough, working a problem through with precision, utilizing many facts and tables.

. . . Planners in the upper [levels of management and large organizations] will have to be . . . deductive thinkers, rather than the empirical investigators, whose mental predisposition is more [that of] a philosopher than an empirical scientist. They will have less patience with facts, and a higher tolerance of ambiguity; otherwise their minds would be unwilling to take the risk of making decisions with broad, less precise (and what appears to the scientist as ambiguous) variables. . . .

For the companies and industries where fast change is vital, . . . we will see greater centralization of the planning role, and in some cases the staff men will be given official authority, rather than held only to an advisory status. . . .

On the other hand, in those companies where change is less frequent and drastic, and where the company lives a more comfortable life, not bombarded so heavily or frequently from the environment, . . . planners will continue to be advisors. . . .

Provision for orderly change can be made by establishment of long-range planning positions, if the man in the position has the time and interest to watch future developments in the company and environment, and think through the effects of these on company operations; has stronger than average characteristics of independence, a kind of natural dissatisfaction with the status quo, and a critical and inquiring mind; is rewarded on the basis of creativity and intelligence in balancing long-run company goals, rather than concentrating exclusively on profits this year.[5]

RELATED FIELDS

Directly and indirectly, corporate planning will draw from numerous disciplines. *Mathematics* must supply the more precise statement of interrelationships needed in the analysis of everyday operating activities. It is the potential means of expressing the dynamics of the corporate situation and its projection into the future. It is the language of probability and of computers. Mathematical statistics support the use of samples representing large populations of data: from market information and quality control to employee opinion. New formulations such as information theory and symbolic logic suggest new ways of handling data and new analogic simulation; and game and decision theory seek to encompass enough elements of business situations in real life to assist in resolving questions of corporate strategy and management choice. Increasingly, decisions subject to routinization are derived from mathematical statements which supply the answer in terms of the instructions incorporated within them, or reveal when significant exceptions are present.

Calculating such system solutions as the combination of different means of transport which best compromises low transportation costs and prompt delivery, or minimum safe bank balances for diverse operations at different locations, is the type of mathematical programing emphasized in *operations research—or operations analysis,* as it is also called. Linear programing and queueing theory are illustrative developments associated with this area of emphasis.

Through national income and related statistics, and more detailed regional studies by government and other organizations, *economics* describes the background situation against which companies estimate their business prospects. Economic policy shapes federal actions designed to lessen the business cycle, reduce unemployment, or subsidize private enterprise. Economic techniques are exemplified in financial forecasting, market analysis, cash flow, and return on investment. Classical concepts such as price as a function of marginal cost and return, or value theory, seek to extend their descriptive validity and practical usefulness. With the aid of electronic computation, more and better economic analysis is possible for the individual firm—especially in connection with the basic economic objective of determining the optimum allocation of corporate resources. Reliable methods will be developed for relating—in one quantitative model—sales, inventories, material flow, employment, production, and distribution for a single company, division, or product. Representing a combination of economics and mathematics, modifications of customary *accounting* are being advanced to show more clearly the financial interactions most vital for continuous planning review.

The relevance to corporate planning of developments in the various fields of *psychology* was implied in the previous section. For example, under continual study are the predictive accuracy of individual psychological testing and the appraisal and forecast of group reactions. As a partner in human engineering, psychology throws light on the precise interrelationships between man and machine affecting the efficiency of production processes. Psychosomatic medicine elucidates the connections between environmental stress and strain, personality characteristics, and specific incapacity or illness. Psychiatry and psychoanalysis explore the inner workings of mind and emotions, which influence man's every thought and action.

By extending its scope of consideration, *engineering* broadens its impact on corporate planning. *Systems engineering* aims to define the set of principal elements which constitute an integrated operation such as technologically complex production. Men, machines, facilities, output, inventory, storage, shipping, cost, plant layout, and research and development are viewed all together, and each is analyzed with respect to its interactions with the others and its role in the total system. Concepts from mathematics, physics, and other fields are very much involved. At the same time, specific knowledge of the characteristics and use of materials, the measurement of physical forces, engineering design, and other traditional applications is being extended. In expanding its specification of production processes, exemplified in the past by time-motion studies and plant layout, *industrial engineering* will apply a broad range of mathematical-statistical method and interrelate more closely with physics, physiology, and psychology.

Relevant knowledge from many disciplines is being employed in *business administration* for its purposes. *Management science* is evolving as a professional field emphasizing, as its name suggests, scientific methods and mathematical statement. *Sociology* and *political science* provide perceptions which will lead to specific methodologies applicable in business. Most physical and behavioral sciences relate to management and corporate planning in one way or another, providing background knowledge, insight, or technique. Any field of endeavor can provide a suggestive analogy which—although not directly applicable—triggers a constructive thought or awareness which is put to use in planning. "More and more the really striking advances come from men who have the imagination and adventuresomeness to bring other men's notions to their problems at a moment of decisive relevance."[6]

The fields most closely related to *corporate planning* are trending in the same direction. To expand its own area of knowledge, each has found it necessary to consider aspects of the others. Information and techniques have been widely exchanged; in particular, advances in mathematical theory and new achievements in experimental method are quickly applied wherever they are suggestive or specifically helpful. In general, these fields display an increasing body of common knowledge and technique.

An ultimate objective of *comprehensive planning*—as well as a number of other fields—is a systematic expression of the interactions between numerous and diverse elements which embodies both the scientifically quantitative and the behaviorally qualitative. It must have sufficient precision to support its use as an analogue or model for planning purposes in real-life situations. Almost certainly, it will incorporate contributions from various fields, and its difficulty suggests that it will not be attained for some time. However, its realization will constitute a milestone in the advancement of knowledge, and a final confirmation that comprehensive planning is a distinctive discipline as well as field of study.

REFERENCES CITED

[1] Herbert A. Simon, *The New Science of Management Decision,* 1960 (Harper & Brothers), 50 pp.

[2] Ramo Wooldridge, A Division of Thompson Ramo Wooldridge Inc., Canoga Park, California, *Demonstration Models of Intellectronic Management Planning and Control Techniques,* 1961, 65 pp.

[3] Solomon E. Asch, "Opinion and Social Pressure," *Scientific American,* November 1955 (Vol. 193, No. 5), pp. 31–35.

[4] Robert W. Austin, "Code of Conduct for Executives," *Harvard Business Review,* September–October 1961 (Vol. 39, No. 5), pp. 53–61.

Wilbert E. Moore, "Management in Moral Crisis," *Princeton Alumni Weekly,* 23 February 1962 (Vol. LXII, No. 19), pp. 8–11, 15. [Chapter 1 in *The Conduct of the Corporation,* New York (Random House), forthcoming 1962.]

[5] Charles E. Summer, Jr. (Associate Professor of Management, Graduate School of Business, Columbia University; formerly, Manager of Research, Booz, Allen and Hamilton), "The Future Role of the Corporate Planner," *California Management Review,* Winter 1961 (Vol. III, No. 2), pp. 20–31.

[6] McGeorge Bundy, "Science as a Way of Life," *Harvard Today,* Autumn 1961, p. 21.